The Best of
Books for Keeps

*Highlights from the leading
children's book magazine*

The Best of
Books for Keeps

*Highlights from the leading
children's book magazine*

Edited by Chris Powling

The Bodley Head
London

For All Members of the BfK Team
(Past, Present and Future)

1 3 5 7 9 10 8 6 4 2

Copyright © in this collection *Books for Keeps* 1994
Chris Powling has asserted his right under the Copyright, Designs and Patents
Act, 1988 to be identified as the editor of this work

First published in the United Kingdom 1994
by The Bodley Head Children's Books
Random House, 20 Vauxhall Bridge Road, London SW1V 2SA
Random House Australia (Pty) Limited
20 Alfred Street, Milsons Point, Sydney,
New South Wales 2061, Australia
Random House New Zealand Limited
18 Poland Road, Glenfield,
Auckland 10, New Zealand
Random House South Africa (Pty) Limited
PO Box 337, Bergvlei 2012, South Africa
Random House UK Limited Reg. No. 954009

A CIP catalogue record for this book is available from the British Library

ISBN 0 370 31905 2

Designed by Rowan Seymour
Printed and bound in Great Britain by Clays Ltd, St Ives plc

Contents

Foreword

More children's books are published in a year nowadays than any one child could ever read. As a magazine, *Books For Keeps* is a vital part of this publishing scene – it deals with what's afoot, with discussions and debates, with the kind of recommendations that are open invitations, not fixed critical certainties, leaving buyers and borrowers free to decide for themselves.

Given the ephemeral nature of magazine writing and production, the editors are bound always to press on with the next event, challenge, order, initiative. But it is clear that some pieces, articles particularly, are a kind of social history of books, reading and childhood. In this volume, they are given their own chance of being 'for keeps'. In addition, as all good anthologists know, bringing them together creates not just a collection but also a unity, an argument, an interweaving of convictions to demonstrate what is at issue in children's literature and children's growth in literacy. The lightness of the editorial tone does not preclude the seriousness of its purpose.

There is room and need for more of this, especially when, as now, the conditions of reading and the nature of texts change. Hence the importance of this book.

Margaret Meek

Introduction

This compilation is offered in the same spirit with which Pat Triggs, the founding editor of *Books for Keeps*, introduced Issue Number One in March 1980:

> 'Helpful, practical, stimulating, informative, entertaining, sometimes provocative and always enjoyable to read – this is what we intend *Books for Keeps* to be.'

It's our intention still . . . and is reflected, we hope, in the pages that follow. What they also provide, at least potentially, is an overview. By bringing together in one publication pieces written years apart, often in response to particular pressures and circumstances, there's a chance we'll mirror the shifts and sticking points of a decade or more – and a pretty crucial decade at that. All too often *BfK*'s bi-monthly celebration of the pleasures of reading has felt like a sideshow – the main event being a slugging match between market forces, diminishing public provision and the imperatives of political orthodoxy. Nevertheless, should some future historian choose to plot the course of children's reading in the 1980s and beyond, it's hard to believe *BfK* won't provide much of the foreground and background detail. Here, in a handy form, is some of it.

Of course, this documentary approach is not without risk. 'I'm a bit concerned at the sexist-seeming references to the author as "him" throughout,' said Bernard Ashley of his article on page 161 which dates from July 1980. We are, too. After all, we printed it that way. Any change now, though, would blunt one of the points of the enterprise which is why, by permission of the author 'herself', every piece appears here in its original state.

Common to them all, whatever their subject, is a keen interest in the way books are best assessed and mediated to children in real-life classrooms, libraries, bookshops and homes. The changes we've seen in the School Bookshop Movement, still central to *BfK*'s concerns, have only reinforced our belief in book *ownership* – not to mention our admiration for the parents and teachers who promote it. Their good-humoured, up-to-the-armpits involvement is something we try to catch in our tone-of-voice:

The Friendly Robin
Enid Blyton, ill. Constance Marshall, Knight
(Jan 93), 0 340 18741 7, 2.50

Once there was a little girl called Elizabeth. Every day she went to Infant School. Her favourite lesson was Nature Study and she specially liked it when her teacher, Miss Cathey, told the children a story out of a big book called *Enid Blyton's Nature Reader*. The stories were all about birds, animals and plants. Quite often the creatures told each other about their lives or sometimes there were some children in the story who helped to look after them. That was all a long time ago, in the 1950s, so you can imagine Elizabeth's surprise when, one day when she was quite grown up, she was sent a book with some of those very same stories in it!

' Goodness,' she said to herself, 'I remember these almost word for word. How very old-fashioned they seem to be now. I'll take them to read to the children in my own Infant School.'

The little girls and boys she read them to liked them very much, and said 'Can we hear them again?' This really took the wind out of Elizabeth's sails, I can tell you.

(*BfK* 80, May 1993)

Liz Waterland, ruefully open-minded.

For open-mindedness is very much a *BfK* requirement. However awkward or unpredictable its outcome, what we've always been after is a personal engagement with reading – enriched, preferably, by a healthy respect for other people's personal engagements. Hence our commitment to the inter-cultural, to the full range of reading methods (including the 'apprenticeship' approaches so misrepresented by politicians) to the fictive aspects of non-fiction. Underpinning it all is a fierce opposition to *lists*. From their first appearance, *BfK* has challenged these corrupting substitutes for a proper literary pedagogy and we'll go on challenging them for as long as turns out to be necessary.

Mind you, we're bound to win in the end. Richard Hill, *BfK*'s managing director and sole full-timer, never tires of pointing out that our network reaches beyond our five part-timers in London and Winchester; beyond our two dozen regular reviewers and ever-increasing contributors nationwide, beyond even our thousands of subscribers throughout the world since many an individual copy will be passed on to five or six different readers. What official order, he asks, can withstand an army of enthusiasts like that?

Of course, it will be obvious to these same enthusiasts that *The Best of Books for Keeps* is a very different entity from *BfK* itself. Gone are the colour spreads, the news pages, the forty per cent of every issue we assign to reviews – our 'magazine-ness', in short. In its place, though, brought into sharp focus by this change of format, is the chance to see how well our feature material has worn over the years . . . to balance the benefits of hindsight against the freshness of catching the world of children's books on the wing. This kept me reading long after I'd despaired of arriving at that final, indisputable selection all editors dream about. I hope everyone who picks up this book will share my fascination.

Enjoy the Anthology!

Chris Powling

PART ONE

Classics, Folk and Fairy Tales

Needle on Treasure Island

For JAN NEEDLE Treasure Island *has always been a very special book, one which he returns to often. Here he makes us a present of his thoughts about why it fascinates him and why he believes it has much to teach us about writing for children*

EVER SINCE IT WAS PUBLISHED almost a hundred years ago, *Treasure Island*, by Robert Louis Stevenson, has been recognised as one of the best children's books ever written. On the surface, the reasons for its success seem obvious. The map, the treasure, the pirates, the brave young hero; they are, simply, classic ingredients for an adventure yarn. But *Treasure Island*, I think, is far far more than *just* an adventure yarn. I reread it quite frequently – the last time before I started writing this – and I remain convinced that it is a deeply important book in terms of children's literature, both for readers and practitioners.

Even at its simplest level of success, its story, *Treasure Island* has much to teach us about writing for children. Many, many other books, of course, have the 'classic ingredients' I mentioned before, but I know of no other that deploys them with such unremitting intensity. After only 8,000 words, at the end of a mere six out of thirty-four chapters, we have seen the quiet life of a simple country boy transformed. Jim Hawkins has met and been terrorised by three appalling villains – Billy Bones, Black Dog and Blind Pew. He has shared in the deaths of two of them, as well as that of his father. His livelihood (the inn) has been smashed, and his thirst for adventure – and treasure – has been aroused. Six chapters further on, and Jim is faced with the awareness that the 'adventure' is a nightmare that will almost certainly end in torture, degradation and death.

In *adventure* terms, the way the story works through and on Jim Hawkins is vital. Everything (except three chapters necessarily told by Dr Livesey) happens to him. But because of his character – a magic mixture of naivety, intelligence, stupidity, impatience, modesty and self-congratulation – it also usually happens *because* of him. A good example is the sequence of events that forms Part Five: Jim's 'Sea Adventure'. After the bloody and terrifying attack on the stockade is over, Jim – like the mere boy he is – gets fed up and goes walkabout. This utterly stupid action quickly runs away with him and he finds himself cutting free the *Hispaniola*, which is at anchor in the hands of the pirates. In a rush of events totally beyond his control he is forced to kill a man, gets pinned to a mast by a knife in the process, then 'escapes' back to the stockade only to walk into the arms of the enemy. Like almost every other twist in the narrative (and there are plenty more to come, well after the point where most writers would have begun to cruise towards their conclusion) it is entirely organic, entirely uncontrived.

It is the organic nature of the narrative, the fact that it is a natural progression of events which come about through the actions of the characters, that lifts Stevenson's story into far more complex areas of success than as a mere adventure. For what he did was to write a book about a child, ostensibly for children, which utterly refuses to fudge the issues raised by its basic situation. The hero is young, but nothing that happens is allowed to be softened by this fact. *Treasure Island* is the story of a child in a world not just of adults, but of totally ruthless, indeed mentally crippled, adults. And Stevenson was prepared to stare this fact in the face.

The violence of this world is at first handled with subtlety. Horrible as Bones and Pew are, they are kept firmly in check. You marvel at their nastiness, but you are not made to fear it; it is nastiness at a remove. But as soon as Jim is on the island, his escape routes cut off, Stevenson drives home his point. It is a hammer-blow; a stark and startling revelation of just what the expedition means and where it will all quite possibly end.

The revelation comes – as it must to achieve its complex effect – through the agency of the real giant of the book, John Silver. From the moment we have met him, we have been seduced. Like Squire Trelawney, like Dr Livesey, like young Jim, we love him. Here, the brilliance of Stevenson's writing is amazing – because we have been told time and again (as has Jim) that Silver is a villain. He himself has even stated, without equivocation, that when the time comes for the mutineers to rise, his 'vote' (for the others) is death, and that he will personally tear Trelawney's 'calf's head off his body with these hands'. His charisma, strangely, is undiminished.

It is Silver, then, who strikes 'the first blow'. He is trying to persuade a loyal man called Tom to join the pirates. Jim is watching from a bush, and all three of them hear the death cries of another 'loyal' who is being killed elsewhere. At this Tom, in disgust, bravely turns his back on Silver and storms off.

> But he was not destined to go far. With a cry, John seized
> the branch of a tree, whipped the crutch out of his armpit,
> and sent that uncouth missile hurtling through the air. It
> struck poor Tom point foremost, and with stunning
> violence, right between the shoulders in the middle of his
> back. His hands flew up, he gave a sort of gasp, and fell.

Then, before Jim's horrified eyes, Silver leaps on to the man and – panting – stabs him to death.

From this moment forward, the violence and villainy accelerate. In one extraordinary sequence, Hawkins has a philosophical conversation with Israel Hands, the ship's coxswain whom he is soon to kill, in which he says that dead people, he believes, live on in another world. Hands replies: 'Well, that's unfort'nate – appears as if killing parties was a waste of time.' Right until the very end, too, Silver seeks the greatest success for himself alone, and is prepared to murder anyone, including Jim, to achieve it. The death toll, in fact, is amazing.

Because Jim is narrator, and because Jim is a child, the other strand of moral viciousness in the story goes unremarked. But it is there, and it is not deeply buried. This is the undercurrent of greed that motivates the 'good' camp. Almost at the beginning Jim notes that his mother has risked their lives through greed, and he reflects, as narrator, on the stupidity and stubbornness of Squire Trelawney. Even more fascinating, perhaps, is the background which Stevenson (a Scot) gave to Livesey (one of the very 'best' of the 'good' characters): 'I was not new to violent death,' the doctor tells us. 'I have served his Royal Highness the Duke of Cumberland.' Livesey, in fact, served the butcher of the Scots.

It is a chilling point, but not one that should be made too much of. Stevenson was certainly aware of the moral ambiguities in his story and characters, but far more importantly he was prepared to write about the evil in mankind in its most naked manifestations. He was writing about a time in which a boy could quite easily have become enmeshed in such a situation, and he wanted him to survive it. But it is worth remembering that Jim alone of the characters is never deeply interested in the treasure. From the moment the island is sighted he hates it, and at the end he has nightmares about a place that 'oxen and wainropes' would not drag him back to. He does not even bother to mention how he used his share of the loot.

Jim saves the adults in his camp, and they in turn recover the treasure, through a series of adventures that are extremely exciting. But the process is hardly a romp, and it is certainly not a game. At the end, seventeen men have died, many of them horribly and in full view, a charismatic mass-murderer has been allowed to escape, and a boy has had his taste for adventure shattered. As to the treasure itself, Jim writes:

> How many [lives] it had cost in the amassing, what blood and sorrow . . . what shame and lies and cruelty, perhaps no man alive could tell.

It is a strange feeling to be left with at the end of a 'good pirate yarn'.

One must never forget, though, that the extraordinary success of *Treasure Island*, its many levels and moral complexities, are a product, first and foremost, of the fact that it *is* a rattling good yarn. It has a superb story, and a host of brilliantly achieved characters (even minor ones, like Ben Gunn, Hands, Pew, and so on, are vivid with life) who are totally at one with it. For a reader, that's a lot to be thankful for. For a writer, it's a lot to try to achieve!

BfK 11
November 1981

I first met *The Wind in the Willows* in primary school, when I was nine. Our teacher was a severe, yet kind and enlightened, maiden lady called Miss Annie Cox. Every Friday afternoon she used to read aloud to us from a children's classic. We had some say in her choice of books, for she would suggest a title and we could either approve or veto it. None of us had ever read any of the books beforehand – ours wasn't that kind of district – but we applied a simple test: did the title promise plenty of action? We firmly rejected *Little Women* and *A Little Princess*, which we were sure would be soppy, but we all voted in favour of *The Jungle Book* and *Treasure Island* . . .

(John Rowe Townsend, 'The Best Bargain I Ever Made', in *BfK* 17, November 1982)

JAMES RIORDAN ASKS

Where Have All the Folk Heroines Gone?

MOST FOLK AND FAIRY TALES are about boys, men and male adventures. In the major fairy-tale collections, the ratio of titles featuring males to those featuring females is as follows: 81:25 in the Grimms, with six mixed (though the male always comes first); 65:22 in Jacobs' collection of British fairy tales; 34:16 in Andersen; and 17:1 in Lang's version of the *Arabian Nights*.

When females do feature in the tales, they often play insignificant, passive roles, or are portrayed as evil, ugly temptresses. Loving, watching, serving or hatching evil are the main activities permitted to women in fairy tales. In the Grimm tales, for example, 80 per cent of the negative characters are female.

So what? Surely no one takes fairy tales seriously? Or do they? There is plenty of evidence to show that children learn a great deal about the world through stories, about what is expected of children of their age, and what they can and ought to be when they grow up. Fairy tales play an especially important part in the early development of ideas simply because of their immense popularity. They are read and told over and over again to children in the process of developing their own identity and future expectations by teachers and parents whom they trust above all others; and they are usually the first stories and films that children come into contact with.

And what do the stories say? That girls are not very important or positive characters, that females are empty creatures who do less exciting, less varied, less independent, and less intelligent things than males. Even heroines like Cinderella, Sleeping Beauty and Snow White remain subservient females –

prizes for male adventure. Females serve, males lead; and, the fairy tales imply, the former cannot exist without the latter.

The irony of fairy tales is that, although the main collectors were professional men, the original storytellers were mostly women – and humble, working women at that. Charles Perrault called his tales *contes de vieilles* (old wives' tales). They came from ordinary people, such as children's nurses, farming women, servants and village sages who themselves often led active and robust lives. The *Arabian Nights*, it may be recalled, are recounted by a woman, Shaharazade, and during research into their origins I was surprised to find as many heroines as heroes.

When such fairy tales came to be recorded, published and 'mass-marketed', mainly in the last century, however, they were fitted to polite society's prevailing ideology, including the contemporary view of women. The published collections of fairy tales were originally intended for the literate; the values and aspirations presented were therefore those of the middle class. And when they came to be extended to the common people (after the 1870 Education Act) they naturally bore the dominant values of thrift, hard work, acquisitiveness and rugged individualism, as well as censorious attitudes to drink, gambling and sexual promiscuity (by women). Since there was virtually no call for educated Victorian girls to earn a living, they were expected to marry early and set their sights firmly on the domestic hearth. So it was in a girl's interest to make herself an attractive marriage proposition by acquiring certain social graces while still a child – singing, dancing, music, embroidery, pretty manners. And the prescribed feminine attributes had to be displayed: females were to be wan, decorative, quiet, gentle, neat and tidy, fearful, and helpful to the male.

On the other hand, the acceptable Victorian image to fit educated males for their roles as captains of industry and Empire was quite different from ideals of femininity: boys had to be daring, vigorous, courageous, energetic, masterful, wild, unemotional and naughty (though not rebellious). The concept of a double standard of morality condoned sexual promiscuity in men as a display of 'masculinity' and male aggression, whilst condemning it in women as a sign of 'unfeminine', shameful behaviour. The princes of fairy tales, as of real life, could therefore sow their wild oats, while their blushing brides had to be delivered up pure and unsullied. Fairy tales were thus adapted and selected by their collectors and publishers to reflect the prevailing mores of an industrial ruling class establishing its power over the rest of society.

While social conditions down the ages have demeaned females, making them mere handservants of the man, fairy tales are fiction; as such *they do not have to* reproduce injustice and inequality. Those who tell the tales today have the opportunity, the duty even, to select tales and images that can help to counteract centuries of literary abuse of the female sex. They can provide girls with all manner of exciting models, thereby helping to combat deep-rooted prejudices fostered by the much-read tales.

Such fairy tales are not easy to come by after so much neglect. *But they are there.* I have found plenty in our own heritage of folk tales from around the British Isles. Typically, the tales of the British people contain no splendid palaces or pretty, elegant fairies; no handsome princes and aspiring peasant brides; no wicked stepmothers and ugly sisters; no noble knights and decorative *belles dames* waiting to be saved. Everything is popular and from the familiar lore of these islands. Heroines and heroes are as wild, unkempt, simple, hardworking and superstitious as they probably were in fact. And bold heroines are about the land, from Cornwall's Cherry of Zennor to Wales's Maid of Llyn y Fan Fach, from East Anglia's Cap o' Rushes and Mary Who Were Afeard o' Nothin' to the Lancashire Witches, from Yorkshire's Old Mother Shipton to Lincolnshire's *Pottle of Brains*; but especially in Scotland: *The Black Bull of Norroway* (where the heroine has adventures in search of her beloved and awakens him with a kiss, unlike the French Sleeping Beauty or the German Snow White), Kate Krakernuts, Mollie Whuppie and *The Well at World's End*. Here are heroines in plenty to stir the heart and blur the eye, even curdle the blood.

Beyond our shores, the abiding matriarchal influence is readily apparent even today in East European folk tales. Slav tales, for example, feature the Frog Princess, not Frog Prince, the ubiquitous Vixen (Liza) rather than the Western Fox (Reynard), the adventurous heroine of the Bohemian Twelve Months or the Russian Fenist the Falcon, with her helpful, and often beautiful, Baba Yagás (witches).

But it is not only a matter of locating forgotten tales; it is necessary to trace back and locate stories in their original versions – before they were subverted by men's fear of and lust for women's power as observers and instruments of life and death. Let me illustrate. In my researches into original *Arabian Nights* stories, I was not surprised to find the oft-quoted lines from Prince Camaralzaman and Princess Budoor as spoken by the misogynist Prince:

> If you ask my mind of women
> I will tell you; I know them well.
> When a man's head is grey and his wealth declines,
> Their love will turn to scorn.

And further,

> With their fingers dyed with henna
> And their hair arranged in plaits,
> With their painted lids and honeyed lips
> They trap unwary men in the web they spin
> And suck out his life's blood until he is dry.

Among all the modern versions of the tales, only dear old Sir Richard Burton permits the Princess to respond in kind as she does in the original fifteenth-century version:

> Men are vain and cruel
> And cannot love one wife alone.

And then,

> Beware of men, for they will force you to obey.
> The maid will not prosper who gives men their rein.
> They will close her mind to life and science,
> For they fear above all the liberation of her mind.

Why have so many male collectors ignored these lines?

There *is* a small number of collectors who have set out to

redress the balance: Alison Lurie (*Clever Gretchen and Other Forgotten Folktales* – Heinemann), Ethel Johnson Phelps (*The Maid of the North and Other Folk Tale Heroines* – Henry Holt) and Jay Williams (*The Practical Princess and Other Liberating Fairy Tales* – Chatto). It is an interesting comment on British publishing that the response from two publishers to my own unpublished collection of 'feminist' folk tales was that it might 'upset parents and librarians more used to traditional images'! All the same, the challenge is there to those authors and publishers who wish to take it up. And take it up we must, for the price of rigidity in sex roles portrayed in folk and fairy tales is paid by males as well as females. Boys are equally constrained by the need to be strong, brave and clever, fearing to express themselves emotionally, to take on and enjoy roles defined as 'feminine'. The oppression and exploitation of one sex inevitably inhibits the fulfilment of human potential in the other. Fairy tales can and should encourage the imagination and creativity of all children . . . at the expense of none.

BfK 16
September 1982

> When things go well, Anansi is a man, but when he is in great danger, he becomes a spider, safe in his web high up on the ceiling and often called 'Ceiling Thomas'. Brer Anansi usually manages to triumph over the bigger and stronger animals by using his wits. The stories poke fun at human failings such as greed, selfishness and vanity, and at the very individual characters of the animals themselves. During slavery times, the Anansi stories were as much part of the ethics of life as the control of the masters, showing the weak and small outmanoeuvring the mighty so that the flame of hope was constantly rekindled in the slaves . . .
>
> (Judith Elkin, 'Traditional Tales in a Multi-Cultural Society', in *BfK 20*, May 1983)

Most folk tales are set in a timeless time, but some – usually known as 'historical tales' – take place at a specific moment and in a specific locality. I'm thinking of stories such as 'Dick Whittington' and 'The Pedlar of Swaffham' in which a piece of verifiable historical grit is clothed in fantastic pearl. We know, after all, that there was an historical character called Richard Whittington. He came from Gloucestershire, and was three times Lord Mayor of London, but how on earth did he get mixed up with a wealth-giving cat?

Stories like these seem to call out for full period costume, and that is what I have sometimes given them: an historical setting with much more attention to the details of day-to-day life than one finds in stories collected from the oral tradition. In retelling tales in this quite leisurely (up to 5000 or 6000 words) way, I am recognising that while I write my tales with keen awareness of how they will sound, and in the hope that they will be shared by parent or grandparent and child, they are firstly literary compositions.

(Kevin Crossley-Holland, 'Restraints and Possibilities', in *BfK 65*, November 1990)

Hans Christian Andersen

ERIK HAUGAARD writes
about a unique and
original storyteller

'MY LIFE HAS BEEN a beautiful fairy tale, rich and happy.' With these words Andersen described his own life. He was born amidst the squalor which you can find today only in the poverty-stricken villages of the Third World. His father was a journeyman shoemaker who patched the shoes of those so poor that they often could not pay him. His mother was a washerwoman who stood in the cold river washing the clothes of others. But in the fairy tale it is often the poorest of boys who marries the princess! In the fairy tale, good fortune can be the lot of those born the meanest. At the end of *The Ugly Duckling* Andersen says: 'It does not matter that one has been born in the henyard as long as one has lain in a swan's egg.' Even as a small child Andersen believed that he was different, not like other children, and it was true – he had lain in a swan's egg.

Many people took an interest in the extraordinary child, but most thought that learning a trade was enough of an advancement for the washerwoman's son. Little Hans Christian did not agree; in the fairy tale of his life there was no room for his becoming a tailor or a carpenter.

Fourteen years old, with little money in his pocket, he set out from his native town of Odense for Copenhagen. True to the heroes of romance and the fairy tale, the goal he sought was fame. Foolish perhaps, but had his ambition been less, he would never have succeeded. It was that very fever of ambition burning within him which made people help him, even, as in a fairy tale, the King of Denmark.

But ambition was not enough; hard work and – terribly important – the ability to overcome defeat and not to be destroyed by it were necessary too. The latter was the hardest, for almost any criticism of his work reduced Andersen to tears. As a child he had described the poet's lot in these words: 'First you suffer so terribly, and then you become famous.' He was to achieve fame, but he was also to learn that suffering did not stop because of this.

Cameo of Hans Christian Andersen

He was thirty years old when the first little pamphlet appeared containing five fairy tales, among them *The Tinder-box*, *Little Claus and Big Claus* and *Thumbelina*. He had already written plays, poetry and novels, but it was his fairy tales which would attain for Andersen the success he had dreamt of when he was a little barefoot urchin in Odense.

The first fairy tales were written 'for children in such a manner that adults could listen to them as well'. (I wish that this sentence would be kept in mind by all authors who write for children.) The later fairy tales and stories were composed 'for adults but written in such a manner that children could listen to them as well'.

In an Andersen story, Dame Fairy Tale herself appears and says: 'One ought to call everything by its right name, and if one doesn't dare to do it in everyday life, then at least one should do it in a fairy tale.' This may sound like nonsense to those who believe that such tales are merely idle rubbish created to amuse children. True, the fairy tale contains plenty of fantasy, witches, giants and evil dwarfs but its backbone is reality, truth. The purpose of the fairy tale is to express something which needs to be told in such a manner that it will be heard.

During the German occupation of Denmark, an actor decided to read in public a story by Andersen called *The Evil King*. The Nazis had no doubt about whom the evil king was supposed to portray, and the actor found himself in jail. The little fairy tale had contained enough truth to offend the despot.

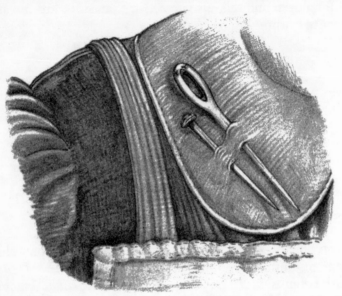

Illustration by Michael Foreman from *Hans Andersen: His Classic Fairy Tales*

In fairy tales, animals are often given speech but that inanimate objects – such as darning needles, collars or an iron – also possess a soul is, I believe, Andersen's own discovery. He made them speak with human voices about their experience as objects. The darning needle has only the memory of a needle and the ambitions of such a humble tool. He deals in a similar manner with animals: a duck does not question that fatness is beauty any more than a rat would question that a larder is para-dise. They have desires and are frustrated when they cannot fulfil them, but their desires are reasonable for their kind. Therefore, they are at times tragic and sometimes funny, but they are never sweet and sentimentalised.

Like many authors in the nineteenth century, Andersen was

fascinated by science and technology. In 1850 he foresaw that travel by air would eventually surpass other forms of transportation. In one little sketch, he has the future citizens of America who are visiting the 'old countries' clutch in their hands the best-seller of the day – *Europe Seen in Eight Days*.

But it still came as a surprise to me, when I translated a fairy tale called *The Philosopher's Stone*, to find that he had an opinion about children and television as well. In that tale 'the wisest man in the world' lives in a castle where, in one of the lower chambers, is a room with glass walls which mirror the whole world and enable him to see what is happening everywhere. 'The pictures on the walls were alive and moving; they showed everything that was taking place, no matter where it was happening; all one had to have were the time and desire to look.' The wise man did not even bother to glance at the pictures, but he had children who did! They were very fond of spending their time in this room in the castle. Then their father would sigh and say to them: 'The ways of the world are bitter and filled with grief. What you see is not reality, for you watch it from the safe world of childhood and that makes all the difference.' Indeed it does; reality and what appears on the TV screen are not the same, for you are merely seeing it, not participating in and experiencing what is being shown.

Books written for children are relatively new, only a couple of hundred years old, and the fairy tale is much older than that. It is probably the most ancient form of literature, but just because it was a little late in being written down this might be hard to prove. But does the fairy tale have anything to say to the modern child? After all, the world has changed; grandmother, who used to tell such tales, is no longer sitting in the chimney corner.

The literature which amuses the child of today is derived from the fairy tale. Science fiction deals, if not with witches and giants, with archetypes; it is a member of the family though not quite a respectable one. Are Professor Tolkien's books not fairy tales? I believe that the fairy tale fills a need in a child's life, and only if that need ceases to be will the fairy tale vanish. We grown-ups often forget what it was like to be a child. If you recall your childhood, you will become aware how much its world resembled the fairy tale's. Good fairies could appear suddenly and save you, just as ogres could pop up too. Sometimes persons whom you loved and knew well – like your own mother – could be the good fairy and a witch almost at the same time. The wonderful and the horrible were never far apart, and so much that happened was, like magic, past understanding.

The child conceives of its world as surrounded by a wall containing a gate which leads to the much larger world of the adults. Through that gate he will have to pass, and the child both longs for and is frightened by this. In the land of grown-ups, things may be acquired by a mere act of will, whereas a child can only wish for things. How fervently one could wish then! The gift of three wishes which the good fairy often bestowed on the hero of the fairy tale was meaningful when one was a child.

If children like fairy tales because they resemble their own world and portray their situation, why do adults like them too? I think it is because the fairy tale deals in archetypes: it is a world of good and evil without those embarrassing shades in between. Good triumphs and evil is summarily punished. This is refreshing in a world as sophisticated as ours, and it is pleasant to return through the gate to the land of one's childhood. But suddenly one can sometimes wonder if the fairy tale is not closer to the truth than all the books one has ploughed through since one was deemed a grown-up. Are evil and good relative, or are they absolute as in a fairy tale? Those who perished in the concentration camps of Nazi Germany and Siberia would probably have tended to agree with the fairy tale.

'Once upon a time' is no time, just as east of the sun and west of the moon, or the end of the world, is no place. In reality, however, it means 'at all times, in all places'. It is a declaration announcing that what you are going to hear is the truth – both in time and in space. And everyone, be he king or beggar, needs to hear the truth once in a while at least, and that is why I most fervently hope that the fairy tale will always be with us.

BfK 25
March 1984

Fortune gave me two cards. Firstly, it happened that my little charge, a sweet and biddable child, with the currently popular name of Alice, has a close resemblance to the little Alice Liddell whose photograph ends the recently published facsimile edition of the first draft of the tale, 'Alice's Adventures under Ground'. Her hair, which is dark brown (unlike the fair-haired girl of Mr Tenniel's pictures), is cut in the same way, fairly short with a fringe over her forehead. Secondly, I lately acquired a sympathetic friend, a Miss Gertrude Thomson, whose drawings of children have made her both friend and assistant to Mr Carroll, as I shall call him here. She informed me where he usually took his afternoon walk, and so it chanced that he came face to face with little Alice and myself, also taking a stroll . . .

(Naomi Lewis, 'Authorgraph of Lewis Carroll', in *BfK 71*, November 1991)

To mark the sixtieth anniversary of the first appearance of A A Milne's famous bear, CHRIS POWLING offers an essay

On the Permanence of Pooh

WHEN DID YOU last play Pooh-sticks?

As you'll recall, it's not a complicated game. All you need is a bridge, a handful of twigs and a river whose speed-of-flow urgently requires testing. After this, Nature can safely be left to take its course. Like conkers, pillow-fights and seashore pebbles flat enough for skimming, Pooh-sticks brings about a response so obvious nobody has ever spelled out the rules in any detail. Literary historians, however, being bores of little brain, may try to tell you it was invented by A A Milne and cite chapter and verse (or hum) to prove it. Well, that's their story. His story is rather better. It simply documents a phenomenon that's timeless and universal. Pooh-sticks has *always* existed.

Like Pooh himself, of course. Or Piglet. Or Rabbit. Or Owl. Or Kanga. Or Roo. Or Tigger.

What?

Oh yes. Or Eeyore.

Who, except on purpose to establish essential Eeyore-ness, could possibly forget Eeyore? Haven't we known him, or someone exactly like him, all our lives? For the Pooh books introduce us to what's already perfectly familiar, that's all. Well, almost all. The permanence of Pooh is certainly rooted in recognition-at-first-sight, but it's the freshness built into every subsequent encounter by sheer literary craftsmanship which keeps us hooked. Take this, for instance:

Illustration by E H Shepard of Pooh and Christopher Robin playing Pooh-sticks

> Before he knew where he was, Piglet was in the bath, and Kanga was scrubbing him firmly with a large, lathery flannel.
> 'Ow!' cried Piglet. 'Let me out! I'm Piglet!'
> 'Don't open the mouth, dear, or the soap goes in,' said Kanga. 'There! What did I tell you?'

All the Pooh stories have this luminous what-did-I-tell-you quality. They're a celebration of the obvious made suddenly less blinding. Yet, over and over again, the revelation is kept sharp by the author's verbal deftness.

Of course, as the years go by we have to work a little harder at the text. Time casts a stumbling block or two into the passage of most books and Pooh is no exception. The biggest obstacle here, undeniably, is Christopher Robin.

Was there ever a more insufferable child than Christopher Robin?

Every inch of him exudes smugness – from the top of that curious bobbed haircut to the tip of those tiny-tot sandals (and the smock and shorts in between are just as irritating). Okay, so we shouldn't take him at face value. Maybe there *is* deep irony in this twentieth-century version of the Victorian Beautiful Child. In Christopher Robin's case, however, we must certainly heed the wise advice of Oscar Wilde that it's only a superficial person who does *not* judge by appearances. With Milne's prose reinforced by E H Shepard's superb line-drawings, Christopher Robin must surely be just what he seems. And what he seems is a serious affront to anyone who believes children are simply people who haven't lived very long. My favourite literary fantasy is a confrontation between Pooh's celebrated owner and that alternative emblem of childhood, the hardly less celebrated William Brown – amazingly in fact and fiction, some half-dozen years the elder. The outcome, as satisfying as it is pre-dictable, might be summarised thus:

'How did you fall in, Christopher Robin?' asked Rabbit, as he dried him with Piglet's handkerchief.
'I didn't,' said Christopher Robin.
'But how –'
'I was BOUNCED,' said Christopher Robin.
'Oo,' said Roo, excitedly, 'Did somebody push you?'
'Somebody BOUNCED me. I was just thinking by the side of the river – thinking, if any of you know what that means – when I received a loud BOUNCE.'
'Oh, Christopher Robin!' said everybody.

Actually, they said it to Eeyore, but few adults today won't relish my substitution.

Today's children, on the other hand, would probably wonder why I'm making such a fuss. Like Heffalumps and North Pole Expositions and Crustimoney Proseedcake and the 'useful pot to put things in' which grown-up critics now shrink from for fear of seeming to endorse nostalgia, Christopher Robin now-adays is self-evidently a period-piece – part of a continuing costume drama of no greater handicap than the Eton collars and gob-stoppers and dinner-gongs in the early William stories. What still counts for youngsters, in my experience, is what should count for us: the toy-animals who are almost people. They're far more important than the twee human who is nowhere near a child.

And it's not hard to see why. That 'almost' is crucial. For Pooh and company are magnificently full-of-life only so far as *comedy* allows. They don't grow, for example. That's not their function. To grumble, as a recent critic has done, that 'the narrative derives . . . from the conjunction and opposition of known qualities. No one, not even the comparatively imaginative Pooh, changes or develops' is to miss the point by a mile. The same is true of William, Henry, Douglas and Ginger, over the course of three hundred or more Richmal Crompton stories. The known qualities deployed by comedy are static because the pain of being otherwise would foul up the plot. Children are free to laugh at what happens to Eeyore precisely because they recognise at once there's no need to feel sorry for him: he's so good at feeling sorry for himself. None better, in fact – just as Rabbit's bossiness can't be topped, nor Piglet's timidity, nor Tigger's bounce, nor Owl's pomposity.

Hence attention can be focussed right where Milne wants it – on a series of the most gentle come-uppances ever devised: 'There! What did I tell you?'

The permanence of the Pooh books, then, has nothing whatsoever to do with their psychological depth or the sharpness of their social comment or their status as morality. These don't matter a jot. What's important, through and through, is their success as storytelling. And this is a triumph. It survives shifts in fashion. It survives Christopher Robin. It even survives that odd tone of voice which, for all Milne's simple language, never quite settles for a child audience. The world Pooh creates is completely unique and utterly self-sustaining. Yes, it is a world that's very like ours . . . but much, much more like itself.

A Proliferation of Pooh

Winnie-the-Pooh first appeared in print in 1926 in the book which bears (sorry!) his name. Two years later came the second set of stories about Christopher Robin and his friends, *The House at Pooh Corner*. Those two books, discounting isolated and disguised brief appearances in verse in *When We Were Very Young* and *Now We Are Six*, are the sum total of Milne-created

Pooh literature. This year Pooh, in publishing terms, is sixty. Birthday parties and bear rallies have been held across the country, Pooh has been presented with an OAP bus pass and been featured on the Nine O'Clock News: hype on a scale that could only be mounted on the back of a national institution. Those two modest books with their charming black and white Shepard illustrations are still in print. So also are over fifty other 'Pooh books' on the Methuen and Magnet lists.

You can have the stories themselves in hardback or paperback, full colour or black and white, collected or selected, mixed or singly, miniaturised, boxed or packaged, in English or Latin. And then you can have all the spin-offs: 'inspired by', 'based on', 'in the style of', 'after the style of'. There are two pop-up books 'after the style of E H Shepard'. A very long way after! And with extracts from Milne's original text edited to near nonsense. There's an alphabet book, a counting book, board books with new titles (*Pooh's Rainy Day*), a painting book, a song book, a craft book, a recorder book and no less than *four* cookery books (a bit tactless to put the risotto with bacon in Piglet's section of *The Pooh Corner Cookbook*).

You can have a Pooh frieze, or Pooh posters, a Pooh address book or birthday book. You can even get philosophical with *The Tao of Pooh* or tone up your muscles with *Pooh's Workout Book*, paperbacked this year because Now We Are Sixty. Apart from a few extracts from the genuine Milne, the entire text of this last paperback is written by Ethan Mordden after the style of A A Milne – and if you want convincing that there is more to Milne's deceptively simple style than meets the eye, read Ethan Mordden.

Specially for the birthday/Christmas season are some new publications. *The Winnie-the-Pooh Journal*, a book of lined pages each headed with a Pooh quotation 'For Writing Your Special Thoughts in Your Own Words'; four *Pooh Sticker Books*, containing a story and four pages of reusable self-adhesive stickers to move around the pages; and *The Pooh Book of Quotations*, compiled by Brian Sibley, which should find a place on the bookshelf in anybody's loo.

A special award to Methuen for making a little go a very long way! And that's not saying anything about the Disney versions of Pooh – which is probably the best thing to do with them. Except to repeat the story of Suzanne told by Liz Waterland in the latest issue of *Signal* (No. 51). Suzanne was watching the Disney *Winnie-the-Pooh and the Honey Tree*. 'Halfway through she turned to her mother in indignation. "That's not what really happened," she exclaimed. "That's not *true*." "What did really happen? What is true?" her mother asked. "The book, the book is," said Suzanne. "The book's true. *I* know what happened. We read it."'

Pooh, confused by all this Proliferation, may well be cheering.

BfK 41
November 1986

These classic stories have been presented in so many different ways since Kipling wrote them, but Ian Richardson's reading must be one of the most faithful and evocative. His voice is rich in tempo and modulation, absorbing the listener into Mowgli's jungle world. His narrative voice is leisurely, lyrical and deep, drawing out Kipling's poetry, or dramatic and fast when the action demands. His character voices range from Mowgli's high-pitched, man-cub's voice to the roars of the Tiger and the threatening, measured tones of the Panther. This is a writer whose appeal to today's children is widened through abridgement.

(Rachel Redford reviewing an audiotape of *The Jungle Book Stories* in *BfK 63*, July 1990)

Kenneth Grahame once wrote, 'What the Boy chiefly dabbled in was natural history and fairy tales and he just took them as they came, in a sandwichy sort of way, without any distinctions; and really his course of reading strikes me as rather sensible.' I agree. The 'classics' should be tossed to children as interesting food to be sampled not virtuously but as sandwiches whose fillings must surprise them.

(Margery Fisher, 'Surprise Sandwiches', in *BfK 71*, November 1991)

The Limits of Delight

MARGARET MEEK

Must we love 'great' books? Should the acknowledged quality of text preclude personal dislike? BfK launches an occasional series in which established figures in the children's book world admit to . . . well, a blind spot. We begin with one of the most celebrated of all children's classics, The Wind in the Willows

MY LONG-DRAWN-OUT unease about *The Wind in the Willows* stems from the same roots as the pleasure of more discerning readers. Those who tell me they like the book, and many genuinely love it, praise the very features of it which give me a frisson of mild disgust. The prejudices which survive my every re-reading (I try hard, once a decade) reveal the boundaries of my conscious awareness of reading as *desire*. So, let me confront the limits of my delight in books for children, remembering always that both author and reader are subject to the laws of the unconscious, where time doesn't exist.

Bordering the garden of the house where I lived until I was twelve was a small but fast-moving stream – a 'burn' in my dialect. To play on the bank was forbidden, therefore always attractive. In summer, when the water level was lower, crawling along the branches of an overhanging elder and catching minnows in jam jars were tolerated activities. Raucously bad-tempered ducks sometimes appeared, but for the most part the burn belonged to skinny, slimy boot-button-eyed water rats who

darted and scrambled out of holes with noises like soup-slurp-
ing. I was fascinated and appalled. I recall the nauseous horror
of their presence in a second. I cannot love a rat, nor can I imagine one as the wise, tolerant, poetry-writing, picnic-provisioning
hero of this particular arcadian novel.

Perhaps I could have grown into a tolerance of the bizarre
behaviours, the language and snobbery of Rat, Mole, Badger
and Toad had I met them in the early days when I enjoyed the
naughtiness of Peter Rabbit, the bad temper of Squirrel Nutkin,
and the vague menace of Mrs Tiggy-Winkle. Or, when, as an
adult, I first admired the matter-of-factness of *Charlotte's Web*,
and the fabulation of *The Sheep Pig*, I should have taken the
trouble to understand more of the late adolescent boy's attachment to Toad, Winnie the Pooh and the Hobbit. I *could* have
found my way into the world of the River Bank and the Wild
Wood if I'd followed Jan Needle's retelling of the tale as a social
satire, but none of these options takes away my feelings of utter
exclusion from this fictive universe. True, I was reading boys'
comics and Elinor Brent-Dyer when the librarian offered me a
fine, clearly unread copy of *The Wind in the Willows* as a special treat. But it was already too late. Not even the enchantment
of Ernest Shepard's drawings could entice me into that world. I
knew exactly how Badger in his long dressing-gown and down-
at-heel slippers would smell. At no time did I want any of that
male company; it represented too many kinds of social exclu-
sions. Three bachelors of a certain (or rather, uncertain) age,
free from any real responsibilities, spending their days messing
about in boats, and gossiping about the intolerable social habits
of Toad whom they consider to be their friend just made me
embarrassed. I knew what boys did in corners. They formed
exclusive clubs, discussed girls whom they looked at sideways
without turning round, and taught each other how to exploit
the superiority they recognised as theirs by right.

The world of the River Bank is a men's club, with Fortnum
and Mason picnics for luncheon, and suppers in warm kitchens
underground without the problems of shopping or washing up.
When the Otter child goes missing, his father 'lonely and heart-
sore' watches by the ford where he taught the little one to swim.
Mrs Otter appears only as the 'they' of 'the Otters' who insisted Rat should stay to supper, and 'keep it up late with his old

comrade'. To believe in the artistic success of *The Wind in the Willows*, one has to enter this enchanted circle of friends. Grahame's careful, devoted biographer, Peter Green, and his most important and discerning apologist, Humphrey Carpenter, do this well.

So my readings of *The Wind in the Willows* are those of a pagan, an outsider. I can't believe in the Piper at the Gates of Dawn, but I have learned a great deal about the embarrassment suffered by agnostics. The more I read about Grahame as a person, the more I see in this text the psyche of its author. The words open up an adult's longing to be a child granted an adult's freedom to do what he likes.

As for the famed humour of Toad's adventures, they are more irresponsible than funny. Most enthusiasts don't recollect the details of the text, but remember well-staged versions of *Toad of Toad Hall*. When John Betjeman explored, on television, the delights of going up the Thames Valley by rail, I caught a glimpse of irony and nostalgia that reminded me of Toad's social upstartness. But I'm not enticed by any commentator's attempt to turn the story into an allegory or social fable. It hasn't the required depth. So Toad remains a creature of stagey pranks (what my parents called 'carrying on'), which seem now a kind of *fin de siècle* buffoonery, like charades. I wonder if the laughter they provoke is ever less than caustic. Far from sustaining the illusion of an animal world that is preferable to that of humans, or even of one that, post Aesop, judges our frailties, Toad simply highlights his creator's ambivalences about the relations of animals and people. He is a pantomime personality. This is not the case with any of Beatrix Potter's subtler creations. I am never afraid for Toad, but Jemima Puddleduck provokes every scrap of my protective instinct.

My perpetual difficulty is with the actual language of the text, not the quotations, references, allusions, all of which stroke any reader's sensibilities with prideful pleasure at knowing a little Latin, nor yet the 'ornateness and wit' that Humphrey Carpenter says makes it difficult for the young. There's a hollow tone in the way the author handles the implications of social distinctions that is different from Lewis Carroll's steely shots. For example, Rat rummaging in Mole's house for things to eat encourages Mole to explain 'how that was thought out, and how this was got as a windfall from an aunt, and that was a wonderful find and a bargain, and this other thing was bought out of laborious savings and a certain amount of going without'. You can hear the rise and fall exactly, the implication being that Rat's tact made up for Mole's bad taste, when in fact Mole's lack of subtlety is exposed quite cruelly. Grahame knew as well as anyone about these economic devices, but here, as elsewhere, disdain wins out. The sentimental nonsense of the Piper at the Gates of Dawn put me off for years. Compared with any genuine panic in deep Highland forests, this rural deity makes me turn the page to avoid what now comes across in Shepard's illustration and Grahame's text as an advertisement for shampoo. Rat's longing to go south, repressed by Mole's fisticuffs, makes it seem that the author is, in this scene, being too hard on himself. Gauguin had already made such a trip respectable.

My particular interest is in the kind of reading experience *The Wind in the Willows* provides for children who have little contact with Victorian children's books and are outside the charmed circle of the author's friends. Humphrey Carpenter suggests that younger children like the 'story parts' and read the book 'for themselves with *complete enjoyment* [my emphasis] in adolescence'. His case that the River and the Wild Wood are 'more than adequate symbols for the deepest level of the artistic imagination' is, I think, over-generous. The book, as a whole, offers an image of childhood, as does *Peter Pan*, but not a general account of all childhoods. I guess it creates for some readers in each generation, notably those boys of quietist taste who are tentative about growing up, a place of reverie. Grahame was clearly ambivalent about adulthood, so his escape was to revisit this alternative world where he was safe from the responsibilities and demands of the everyday (his wife and his duties at the Bank of England), as he told the stories to his son. The much-vaunted wisdom of the characters is too uncomplicated, so the book is less mature than is often claimed. It also has, for me at least, deep deceits, which careful scholarship may even perpetuate as examples of poetic skill.

Carpenter's view that *The Wind in the Willows* is 'the finest achievement of children's literature up to the date it was written and perhaps afterwards' seems excessive, although by now my limitations as a critic of it are clear. In the small, enclosed, excluding and exclusive world of the River Bank and the Wild Wood, even allowing for Toad's outbreaks and the threat of the ill-mannered weasels, and accepting the mock-heroic endeavours of Rat and his friends to emulate the champions of old, young readers meet a storyteller of distinct verbal felicity, in parts, but of clearly limited range for modern children. The excitement of reading is a dialogue with their future. Here they encounter the author's imagined past. For a time it may prove delightful, even re-creative. But this arcadian world is neither brave nor new; it has too few people in it. To meet them is to encounter the same person, the author, variously disguised as a Rat, a Mole, a Badger and a Toad, all equally egocentric and self-regarding. Pity.

BfK 68
May 1991

What, I wonder, are Puffin's motives in collecting these titles into a new series? Do they presume that young readers wish to add these so-called classics to their collections on a sort of 'yard-of-children's-books' principle? Will it simply work out as an economical proposition due to copyright considerations? Are these books aimed at the doting aunties' and ill-informed grannies' market, who generally like to buy familiar and safe-sounding books for their young relatives?

Given that they have arrived, who will read them? My librarian considers that children (and teachers) have enough on to keep up with newer and perhaps more meaningful books; they do not need to be 'cluttered' (her word) with some of the older titles, especially when not all are strictly children's classics anyway. I personally doubt whether they cannot be matched in style by more modern authors. Most make good stories, but not all so great as to be an indispensable part of literary growth . . .

(David Bennett reviewing *Puffin Classics*, in *BfK* 16, September 1982)

What Makes a Children's Classic?

VICTOR WATSON

I WAS RELIEVED that the question I have to consider is: *What makes a children's classic?* – and not: *What are the children's classics?* On the second question, no two readers would ever agree.

Let's try some definitions. 'Books written by dead people' was suggested by a group of ten-year-olds, but when asked for some examples they suggested *Tom's Midnight Garden*, *The BFG* and *The Snowman*. But their judgement was not as confused as it seems, for they clearly knew that the word 'classic' in its many contexts almost always suggests an excellence surviving from a past age. That's not a bad idea to begin with: a children's classic is a book whose popularity has survived the age in which it was written. And I would add that such a book does not simply endure like a fossil in a glass case, but is constantly re-made and improvised upon so that its qualities and its appeal are transformed and revealed to new generations of readers.

But I know there are doubters who point out that whether a book is continually re-issued has more to do with the economics of publishing than with a serious concern for young readers. For if publishers re-issue attractive books from the past, well-meaning adults can hardly be blamed for buying them.

Take *Alice*, for example. The two stories, *Alice's Adventures in Wonderland* and *Through the Looking-Glass*, were published in 1866 and 1871–2 and they have been in print ever since. Yet it's undoubtedly the case that more copies are purchased by adults than read by children. But children *did* read

Alice in the past. We can generalise from that and suggest that no children's book has become a classic unless it was first enjoyed by a whole generation of young readers. It may be true that the status of the two *Alice* stories as classics is today sustained by adult conviction, but it was established in the first place by the commitment of children.

Our secondhand bookshops are full of the abandoned relics of an age devoted to didacticism upholding the pieties and properties of the Victorian middle classes. Their instructional authority was reinforced by the fact that most of those stories were given as Sunday School prizes. So what a breath of fresh air *Alice* must have brought to those Victorian nurseries! Here was a young heroine who did what little girls were not permitted to do: she spoke her mind *and turned didacticism the other way round*. It is the adults who get corrected and rebuked. In a world of lunacies and cruelties, Alice is brave, forthright and intelligent. *Alice's Adventures in Wonderland* and *Through the Looking-Glass* have been analysed by mathematicians, philosophers, clergymen, Freudian psychologists and literary historians, and their views have helped to confirm the books as enduring children's classics. But they would not have become classics in the first place if the children of the 1860s and 1870s had not taken Alice to their hearts.

Illustrations by Tenniel of Alice

Subsequently the two stories have attracted the imaginative inventiveness of illustrators, from Tenniel and Rackham to – most recently – Anthony Browne. A children's classic is repeatedly brought to life afresh by later artists, not only illustrators but also dramatists and directors of film and television. Stories are made into plays – or, in the case of *Peter Pan and Wendy*, a play is made into a story; or they are made into full-length feature films (*The Railway Children*, *The BFG*, *Danny the Champion of the World*), or adapted and serialised for television (*Tom's Midnight Garden*, *A Little Princess*). A characteristic of the classic children's story is its capacity to offer from within itself new meanings and fresh emphases while retaining its original integrity. I am cautious about proclaiming that too confidently, for I have in mind the example of Beatrix Potter, whose books are like tiny fortresses resisting all attempts to meddle with their self-contained completeness.

I believe our literature is composed of the books we set aside for re-reading. If that's true of individuals, it is probably true of the whole culture. The great children's classics are those books our national consciousness cannot leave alone. We keep remaking them and reading them afresh. While it is certainly true that thousands of British children have not read them, the two *Alice* stories have become part of the language. Children who have never opened the books know about the Mad Hatter's tea-party, the Queen of Hearts and Tweedledum and Tweedledee. All children who have access to the full cultural possibilities of the varieties of language in our country have access to those images, whether they've read the books or not. The classics are part of our national vocabulary – metaphors, perhaps – reverberating in the wider cultural language which we all share (though not equally, more's the pity). Eeyore, with his melancholy burst balloon and empty honeypot, is an *idea*, an enactment of meaning, more subtly dramatic than any abstraction could ever be. And so are Ratty and Mole remonstrating with the impossible Toad; and Wendy and the Lost Children in their underground house; and the foolishly trusting Jemima Puddleduck.

I've tried so far to explain children's books in terms of their popularity and significance to the culture. But have they any recognisable characteristics in common? I believe they have.

Among the thousands of books written for children, there appears now and again one which, through some mysterious alchemy, the author has transformed into a metaphor expressing the ways in which children and adults love one another.

Children's classics are love stories.

Lewis Carroll was the first to do it. His two stories are not simply stories for children, or stories about Alice Liddell; they express and embody his love for her. There is no doubt that he loved her – he told his readers about the effect she still had upon him:

> Still she haunts me, phantom wise,
> Alice moving under skies
> Never seen by waking eyes . . .

Perhaps the stories – especially the second, written when she was no longer a child – were for him a treasuring-up for the future of his memories of her. There is no sentimentalising, just a sustained, witty and affectionate tribute to her good sense, which is at the same time a story – a *gift* – for her.

Every adult who has loved a child understands that the intimacy which can exist between them has within it a potential poignancy. We may set it aside and refuse to think about it, but we know that loving a child is menaced even more than other relationships are by the processes of change. An intimacy with a child is never an equal one because there is an acute difference of understanding: John Burningham's Granpa *knows more* than his granddaughter about the future and its likely outcomes. *Granpa* is a wise book; it arises from that intimate space that an old man and a little girl create between them. For adults, such spaces are beset with expectations of sadness and loss. Furthermore, their inarticulate dynamics can involve fear, nostalgia, longing and perhaps sexuality.

The analysis of these dynamics must be left to psychologists and social historians. But I believe the stories we regard as classics have this in common: they are born out of that sensitive and problematic area of need and longing. They continue to appeal to us because it is an area that is at the heart of family life. Any good novelist, I suppose, could write about it. But a children's classic is not just *about* a love for the child; it is simultaneously a story *for* the child, an acknowledgement and welcoming of the child. The great children's classics are stories for children powered by an adult's sense of loss. They enact the relationships they serve.

Frances Hodgson Burnett's *A Little Princess* is overtly a story about a little girl's courage and generosity in humiliating circumstances. But the scenes which have the greatest emotional power are those when Sara says her last goodbye to her father, and when the Indian Gentleman arrives to restore her father's wealth and reputation, and offer himself as a surrogate. The novel is at a deep level a story of a little girl's loss and recovery of her father – an unlikely series of events but profoundly satisfying. It has a great deal in common with E Nesbit's *The Railway Children.* Here is a tale of trains and tunnels and porters, but what makes an ordinary story into an extraordinary classic is that it's driven by another, deeper story about a daughter rescuing her father. This is a story of passionate wish-fulfilment – and if you think 'passionate' is too strong a word, re-read the chapter in which Bobbie is reunited with her father at the railway station (or watch your video of the film). In just that brief episode, an authorial yearning surfaces and becomes visible.

Illustration by Mabel Lucie Attwell of Peter Pan

Most of the classic tales started as stories for real children. This brings us to *Peter Pan and Wendy, The Wind in the Willows,* the two *Pooh Bear* books, and the tales of Beatrix Potter, and, in the case of J M Barrie and A A Milne, we know that the adult's love for the child was problematical. C S Lewis wrote his books for real children too, but, although they have achieved a cult status, especially in the US, I do not think the *Narnia* books are classics. Despite his undoubted brilliance as a storymaker, Lewis' conception of children is distant and narrow. The perfect union of an adult's love and a storymaker's tact is to be found in the best of the *Swallows and Amazons* stories; Arthur Ransome's affectionate respect for his half-real, half-imagined children is everywhere felt and nowhere proclaimed.

I believe *Tom's Midnight Garden* is a classic. Furthermore, it exemplifies exactly what I believe the great classics have in common. It has no hint of authorial distress, or sadness, but it is a story about old and young, and how their mutual – but different – needs come together in the form of a story. In this narrative, both are participants, though one is more in control than the other. The old woman becomes young again in the storying of her memories – but not perfectly, and not for long. Although Philippa Pearce allows no cheating of the realities of time, in her making of the narrative past, present and future lose their firmness, and the difference of generations is only a difference, not an apartness.

Hattie needs the story because in old age her childhood has come to seem important; Tom knows little of that – he needs the story because he is lonely. In *Tom's Midnight Garden*, it is implicitly acknowledged that the child and the adult regard the story with equal seriousness but from different perspectives. For a child, a story is an inviting signal from further along the road; it satisfies immediate needs and predictive interests. But for the adult who's telling it, a story can never be a sign of what lies ahead. The great classics are written by people who understand that difference, and who know how to write a story which welcomes and respects it without making a fuss.

I believe that the classics are stories which appeal, differently, to both children and adults because they arise out of the love that can exist between them. In the very best – as in Philippa Pearce – the writer's firm authorial tact protects the child-reader from an adult's understanding of time and change. A great classic is simultaneously a joyous greeting and a valediction. *Tom's Midnight Garden* ends with a goodbye.

I know this account leaves many questions unanswered and I

propose to be honest about that. In particular, several of Beatrix Potter's stories are surely classics – but I cannot accommodate them in the account I have tried to give. There are other anomalies too. Is *The Wizard of Oz* a classic? And if your answer is Yes, are you thinking of the book or the film? Can a poem be a classic? Or an anthology? Can a continuing sequence of stories (Rupert Bear?) earn classical status? Can a novel for young adults become a classic? (I think not – they are usually too remorselessly self-conscious and explicit.) Then there are the great novels which were not written especially for children – *Robinson Crusoe, Jane Eyre, David Copperfield, Treasure Island* – what about them? And *Rosie's Walk* is probably as familiar to infants today as the First Chapter of Genesis was in the seventeenth century – is it, or will it become, a classic? I leave you with one more question: Roald Dahl is (after Enid Blyton) the most popular children's writer at present; so which of his novels, if any, do you think deserves to become a classic?

BfK 71
November 1991

Sir Gawain is one of King Arthur's more gallant and romantic knights. This version is a rich introduction to a time-honoured tale. As a rule I avoid adaptations of classics, but this is retold with skill and sensitivity and much of the glory of the original is retained.

The illustrations, in the style of ancient, illuminated manuscripts, are overwhelmingly beautiful; like glowing jewels they vie strongly with the text for first attention and give an air of authenticity. Incidentally, they're a wonderful stimulus for art lessons.

(Pam Harwood reviewing *Sir Gawain and the Green Knight*, retold by Selina Hastings, and illustrated by Juan Wijngaard, in *BfK 71*, November 1991)

PART TWO

Picture Books

A Question of Images

*LISA KOPPER thinking aloud about
'drawing black people'*

MULTI-CULTURAL BOOKS for children are a complex issue. Even
the word 'multi-cultural' rankles. Nobody really knows what
to call anything in this sensitive area – the 'correct' phraseology
is always changing. I'm an illustrator and involved with images
so I'll just call it drawing black people, Indians, East Asians or
whomsoever I am depicting.*

I'm forever being asked two questions about this field of
illustration: Why can't people draw black people and why aren't
there more black illustrators? Now, as the 'multi-cultural' book
becomes a more established part of children's literature, I think
there is a third question: What is the role of white artists and
writers in the production of books about black people?

I'm a white artist but have done a number of books about
people from all parts of the world. I often wonder whether I am
right to do this work when more and more books are being
published but, in percentage terms, fewer and fewer are illustrated by black artists.

When I was first asked in 1979 to illustrate a children's series
about an African child, my response was, 'But don't you really
think a black artist should do this?' The publisher replied, 'We
can't find them.' I did the books (the *Jafta Family* series) and
the experience was wonderful for me; it opened up whole new
worlds literally.

When I consider how my career came to take this direction, it
wasn't really an accident. I was made aware of social issues,
poverty and discrimination, early in life because my parents

*For the purposes of simplicity, I have spoken about black people in this article
but much of what I say also applies to Indians, East Asians and other groups.

were involved with the emerging Civil Rights Movement in the United States. In the late fifties you never saw a black face anywhere in the media; not on TV, not on posters and in only one picture book – and we all know what that was! Later I had a book for older children about a black girl growing up in the South. I remember looking and looking at the small line and wash drawings – they weren't very special but they were the first pictures I'd seen that attempted to portray black people in a sympathetic way.

In the mid-seventies, I did some work for the Anti-Apartheid Movement in this country. Despite my awareness of the bad representations of black people, I found it difficult to draw the kind of image I wanted. It was hard for me to see what was good and what wasn't. The old stereotypes just kept sneaking on to the paper. I decided that I would have to make gradual progress and go for a good 'feeling' before fine drawing as I was having problems with features. I used a lot of silhouette and did my first small book (*Children of Soweto*) in woodcut – strong and effective but without detail.

I started thinking about the kind of difficulties I was experiencing and why I was so uncertain of my images. After all, artists draw many things they don't know intimately – elephants, tigers, outer space . . . It was then that I realised that I, and probably most other children, had learned to draw both familiar and unfamiliar things from looking at pictures. That's how I knew that girls on horses had long flowing hair and they certainly didn't wear glasses or have big noses. But what pictures had I seen of black people? Virtually none. So if children learn to draw and see not so much from life as from other people's drawing, then we were a whole generation grown up on *Little Black Sambo*.

We all learn from our own visual traditions. It's the same for black and white children and worse for black artists in many other parts of the world where our shoddy traditions have replaced their own. Many African illustrators continue to draw themselves in the distorted way they learned from the books we made for them.

When I tackled the *Jafta* series, I was determined to break the pattern of my learned imagery. I decided that my child had to be as beautiful and appealing as I could possibly make him. I

Illustration by Lisa Kopper from *Jafta – The Wedding*

looked at photo after photo, spoke to numerous people from
that part of Africa and made more mistakes for every finished
piece of artwork than anyone could imagine. I can still see
things I'd like to change, more as time passes, but I like to think
my work is progressing with every book. *Jafta* will always be
special to me because it really taught me how to draw. It also
helped me to see in a less superficial way. People have looked
different since then – more individual.

Then and now I always work with an author who knows his
or her subject well. Not only does this help me to authenticate
my drawings but, being something of a traditionalist, I still
believe that the words are the heart of a book no matter how
simple.

I hope that some of the books I have done will encourage
other artists to break the mould in their own way so that we
can establish new and varied images. I believe that what we see
when we are very young is firmly fixed in our subconscious and

hard to change. This is why picture-book images are so important. People can't draw black people because they haven't had
the visual resources to learn from. And perhaps also black people do not take seriously a profession which has represented
them so badly. Most talented African artists select to do painting or sculpture which are more firmly rooted in their own traditions. I suspect the same might be true here.

To try and find out what happens to black art students, I did
a telephone survey of the design and illustration departments of
a number of London art colleges and polytechnics. The results
were fairly grim. Again and again I was told, 'We do not operate a discriminatory policy; we simply don't get the applications
from black and Asian students. We would welcome more.'
Some percentages were too small to count. Even in predominantly black colleges, the art departments were white ghettos.
The few black students that there were (almost always boys)
frequently did well and several were prize winners. These, however, did not generally choose book illustration as a profession

Illustration by Lisa Kopper from *Amber's Other Grandparents*

but opted more for fashion, design and advertising. Many teachers thought there was a class problem and black children were not getting the support they needed at home. Those students who actually chose to do children's book illustration tended to be white, middle-class girls.

All agreed that art college stage was too late – children needed to be encouraged and made aware of career possibilities at O- and A-level. I have always believed this and think some effort must be made to reach younger people. I spoke with a couple of black art students and they seemed to feel that, regardless of their colour, they were not encouraged to develop as book illustrators, and were given very little information about this field and the opportunities. My own advice to young gifted black people is to be artists first and make the effort to get into the system, no matter the problems and however painful it is. The black artists and writers I know agree with me on this. We don't want arts apartheid; it won't help anyone in the end.

Those of us who are white and working in this area must tread softly. There is a danger that we could become literary colonialists. All things being equal, it wouldn't matter who wrote or drew what, but unfortunately all things are not equal.

I can understand how black people must feel when so many of the books about them are done by us. Any group in a similar situation would feel uncomfortable and angry, whether Jewish, Irish, Scottish or whatever. So we must guard against any feeling of doing books for 'them', of bestowing a favour. It is not, and no black person would see it as such. I personally feel privileged to have been able to travel around the world through my art and, when what I have done is accepted by those people as good and right, I am honoured. We must always remember that we are guests in someone else's culture. But I hope the day will come when we don't even have to consider these issues; then we'll know there's real integration.

BfK 34
September 1985

I remember, at a parents' evening a few years ago, someone said to me: 'Are you showing us the books *you* like, or the books children like?' It's a difficult question – far too difficult for me to tackle here. For a start I'd have to discuss ponderous matters like the Cox Report's main, and virtually only, criterion for selecting books: 'they should be capable of interpretation at a number of different levels' (7.12). And, then again, I'd have to consider what those 'levels' are supposed to mean, and indeed whether there's not a great deal more to it than 'levels'. In the end, of course, I *can* only choose the books I like and hope children will like them too. Still, it does no harm to get an opinion from the customers sometimes, so I thought I'd ask a few children to help me.

(Jeff Hynds, 'On the Level', a Spring picture-book round-up, in *BfK* 62, May 1990)

Not, we suspect, for us ordinary punters but fascinating nonetheless to report, Sotheby's expect this auction to fetch in excess of £250,000! There's a private American collection of English and American children's books of about 250 titles (valued at £130,000-£160,000) which includes the first account in English of *The Pied Piper* dated 1605, a number of mint-condition first editions, including an English version, dated 1848, of *Shock-headed Peter*. Besides these there are also drawings by Tenniel (the original illustrator of *Alice*), Ardizzone and Kit Williams (*Masquerade*). Let us know how your biddings go.

(Newspage on Sotheby's sale of illustrated and children's books, and related drawings, 1–2 December 1988, in *BfK* 53, November 1988)

Grand Designs

*SHIRLEY HUGHES considers the
state of the art of book design*

'DESIGN' IS A WORD which seems to be on everyone's lips these days. Even the Prime Minister approves of it. Art colleges are encouraging it more than ever and design consultancies are thriving. But, outside specialist circles, there seems to be some confusion about what good design really is, a vague assumption that it's something you spray on to a more-or-less finished product to make people want to buy it.

Book publishing, like the rest of our media, is run at the top by 'word' people; that is, highly articulate people who have been educated from an early age to write essays, pass written examinations, get most of their information (and a lot of their entertainment too) from the printed word. If they have also developed a good eye or any capacity whatsoever for draughtsmanship this will probably be through some accident of birth or happy chance outside the main thrust of their 'serious' education. This, of course, is very proper in an industry in which the most precious raw material is words, not pictures. But where this order of merit applies we tend to get a rather rigid division between verbal and visual communication.

Books will increasingly be required to thrive alongside other media, addressing an audience accustomed to getting stories in a variety of different ways. The design of a page, its attractiveness, clarity and accessibility, is more than ever important if we are not to lose that audience. Originators of children's books know this better than anyone. Young readers require the utmost care in the way their books are designed. This area is of particular interest because, at its best, it can be a spearhead of experiment and innovation for the rest of the book trade.

With longer fiction, the process is still traditional. An author

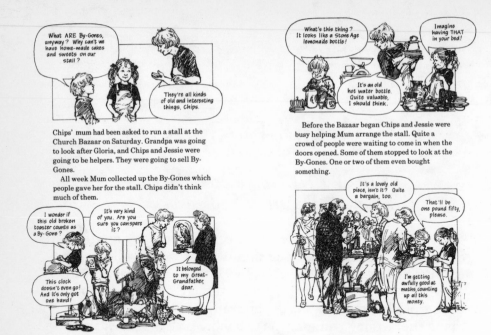

Double page spread from Shirley Hughes' *Chips and Jessie*

may work closely with an editor during the writing of his or her book. When it's accepted he will be consulted about the illustrations if there are to be any. But the main decisions about how the book will actually look, the choice of paper, typeface, cover design, will be made in-house (much of this depends on costing). The members of the design department have nothing to do with the editorial stage and rarely meet the author. This division of skills is often accentuated when the two departments are in different parts of the building, and in very big firms can be totally compartmentalised. Where an enormous number of titles are being put out, pressure of work probably makes it impossible for the designers to read all the books, even if they wanted to. The illustrators, on the other hand, work freelance and, in this situation, it is difficult for them to have a close rapport with the design team.

Picture books are another matter. If they are from the hand of an author/artist they will probably be submitted at the rough-dummy stage with the position of all the type areas already indicated and the illustrations sketched in round them. Not all author/artists, however, have a good eye for typography (if they have it will probably be something they have simply picked up rather than a matter of formal training) and may need a lot of help from the in-house designer. Author/artist collaborations have all too often in the past been vaguely assumed to be made in heaven – or rather, that the two have somehow magically got together to dream up this intimate combination of word and image. As in film-making, the pictures are part of the main ingredients rather than an entrancing afterthought, and have to be conceived as such. Good children's publishers regard it as part of their job to set up a framework in which these ideas can happen, develop and come to fruition as a finished book.

Rona Selby at The Bodley Head has, in spite of her youth, a long experience in this skill. The most important thing about a picture book, she says, is a good plot, whether this is told entirely in pictures, or in words, or any combination of the two. From the enormous number of texts which are submitted she will select the very few which have real visual possibility. Though herself a 'word' person by training, she must carry in her head a large memory bank of possible artists, whose work might marry well with a certain text. She will try to bring the author and artist together at an early stage (if they live a long way from London it isn't always easy). What makes a good story told in words may nevertheless have to be adjusted for a picture book. For instance, a story about a journey with a small child in the back of a car was, after joint discussion, agreed to be visually too static and was changed to a train ride instead. The format of the book having been worked out with the illustrator, the design department will then draw up a grid. The choice of typeface is crucial. Rona must put the needs of her young audience first. She takes meticulous care that the line breaks are of a length that a child can manage, that they relate to natural reading sense and aid reading aloud. This concern takes precedence over, for instance, centred or justified lines of type, however pleasing this may be to the adult eye.

Amelia Edwards at Walker Books was trained in the USA with a sound background in typography and graphic design. In a firm which so successfully specialises in children's picture books, with a reputation for helping and bringing on new illustrators, she also finds herself working closely with authors. The open-plan, atelier-style office facilitates a constant flow of ideas and exchange between the concerns of word and image, with both authors and artists positively encouraged to come in and work on the premises. Amelia says that, if an experienced author/illustrator prefers it, their policy is 'simply to leave them alone', but she has found that when a writer has been brought together with an artist with an idea at an early stage, with 'a designer close by if they need one', the results can be very rewarding. She describes the combination of these open working conditions, with activity and distraction going on all around, with the kind of thoughtful availability the whole team offers to both authors and artists, as 'very hard work, but well worth it in the long run'.

Getting it right...

And getting it wrong.

Page from Shirley Hughes' *Two Shoes, New Shoes*

Children's publishers are much exercised at the moment with the design and illustration of the next stage beyond picture books; that is, short-text stories on which tentative young readers may be encouraged to try their skills in reading to themselves. Just as there is no cut-off age in the enjoyment and use of picture books, inventive design is important in books for any age group, adults included.

Nick Thirkell is one of the most distinguished freelance book designers in the business, with several awards to his credit. He ran the design department at Macmillan for some years and now has his own design consultancy partnership. His style springs from an elegant feeling for typography and a scrupulous attention to the needs of a particular text. Like an illustrator, he aims to give the book a visual pace, a dynamic which flows through from page to page. This, he feels, is what distinguishes design from mere layout. He applies this to non-fiction; art books in which the text may be minimal, such as a stunning boxed set of colour books for the Victoria and Albert Museum on decorative papers. In his design for a luxury edition of *Larkrise to Candleford* (Century), he builds on the evocation of the period with pressed flowers lying alongside the letterpress (they are in reality artfully photographed and designed into the lines of text), and vignetted sepia photographs of turn-of-the-century rural life, offsetting carefully selected colour plates of paintings from that period, dreamily pretty but just on the right side of schmaltz. All this was the work of months, combined with the skills of a picture researcher. It's the kind of job for which a publisher or packager, through pressure of time, would seek to commission a freelance to give it exactly the right treatment.

Nick feels strongly that the amount of care and consideration taken is well worth it and shows up in the sales of the books. Tiny touches really are noticed by the reader and add up to a general feeling of rightness and harmony which is the essence of good design.

Of course, everyone knows about the highly designed book (usually non-fiction) in which the tail is wagging the dog; it looks wonderful in the shop, you take it home thinking that you've found your heart's desire only to find, in addressing the text, that it turns to dust and ashes. This is because the layout designers have disregarded the real essence and sense of the book. Some unfortunate writer has been brought in as an afterthought to fit some words into an already tightly designed grid. But rigorous attention to the right kind of design, one which grows out of the demands of each individual text, combined with exacting printing standards, will increase our reputation abroad and help to create a public at home who are not only readers but want to own and treasure books as desirable artefacts.

I have my own memories of books I had as a child where the design has stuck in my head even longer than the content. In *Bill the Minder*, written and illustrated by Will Heath Robinson (that giant of a draughtsman in both colour and line, lost to classic book illustration by his success in comic magazines), the pages seemed to me so astonishingly striking and intriguing that I never wanted to read the text in case it was a disappointment (most readers, I know, get this feeling the other way round). Who could forget that elegant and deceptive insouciance of Leslie Brook's *Johnny Crow's Garden*, or the guileful way in which E H Shepard gently scattered his line drawings into the pages of *The House at Pooh Corner*, or those garlanded ovals enclosing H Willebeek Le Mair's illustrations for *Little Songs of Long Ago*, with colours like fragile fragments of faded silk, offsetting the austere lines of music on the opposite page? And who has ever equalled the rapturous simplicity of word and image achieved by my hero, William Nicholson, in his *Alphabet*?

More recently Edward Ardizzone's *Diana and her Rhinoceros*, Raymond Briggs' *Father Christmas*, Maurice Sendak's *In the Night Kitchen* and *Higglety Pigglety Pop!* and John Burningham's *Mr Gumpy's Outing* all struck me, from the moment I laid eyes on them and ever since, as a near-perfect blend of text and a strong illustrative style. Some day perhaps someone will write a history of how, in design terms, these actually came about. Speaking for myself, I'm just happy to know that they did, and hope that there will be others to equal them.

BfK 38
May 1986

What more can one say about Shirley Hughes? In the 'Trotter Street' series she produces good stories in an urban setting with illustrations that keep children coming back for more and more. Buy it as a present, buy it for the class book corner or library – buy it wherever you're aiming books at young children! Everything Shirley Hughes writes at the moment has its own special magic and is guaranteed to work for you at every level.

(Judith Sharman reviewing *Wheels: A Tale of Trotter Street*, in *BfK* 75, July 1992)

The Flow of the Images

*BRIAN ALDERSON outlines the
thinking behind 'Sing a Song for
Sixpence' – an exhibition he arranged
at the British Library from October
1986 to January 1987. The purpose of
the exhibition was not just to
commemorate a great illustrator but,
more ambitiously, to demonstrate 'the
integrity of picture book art'*

VERY LITTLE ATTEMPT is made to perceive historical continuities
in picture book art. When therefore the British Library offered
me the chance to put on a small exhibition to commemorate the
centenary of the death of Randolph Caldecott, it struck me that
it might be worth pursuing some of the critical/historical
enquiries that are so often overlooked. For Caldecott may be
seen as a pivotal figure in the development of the English picture book, and it was arguable that his commemoration might
justly take the form of a graphic celebration of this fact rather
than being a 'one-man show'. (Such a show had, in any case,
been perfectly staged at Manchester City Art Gallery only a few
years before.) My hope was to establish the pre-eminence of
Caldecott's place through my selection of books and drawings
with their accompanying captions, and to provide a fuller critical rationale in an illustrated handbook.

The substance of the argument is simple enough, and
nowhere better expressed than by Maurice Sendak when he
talks about 'the rhythmic progression [through the pages of
Caldecott's book] – a sense of music and dance'. Picture books
may come in all shapes and sizes. They may have narrative

unity or be an unconnected sequence of subjects, as in an alphabet book or a collection of nursery rhymes. Their success, however, depends upon the integrity of the illustrator's response
within the covers of the book, and that integrity is most surely
achieved through the illustrator's command of the drawn line.
(I think that I caused some confusion in the argument – both in
the exhibition and in the book – by seeking to add the rather
crude psychological rider: that drawing is also the most natural
way of illustrating. We are all given to it, children and adults
alike, whatever our competence, and to that extent the drawing
of pictures – rather than the making of decorations or the slap-
ping around of paint – answers natural expectations.)

Now it may be coincidental, but from the time that children's
books began to emerge as a definable commercial genre in the
middle of the eighteenth century, English illustrators have
shown themselves to possess a distinctive command of the
drawn line. Undoubtedly the influence of Hogarth was para-
mount, and undoubtedly the Hogarthian style gained variety,
flexibility, and sometimes a coarsening frenzy, through the popularity of caricature prints. The long-term effect, though, was
the establishing of a fertile, non-academic – even amateur – tradition in illustration which was to be especially fruitful in the
making of picture books. It was an hospitable tradition. It
could include the passionate vision of Blake's whole-page prints
for *Songs of Innocence* and the levity of George Cruikshank's
Comic Alphabet. What it insisted on was the fluency of the
illustrator's pen or graver, needle or brush.

Clarifying the technical and stylistic shifts of this tradition
was one of the purposes of 'Sing a Song for Sixpence'. The exhibition attempted to show an enduring family likeness in, let us
say, picture books etched by Rowlandson, or engraved on
wood by the firm of Edmund Evans on behalf of Charles Bennett or Randolph Caldecott, or photographed for printing from
the artwork of Leslie Brooke or Quentin Blake. Frustration was
always at hand, though, for the theme proved to be too large
and too difficult to articulate within the confines of either the
exhibition or the book.

One of the reasons for this is my own penchant for trying to
demonstrate points by making contrasts. I was partly impelled
to set up 'Sing a Song for Sixpence' because it seemed to me that

Illustration by Randolph Caldecott from *Sing a Song for Sixpence*

we are all too easily seduced by the surface impressions of picture books and do not sufficiently consider the inner relationships of the text and the illustrations. I may appear to be labouring the obvious when writing about the English tradition of drawing, but alongside that tradition there have subsisted contrasting modes of illustration whose fuller discussion would have clarified the central argument. With modern work, for instance, how better to counter the *Schwärmerei* that greets each new offering from decorative artists like Errol Le Cain or clever-clever technicians like Anthony Browne, than by reasserting the fluid interaction of picture and text that is present in the less stunning, but altogether more coherent picture books within 'the tradition'.

The impossibility of pursuing these contrasts as fully as I would have liked was matched by what several critics saw as the crucial weakness of the exhibition: the impossibility of turning the pages of the books. For, if 'rhythmic progression' or 'fluid interaction' mean anything at all, they mean the flow of words and pictures through the books as a whole – and looking at the book as a whole is not something that can be contrived in glass cases or within the compass of 112-page manuals. A plan did exist for overcoming this problem by having on display an open rack of modern picture books which everyone attending the exhibition – adults and children alike – could examine at their leisure. This, however, was defeated by Administrative Prudence. It seems that the Warders, upon whom the successful operation of the British Museum entirely depends, were unwilling to permit so radical a departure from convention as to have people reading books in a book exhibition. The only compromise that could be reached was to provide visitors with a list of recommended books which could then be seen and bought in the Museum Shop. That list was a (highly selective) summary of 'the Caldecott tradition' as it manifests itself today, with entries ranging from Beatrix Potter's *Sly Old Cat* to Charlotte Voake's *Over the Moon*.

In books such as these can be seen the delight in picture-book art that prompted the whole enterprise – and fortunately one opportunity did present itself for me to clarify further the points I wished to make.

At a lunch-time lecture in the Museum in January, we were able to 'turn the pages' of a couple of examples to demonstrate the nature and virtues – and fun – of 'the tradition'.

The first book I chose was the little-reckoned Caldecott toy book *Come Lasses and Lads* of 1881. The text, which is a ballad, is not an easy work to illustrate or to come to terms with as something to read to children. But the intelligence and artistry with which Caldecott parallels the May-Day celebrations of the song with a narrative line of his own, the way, for instance, that he characterises participants and creates from hints in the text the sad story of the fiddler – these are as good an example of the integrity of picture-book art as one could wish.

My second example was *The Pirate Twins* by William Nicholson (1929) – a companion piece to *Clever Bill* and a book which it is shameful to find now out of print. Superficially it seems to have little to do with Randolph Caldecott, but it is imbued with the same genius for the complete, harmonious integration of text and picture. This is seen partly in the dynamic way in which Nicholson paces the story through the pages (it is written in his own round-hand script), and the pacing is perfectly complemented by the flow of the images. For, although Nicholson's drawing (for offset lithography) is simpler and chunkier than Caldecott's, it has the same vibrancy of movement and pleasure in off-the-cuff narrative detail.

To the audience it may have seemed coincidental that both these examples included reference to dancing but, in terms of the exhibition and the larger thesis that was present behind it, this was not so. For, when Sendak talked of Caldecott's 'sense of music and dance', he was adumbrating a motif that asserts itself again and again in the progress of the English picture book. From Hogarth, who used a dance scene as an example in his *Analysis of Beauty* (1753), to Quentin Blake, whose Mr Magnolia dances his way from one end of the book to the other, English illustrators (and American illustrators in the English tradition) can almost be judged by their response to the challenge of the dance. For, in the demands that it makes on their powers of drawing – Blake's 'bounding line', Rowlandson's 'bouncing calligraphy', Caldecott's 'art of leaving out' – it symbolises the adequacy with which they can match the tune, the playfulness, the momentum of their subjects.

BfK 44
May 1987

Despite the fact that I don't write with children in mind, I long ago discovered that they make the best audience. They certainly make the best critics. They are more candid and to the point than professional critics. Of course, almost anybody is. But when children love your books, it's, 'I love your book, thank you. I want to marry you when I grow up.' Or it's, 'Dear Mr Sendak: I hate your book. I hope you die soon. Cordially.'

(Maurice Sendak, 'Frightened into Being an Artist' in *BfK* 56, May 1989)

Is it only ten years? I seem to have lived both with the Mother Goose Award and, latterly, without it for a much longer life-time. Conceived on the long drive home from exhausting book exhibitions and lectures, along flat, isolated roads in South Yorkshire, nurtured for nine months, the Award was finally born as a golden egg, designed and executed by a Yorkshire artist, who used a real goose egg as a model for the first hatchings.

Is it only ten years since Jan Pienkowski steamed off a train in Doncaster breathing fire and thunder about printers who couldn't, or wouldn't, carry out his instructions in the printing of the logo and lettering? I think he finally came to rest in Hull, finding there a printer who understood his need for perfection.

And that search for a 'balanced' panel of judges! God help me, how naive I was!

(Clodagh Corcoran, 'Ten Years of Mother Goose', in *BfK* 59, November 1989)

Charles Keeping died on Monday, 16 May 1988. He was one of the most revered and respected illustrators of the last twenty years. Technically in a class of his own, he brought insights into his subject matter that were unique because of the man he was.
RON HEAPY, *his editor at Oxford University Press, remembers what it was like*

Working with Charlie

'ONCE I GOT THE WINDOW, I was okay. Yes, thanks, I'll have a bottle of beer. I always come here 'cos the fish is good. I *love* fish.' And there it was – *The Highwayman*, all stuck together in miniature, in the amazing little concertina Charles always did for his books. 'You must get the horizon line consistent through the book, and print it in warm black. At the end of the book, just reverse it out. Saves work.'

That was the pattern for all our first meetings on a book. Always a bottle of beer, always fish, the concertina and descriptions of where Charlie had eaten fish on the weekend. Anyway, we printed *The Highwayman* in warm black – brown and black actually – and Charles got the Kate Greenaway Medal. 'Yes, it was good to get into black and white again. Stopped me doing my fruit salad effect. But don't ever ask me to draw mice with clothes on.' 'No Charles, we won't.'

In fact we asked Charles to do *Beowulf* next. For all his Cockney manner, Charles was the most intelligent and perceptive

Charles Keeping

artist I've ever worked with. He would get right through to the heart of a text and bring out something unique which no one had ever thought of or will think of again. On *Beowulf*: 'I've got to make the monsters sympathetic, especially the mother. I mean her son's just been bloody killed! No wonder she's angry.' When things went wrong, he was quick on his feet. 'Charles, your concertina hasn't worked. We've got three blank pages here.' 'Don't worry, Ron. Here's what we'll do.' And no one ever spotted the joins in the book.

The idea of *Sammy Streetsinger* had been around for a while, but it wasn't quite right as Sammy was a film star throughout. 'Charles, why not turn him into a rock star? Try watching *Top of the Pops* for three months.' Charles did and hated it, but caught the style and atmosphere of rock and conveyed his hatred in the tone of his words. He had a good ear and we never had to alter his words. That's Charlie's voice in there. In fact the problems he had weren't to do with the rock world. 'I'm sick of drawing bloody tiles, Ron. I've been down in this underpass for weeks, just drawing tiles. And then there's all these bloody heads as well. Two hundred and fifty of them.'

Once he'd got the vision of a book and knew what he wanted to do, he was away and would dig in quite fiercely if he thought you were wrong or didn't understand him. On *The*

Wedding Ghost: 'What's that, Charles?' 'That's a barge, Ron.' 'Sorry, Charles.' But at the same time he was flexible and open to suggestions which he thought made sense. We had some good arguments over *The Lady of Shalott*. 'What's with this falling rose effect, Charles?' Back comes a completely new framework. 'It's like a striptease, sort of. She's lonely and vulnerable. There she is, sitting in that lonely tower, without a stick of furniture.' The book showed Charles's great draughtsmanship and also showed the sexual undertones which would appear in his work, which bothered some critics. 'I always draw the figure nude. Then I put the clothes on.' But again he got right to the heart of the poem.

We argued over the cover of *Shalott*, but in a good-humoured way. 'I think we need a colour, Charles.' 'Yes, a sort of damson,' he said. 'Let's look at all these women's dresses and pick one.'

There she weaves by night and day
A magic web with colours gay.
She has heard a whisper say,
A curse in on her if she stay
  To look down to Camelot.
She knows not what the curse may be,
And so she weaveth steadily,
And little other care hath she,
  The Lady of Shalott.

Illustration by Charles Keeping from *The Lady of Shalott*

(All this was happening at the Kate Greenaway Award which Charles, to his disgust, didn't get for *Sammy*.) So we prowled round eminent lady librarians together, looking at their dresses and raising suspicious glances. Eventually we found the right shade of damson on a lady called Viv. 'Can we borrow your dress a minute?' She took it well.

Charles always had a great passion for the sea and was working on a large 48-page version of *The Ancient Mariner* when he died. This could have been marvellous and now we'll never see it. I was looking forward to our usual arguments over it. 'What's that, Charles?' 'That's an albatross, Ron.' 'Sorry, Charles.'

Ironically, just after he died, the artwork for his new colour book, *Adam and Paradise Island*, came back from the designer with the type on, all ready to go. I sit surrounded by Charlie's artwork and keep on reaching instinctively for the 'phone. There's a problem on the cover and I need to talk to him, but he's not there. The sense of loss I feel for this dear, warm man is appalling and I don't know what to do. I only hope that wherever he is, they serve fish. Good-bye Charlie, and Amen.

BfK 51
July 1988

This gifted young artist has made a poignant and special picture book about Badger, who dies, leaving his friends with fond memories and 'gifts'. There are clever reverberations of *The Wind in the Willows* and other childhood tales. Is the writer/artist giving pastoral tradition a crisp contemporary edge?

The writing is humane, gentle, poetic; the pictures are integral. The telling is slow and not at all morbid. One not to be missed from a talent whose work could become significant.

(Colin Mills reviewing Susan Varley's *Badger's Parting Gifts* in *BfK* 37, March 1986)

Writing Texts for Picture Books

MARTIN WADDELL

A PICTURE BOOK tells a story, at least mine do. Storytelling is what interests me, because I am a storyteller.

The working difference between writing a story and writing a picture book is that when I write a story and finish it, it *is* finished. When I write a picture-book text I am just at the beginning of a long process, in which the whole structure and meaning of the story will be re-interpreted by someone else, an artist who deals in images.

I once boasted to David Lloyd, my editor at Walker Books, that I wrote 'in images'.

'You do,' he replied, 'but you are very bad at it!' It was a neat put-down, but also true. I am a writer, not an image-maker. The danger of thinking you write 'in images' is when it leads to the expectation that the artist will faithfully reproduce *those* images . . . will 'illustrate' the story you have written.

This is the way to produce a *bad* picture book, because the images have been imposed on the artist by a non-specialist – someone who writes. I know this to be so from my own experience, but it is still difficult to come to terms with.

A case in point is *The Hidden House*, recently published by Walker.

I began the story in a bedsit above the Conservative Party Offices in Ladbroke Grove in 1958 (this is not a political statement, I just happened to be camped there). I was in bed with a heavy case of 'flu, and the 'Dollmaker' idea came to me. Out of bed, off with the 'flu, on with the story, back to bed. It was then called 'Dominic'. The manuscript is lost to me, but I suppose it lies within whatever vault holds the rejects from Hutchinson New Authors Ltd, an imprint from which I received great encouragement, short of being published. An old man makes dolls to keep him company, that was roughly the story.

Twenty-five years later, walking up a lane from Tipperary woods towards the Mournes, I discovered the Dollmaker's house, choked with weeds and ivy, grimy windows still intact.

Glorious moment . . . the thing is a picture-book text, full of images! White heat stage . . . lovely . . . the story was written in about an hour.

'Good story!' David Lloyd said.

Happy puffs on pipe from cheery author, expecting big . . . well, biggish . . . cheque.

'You got the end wrong,' he added. 'If it isn't the end, it's something else.'

Distressed puffs on pipe, then excitement. We tweaked the story here and there, working and re-working, until it came right, and it was still *my* story, *my* possession.

'Angela Barrett,' Amelia Edwards, Walker Art Director, said. They showed me *The Snow Queen*.

Two reactions: 'She is good. Very good.'

'What has she got to do with *my* story?' Big Question Mark. (Note the possessive adjective.)

I agreed nervously to go ahead.

Moment of maximum pain. The first pictures laid on the desk, with David and Amelia doing their David-and-Amelia Act, gazing at me gazing at it, and waiting for the pipe to twitch.

Oh, God! I have been nearly thirty years getting *my* story right, a story full of ideas about warmth and togetherness and love and renewal, and look-what-this-woman-has-done-to-it! A strange image, an old child-scaring man on a bench with three huge elongated dolls. Help me somebody! What do I say to them?

'Oh-er,' or words to that effect.

Pipe clenched, while over-heating brain clicks. What is this *Angela* doing? This image is something from inside her, not anything to do with me. Get rid of it! I don't want it in *my* book.

David: 'I think it is brilliant.'

Illustration by Angela Barrett from *The Hidden House*

Pipe puffed furiously.
Amelia, defiantly, as the smoke ascends: 'It *is* brilliant.'
Crushed Author: 'Y-e-s, it is, but . . .'
Chorus (what a double act): '*Look* at it, Martin!'
And I did.
I looked for a long time.
It is brilliant. It is how the book should be, not as I saw it. As I saw it, it would have been a safe book about cuddly dollies, albeit dealing with life and death, but this book is altogether different; it has a whole new dimension. It *works*.

My story became *our* book . . . a picture book, not just a text. 'A perfect blend,' somebody was nice enough to say, but it wasn't just a blend, because blending conveys intermingling, and there is more to it than that. A picture book grows somewhere in the process. In the end it doesn't belong to either the writer or the artist, but both together, and *them* . . . the people whose names are not on the cover: editor, designer, whoever chose the paper, all the people who add the little bits that make it work.

The writer's sense of possessiveness is the first great danger to a picture book. I am, and always will be, very possessive about my picture-book texts, but this can be taken no further than protecting them against the 'wrong' artist. This means the artist who is plain bad, or the artist who is technically good, but brings nothing of his or her self to the story.

The key moment is when you realise that the artist has taken over . . . unfortunately that is usually the moment when the possessive writer feels most hurt. It's a funny mix of feeling, because the hurt is mingled with a feeling of joy and a sense of wonder. '*Look what has happened to it*!' followed by '*It works*!'

More and more I am writing now without indications to the artist that come from my own sense of image . . . it is an inferior sense, it only gets in the way.

The Park in the Dark is an example of the right way to do it.

'Me and Loopy and Little Gee.'

Illustration by Barbara Firth from *The Park in the Dark*

Editor to Writer: 'What are they?'

Writer to Editor: 'Don't know. Just words.'

Neither of us needed to know, we are wordsmen. The toys in *The Park in the Dark* were in Barbara Firth. They came from her own childhood, they belonged to her, and so when she drew them, she felt them, and that feeling comes over in her pictures.

So the writer just writes little stories, and after that it is all up to the artist, and the design department? Not so . . . not 'little' stories; a picture book is often much more than that. A really good picture book is a 'big' story, written in very few words, often layered so that many meanings lie within it.

What does 'big' mean? It can mean 'about-something-that-matters': ideas like the wheel of life, as in *Once There Were Giants* (a terribly difficult book for Penny Dale to make work); ideas like fear of the unknown, as in *Can't You Sleep, Little Bear?* Those are big 'adult' ideas, we recognise them as big easily, and the craft of the thing is to render them comprehensible to very small children.

How about 'Justice'? Children say, 'It isn't fair!' and they mean it, it *matters* to them.

> There once was a duck
> Who had the bad luck
> To live with a lazy old Farmer
> The duck did the work,
> For the farmer stayed all day in bed.

Justice for the Duck! And the right artist! Helen Oxenbury is doing *Farmer Duck*.

There are other 'big' ideas, which are big for the very small. How about splashing? The sheer joy of splash-splash-splashing in cool water on a warm day . . . a big celebration of a very small thing that children love.

> One day Neligan went into town.
> It was hot. It was dry.
> The sun shone in the sky.
> Neligan's pig sat by Neligan's pond.

A fat, steamy pig. A duck and goose splashing in the pond, teasing the pig with quacks and honks of pure pleasure then . . .

>SPLAAASH!
>The pig's in the pond!
>The pig's in the pond!
>The pig's in the pond!
>The word spread about,
>Above and beyond,
>At Neligan's farm,
>The pig's in the pond!

Pig's in the Pond. Jill Barton's pig now.

Noise . . . that's another celebration one. 'Tum-tum-te-tum, diddle-diddle-dum, ratta-tat-tat-boom!' *The Happy Hedgehog Band.* Jill again.

So big ideas can be small from an adult point of view, but then an adult point of view is not very helpful. A 'big' idea is something which instantly interests a child, and if you can shade in some more subtle themes alongside it, so much the better.

I work on the principle that the eventual book will usually be read one-to-one, a shared thing, often at the end of a difficult day. The day may have thrown up barriers between the adult and the child, and the picture book, particularly the old familiar picture book, can bring them together again. It may even open the possibility of airing whatever the matter is.

A picture-book text is a script for performance by the reader, performing to a very personally involved audience that wants to stop, ask questions, look, and point things out. There should be words to work on for that performance, lots of rhythm and rhyme and alliteration and fun and jokes and things happening, a story with a beginning, a middle and an end, a story that often says something about loving relationships between 'big' and 'small'.

No problem! You have three to five hundred words to do it in, ideally less.

Finished?

Get it to the *right* artist.

BfK 68
May 1991

Recently David McKee's *I Hate My Teddy Bear* was attacked by critics as 'difficult', 'surreal' and 'indulgent'. How does Klaus Flugge react to this? 'Sometimes you simply have to do a book. If you believe in an artist you respect his feelings on the matter and believe in what he is doing. Having a special closeness with the artist helps you to understand him, see his point of view. I'm enthusiastic about this book; but it's the sort of book adults find difficult to accept and comprehend *for* children; children don't have that problem, they take what they find. It has sold well abroad.' Another comment on the conservative attitude to children's books of most British adults?

(Pat Triggs, 'The Man Behind the Books – Klaus Flugge', in *BfK 24*, July 1984)

If you are in the habit of stopping off for a cup of coffee at Membury Services on the M4 you might have noticed, from time to time, a man and a woman engaged in animated conversations, very occupied with paper and coloured markers and, among other things, apparently concocting spells. What you were witnessing was a meeting of that unique collaboration between Helen Nicoll and Jan Pienkowski which has produced the very popular and successful *Meg and Mog* series. Membury Services – helpfully situated between London (Jan) and Marlborough (Helen) – provides a good place to work, they say: 'No one disturbs you.'

(Pat Triggs on the *Meg and Mog* books in *BfK 26*, May 1984)

PART THREE

Poetry

Jolly millers, pipers' sons, kings in counting houses, Little Boy Blues blowing horns and sleeping under haycocks, beggars coming to town: what have all these to say to children raised on Saturday Superstore *and the* A-Team? *Is there still a place for nursery rhymes in our high-tech world?* ERIC HADLEY *has an answer*

Sing a Song of Mother Goose

AMONGST THE REMAINDERED STOCK in a second-hand bookshop, I found recently a book by an Italian-American called Alessandro Falassi. It was called *Folklore by the Fireside* (Scolar Press) and in it Falassi gives an account of the tradition of storytelling, song and poetry still alive until recently in the Tuscan villages from which he, his family and relations came.

There is nothing in my own experience or that of people I know which matches his account of a community gathering regularly of an evening in each other's houses. They gathered together around the fireplace – specially prepared for the occasion – to tell stories, sing songs, ask riddles, comment on (and insult) each other through rhymes. The stories and songs, though ancient, were constantly reworked through questions, commentary, topical reference from the audience. That audience (not the passive ones of concerts and plays) included adults, adolescents *and* children. Though there was a special time in the proceedings for them, their stories, songs and rhymes were part of a continuity which led into the mysterious and exciting world of the adults. Before they were hustled off to bed they might just catch one of the young men pouring out his feelings in song for one of the young girls present or insulting the prowess of one of his rivals in her affection. As Maurice O'Sullivan remarks of his own early childhood experience of song in the very similar Irish-speaking ceilidh tradition: 'Every word came out clearly. I did not understand the meaning of the words but the other part of the song was plain to me – the voice, the tremor and the sweetness.'

I don't offer this little account in a spirit of nostalgia. You can't be nostalgic for what you have never had and that kind of society is for us irrevocable and unimaginable. Or is it? Though it may have lost its connections with what came after for adolescents and adults, isn't that tradition still alive in a truncated form every time a parent takes a child upon their knee to sing or say a nursery rhyme? Even more surprising, isn't that 'special place' for song and poetry still made every time an infant teacher invites her pupils to step away from the tables and chairs of conspicuous instruction to gather on the carpet and share a different kind of listening and saying?

The resilience of this part of our story and poetic tradition is all the more surprising when we consider how small a part poetry plays in the lives of the adults and how hard it is to assert its place in learning in our education system – how surprised we would be to see poetry pushed in our classrooms with the same financial expenditure and governmental energy as are lavished on micros.

And yet, to stay with the jargon of that world for a moment, the collection of rhymes, songs, ballads, jokes, riddles, puns and tongue twisters we choose to call 'nursery rhymes' is the most comprehensive 'language development programme' that we have and the user trials have been going on for some hundreds of years now. Those rhymes are not, as their designation now suggests, a random sample of entertaining ditties fit only for the very young. In one sense, they are severely functional – they help the child to become a member of the language community in which eventually they will have to take up their adult place. Unlike some contemporary designers of 'language programmes', the collective wisdom of the historical community understood that *inconspicuous* learning – learning that we do without realising that we are learning – is a very powerful means. Powerful enough, at least, to ensure that we don't have too many remedial talkers. As one eminent linguistician has said: '. . . songs and rhymes help the learner to effortlessly retain the basic patterns of our grammar' – both the spoken and written forms. What he didn't go on to explain was how and why this happens – so I'll make an attempt.

We are saturated as babies and young children in a world of linguistic 'noise'. What the experience of songs and rhymes encourages is attentiveness and alertness to meaning in that 'noise'. It is precisely those qualities which 'mark out' their difference from ordinary discourse which are so important – melody, repetitions, rhythms, cadences, etc. and, of course, their unchangingness amongst constant change. To put it another way, they help children to become 'listeners' – people who attend with the expectation of meaning. It's hard to separate that expectation of meaning from our entry into a world of shared meaning which itself depends upon human relationship. We learn to listen and talk (and eventually to read) in order to share more fully in the human world which surrounds us. As an old Suffolk saying puts it: 'The lil' ol' boy sat on his father's knee while we wor a-telling him a story. And he kept lookin' at him *as though he wor a-pickin' the words out of his mouth*.'

These songs and rhymes offer an invitation to the child – an invitation to participate in and gain mastery over words. Gaining mastery over words involves taking risks and sorting yourself out in this kind of minefield:

> Betty Botter bought some butter
> But, she said, the butter's bitter,
> If I put it in my batter . . .

Are you saying the words or are they saying you? Gaining mastery also involves playing with language, seeing how far you can go – like the infant pupil I met recently who had discovered the power of the word 'very' – especially if you had repeated it five times in the same sentence. Nursery rhymes commit outrages with language – rhyme almost invariably dominates meaning:

> Little Poll Parrot
> Sat in his garret . . .

and they encourage further outrages and improvisations. I won't go into the changes that my son can ring upon the following at the expense of his poor father:

> Bring Daddy home
> With a fiddle and a drum
> A pocket full of spices
> An apple and a plum.

And that brings me indirectly to riddles. I used to think the appeal of riddles lay mainly in their linguistic puzzles. I'm now more inclined to the view that their real appeal lies in the *asking* – power over words is one thing but power over others through words expands the possibilities enormously.

Earlier I stressed the didactic function of nursery rhymes – linguistic rules, conceptual rules, rules for living – but there is a strong critical and subversive strand. They permit what in ordinary discourse would be unspeakable and impermissible to the young child – expressions of rage, anger, disgust, undiluted plain speaking:

> I do not like thee, Doctor Fell,
> The reason why I cannot tell
> But this I know, and know full well
> I do not like thee, Doctor Fell.

This is the area in which institutionalised and collected rhyme begins to shade off into children's own culture with its rich vein of insults, jeering, double entendres and *sotto voce* risky remarks devised to test the adult's 'official' hearing.

But children are not only hard and resilient, they are also susceptible. How else can I explain how my raging, self-willed two-year-old lets himself drift away on:

Hush-a-bye baby on the tree-top
When the wind blows the cradle will rock . . .

Even he can feel 'the voice, the tremor and the sweetness'.

Like all great poetry and unlike so much anaemic verse written for children, nursery rhymes don't moralise. Even the
gallery of monsters which haunt the collections is not primarily
intended to terrorise children to make them good. At two years
old, the pressure came from my son and not me to 'Read
Giant!':

Fee, fi, fo, fum,
I smell the blood of an Englishman
Be he alive or be he dead
I'll grind his bones to make my bread.

Illustration by Tomie de Paola from *Mother Goose*

Just as you have to learn how to listen you have to learn what to be afraid of – passing through the stage of being at the mercy of your generalised fears to that of fearing a specific creature. What more exquisite pleasure can there be than playing out and practising those fears ('What's the time, Mr Wolf?'). Emotions, that is, become more real and more known through the definitions they achieve in metaphor, play and dramatisation. Not that the range of emotions in nursery rhymes is limited to fear and anxiety. How could that be so when they were fashioned, as that great respecter of nursery rhymes, Wordsworth, recognised, for:

> A race of real children; not too wise
> Too learned or too good; but wanton, fresh
> And bandied up and down by love and hate . . .
> May books and Nature be their early joy.

Bill Boyle and Pat Triggs back him up

Speculations about what nursery rhymes mean in the form of scholarly investigations of their historical, political and folklore origins are fascinating – to adults. Children aren't usually concerned to have it explained that *Mary, Mary, Quite Contrary* is probably Mary Queen of Scots, or that the pig stolen by Tom the piper's son was an eighteenth-century sweetmeat and not a real pig as depicted in so many Mother Goose collections. What connects children to this motley collection of songs, chants, prayers, riddles, jokes and jingles which we have accumulated over centuries is the irresistible combination of rhythm, rhyme and story. There can be no better introduction to the world of story than these highly condensed narratives; their very brevity leaves plenty of space for listeners or sayers to roam around in, making of them what they will. And there's no doubt that all human life is here. Little Polly Flinders whipped by her mother for spoiling her nice new clothes, Little Tommy Tittlemouse who caught fishes in other men's ditches and:

> Tommy Trot, a man of law, who
> Sold his bed and lay upon straw,
> Sold the straw and slept on grass
> To buy his wife a looking glass.

There's many a novel which takes longer to say less about the tongue-tied communications of boy-girl relationships than these four lines:

> As Tommy Snooks and Bessy Brooks
> Were walking out one Sunday
> Says Tommy Snooks to Bessy Brooks
> Tomorrow will be Monday.

Nursery rhymes are resonant with possible meanings and the joy is that there is no pressure to 'understand' them. Who is wandering 'upstairs downstairs and in my lady's chamber'? Who is this 'old man who wouldn't say his prayers', who gets 'thrown downstairs' so precisely 'by the *left* leg'? What's he doing in my lady's chamber? Who is telling this story? Why is someone talking to a goose?

One mark of an experienced reader, we are told, is tolerance of uncertainty and ambiguity – three- and four-year-olds seem to be off to a good start.

Sharers of nursery rhymes can feel the sadness of *I Had a Little Pony*, the moral indignation of *Ding Dong Bell*; they can relish nonsense and word play, bounce to *Ride a Cock Horse*, tickle toes with *This Little Piggy* – an involvement of all the senses which is held together by the controlling sense of rhythm.

Rhythm is part of all poetry, from nursery rhyme and witty limerick to the moving love poem. From the banal chant of:

> Tell tale tit
> Your mother can't knit
> Your father can't walk
> With a walking stick.

to the playgroup sound of:

> Dip, dip, dip
> My blue ship
> Sails on the water,
> Like a cup and saucer,
> O-U-T
> Spells OUT!

The common factor is rhythm. Rhythm gives the rhyme or poem its shape, it defines the sound and makes it easier to remember. This sense of rhythm, in the early experience of the child as he is exposed to nursery rhymes, enables him to develop a sensitivity to the musical qualities inherent in any future appreciation of language. The combination of strong rhythms and memorisable rhymes must explain why Mother Goose has stood the test of time.

The words are crafted to provide sounds that give pleasure to the small child. It is in this that the real 'success' of nursery rhymes must be measured. From the attraction of 'Baa Baa Black Sheep' and 'Mary Had a Little Lamb', the progression is natural to the world of narrative poetry and the subtleties of nonsense verse. But without the initial attraction of 'Hey Diddle Diddle' and 'Goosey, Goosey Gander', how many of us would have started on that progression? How many of the youngsters who now relish the 'story style' poetry of Michael Rosen and Roger McGough would have done so without a dose of 'Desperate Dan', that dirtiest of old men, who 'washed his face in a frying pan'? The nonsense verse of such as Colin West and Spike Milligan will be better appreciated by those who have cut their teeth on:

> Diddle, diddle, dumpling, my son John,
> Went to bed with his trousers on.
> One shoe off, and one shoe on,
> Diddle, diddle, dumpling, my son John.

Because of their mesmeric rhythm and simple rhymes, nursery rhymes are easily remembered or memorised by their young audience, which enhances the sense of sharing the fun later. Children can express within their own circle, be it family or nursery group, the pleasure that they feel in the sound of the words. Our adult, more sophisticated (?) reaction to poetry or prose is simply an extension or mature progression of the same feelings, the same responses.

BfK 35
November 1985

Poetry and traditional tales have much in common. Both are ancient in lineage; both are delights to the ear; both explore human emotions, often through story. But whereas traditional tales have lived and changed and travelled through place and time, acquiring local variations, different emphases on their journeys, poetry speaks directly to us in a voice that may be either from ages past or of today.

(Elaine Moss, 'Poetry and Traditional Tales', in *BfK 17*, November 1982)

'The only literature that meant anything to me when I was growing up, except for the rhymes and verses my mother used to sing me as a toddler, was the choral verse we were encouraged to learn to improve our elocution. I was good at this. I got a grade B in a public competition reciting "Jabberwocky" once.' Such triumphs apart, 'any artistic ability didn't show in my school work at all.'

(Roger McGough quoted in *BfK 57*, July 1989)

Any illustrator would relish tackling a collection of nursery rhymes; it's such an obvious and lovable thing to do. After all, the main reason for specialising in children's books at all is the range of subject matter they provide – fantasy, illusion and imagination well beyond what most adult books allow. Not only that, but every rhyme offers something different. You're not shackled to a repetitive likeness for page after page. I don't think people realise how *boring* this can be . . .

(Faith Jaques on her last-ever picture book, *The Orchard Book of Nursery Rhymes*, in *BfK 64*, September 1990)

Taking Care of the Small Box

JACK OUSBEY *on necessary encounters with poetry*

THE POET GEORGE MACBETH and I share an unusual distinction, worth, perhaps, an entry in a book of sporting records. For thirty minutes before the kick-off of a Wembley cup final, I read his collection, *Poems of Love and Death*, and my wife, who was seated alongside me, observed that I must be the only follower in the history of the game to have read poetry on such an occasion. I am, you see, an addict.

I read poetry every day, and always at breakfast time. It is an essential part of my diet and, whilst I can manage without the muesli, I function less well if, for any reason, I am prevented from reading poetry. Often I read a new collection several times, until I feel settled and comfortable with the poems, until they 'fit' well with me, and I with them. Sometimes it is a single poem which demands attention, and then I carry away the book so that I can tune in again when I am lunching, or waiting for an appointment, or having my hair cut. Occasionally, a phrase from a poem jumps into my mind at the breakfast table, and detonates, from time to time during the day, with small explosions of pleasure. The compulsion then is to possess the phrase, to consider its implications and reflect on its unfolding meanings. Poetry sets moving the busy traffic of the imagination and does it in the most surprising and varied ways.

Back, though, to George MacBeth and the Wembley experience. A few minutes before the teams ran on to the pitch in front of a 90,000 crowd, I read 'For the Arrival of a New Cat'. It wasn't enough to read it silently. Once read it had to be sounded. I wanted to hear myself reading it aloud:

> . . . The new cat is
> coming, is coming, the
> roses expect him. Upstairs, in
> the attic, the locked trunks are
> creaking. Their papers and letters
> grip their teeth tightly. The
> new cat is coming, is coming, the
> books on their white shelves are
> scattering leaves to receive him,
> their spines are his servants . . .

and I knew then that this was a poem I wanted to share with the children. Not to study; not to question; not to write about; but to taste, as we allowed it to dance and sing in our agreed orchestration of voices. And, of course, the twelve-year-olds who joined me in this venture accepted, as young children do, that this was a very reasonable way of tackling poetry. Everyone took part; we talked about the way it should be spoken; we kept on trying it out to see how it fitted together; we made decisions about the appropriate number of voices for the different sections; and we moved the desks to the side of the room so that we could feel how much better a poem like this sounds when the speakers become a community of voices. At the end of the session, one boy told me, 'It was good. It wasn't like real learning at all,' and yet he and his classmates now knew, by heart, large chunks of the poem. As that wise poet and teacher Leonard Clark once observed:

> . . . there is much to be said for 'learning by heart', which is another way of saying 'learning by love'. Although poetry should not be used merely as a vehicle for developing powers of memory, there are few young children who can long resist the constant encounters with memorable words and haunting rhythms.

Some time ago a colleague and I worked on a poetry project with the teachers in a junior school. Two co-ordinators were appointed, one for the teachers of younger children and one for those who taught the older pupils. The teachers agreed to use poetry on a daily basis for a term, and set out to find challenging and interesting ways of introducing selected poems to the children. In order to pool their expertise, they did a good deal of corporate planning and, on one occasion, a single poem selected for investigation produced twenty-seven ideas for ways of working. In this way teachers who were less secure about poetry teaching were helped to play a full part in the work.

It was not possible to produce evidence, of the kind favoured by scientific research, to show that these constant encounters affected the way children used language, but at the end of the project the co-ordinators were convinced of the value. One of them felt that the methods that they had adopted led to an active processing of language which was very powerful, and that the regular reading and speaking of poetry had provided many children which a creative stock of language from which they could draw, to transpose and re-shape ideas in words. Children seemed to be able to take hold of language, to possess it for themselves as a result of experiencing the sounds and rhythms of poetry, and one of the most surprising features of the work was the ability of young children to deal with metaphors and images. In describing her experiences with her own daughter, one teacher had this to say:

> This kind of work could be started so much earlier. My daughter is three-and-a-half and everything she remembers, all the things she seems to learn, are to do with poetry or poetic language. I have even read 'Jabberwocky' to her and she has already picked up some of the phrases. She tries to make up things in rhyme and with rhythm because she has such a strong experience of it at a time when she is ready and receptive to it.

This child, not yet four, is having many of the experiences I have when I encounter poetry. We both like listening to poems and trying bits of them out to see what they sound like, and we both pick up phrases and retain them. Her understanding of what language is is derived entirely from her active involvement in its use. It seems more than likely that if her encounters include the intense as well as the routine, the visionary as well as the mundane, and bring her into contact, also, with those strange, surprising conjunctions and patterns of which poetry is

Illustration by Alan Marks from *Something I Remember*

made, she will grow into an effective and confident language user. The difference between us, this young child and me, is that she has no metamemorial capacity. She does not know about knowing, nor know how or why she is remembering things. When I read poetry I am aware that I can select and highlight ideas, that I can shuffle them around to give them further meaning, that I can bring previous experiences into contact with new ones and, from the combination, create a picture of richer or different possibilities. Anne Stevenson describes the process better than I am able to:

> . . . it's the shared comedy of the worst blessed; the sound leading the hand; a wordlife running from mind to mind through the washed rooms of the senses.

This process of transferral – the 'wordlife running from mind to mind' – happened to me a few months ago when I read a poem by Gillian Clarke, called 'My Box'. It was one of those poems I talked about earlier, which had to be carried away to be

re-visited during the vacancy times of a working day. It was so
beautifully wrought, and of such immediate appeal, that I
committed it to memory. If I couldn't be the writer of such a
lovely poem then I would become the next best thing, a part-
owner of it. It begins:

> My box is made of golden oak,
> my lover's gift to me.
> He fitted hinges and a lock
> of brass and a bright key.
> He made it out of winter nights
> sanded and oiled and planed,
> engraved inside the heavy lid
> in brass, a golden tree.

Sometime during that day, by some trick of the imagination
and quite without warning, I found myself thinking about two
other 'box' poems I had read. In *Katerina Brae*, Christopher
Reid has one called 'A Box', and Ted Hughes' *Poetry in the
Making* is prefaced with the poem, 'The Small Box', by Vasco
Popa. You might think that this kind of memory link is not
worth writing about, but I was interested enough to place the
three poems alongside each other and reflect on what each poet
had selected to put inside his box. And some teacher reading
this might be prompted to work with a group of older secondary children on orchestrating the poems for choral presentation (a fascinating job, in itself); might like to use the poems
as models for crafting new ones; might encourage each child to
make a box, place the poem inside, then decorate and seal it. It
would make a good CDT project, but language across the curriculum seems to have died, and whoever heard of a relationship between poetry and technology?

When I started to write this article, it was my intention to call
it 'Bedding the Ear', a phrase from an essay by Seamus Heaney,
but writing about the box poems sent me back to Vasco Popa's
poem to look at it again. The little click of recognition, inside
the head, was almost audible, for 'The Small Box' holds inside
it some of the ideas I have been discussing. Here it is, in full:

> The small box gets its first teeth
> And its small length

Its small width and small emptiness
And all that it has got

The small box is growing bigger
And now the cupboard is in it
That it was in before

And it grows bigger and bigger
And now has in it the room
And the house and the town and the land
And the world it was in before

The small box remembers its childhood
And by overgreat longing
It becomes a small box again

Now in the small box
Is the whole world quite tiny
You can easily put it in a pocket
Easily steal it easily lose it

Take care of the small box

The small box waits for the reader to open it, and what is pulled out depends to a large degree on whose hand it is that dips inside. It seems to me that Popa is telling us about the truth of the inner world, the world of the spirit and the imagination: that area where the brain, working every day as a creative agent, examines and transforms and assesses the input it receives. And where poetry is concerned, it is not just facts that are taken into this inner world, but the emotions conceived by poetic language. I spoke, earlier, of 'small explosions of pleasure' and the 'little click of recognition' which poetry sponsors. If a poem is good enough, I rehearse the feelings it releases, again and again, whenever I read it. And although the poem may not teach me to feel deeply, it allows me to find out about the way I respond and how many emotions are cultivated.

We live in dangerous times for poetry, and for those who love it and know what it can do. The current wave of educational reform is based on an instrumental view of human worth. We are told we must control our children, and each other, by quantification, and if their work and ours doesn't lend itself to measurement criteria, assessment objectives, competency skills, and all the other threadbare trappings of reductionist theory, it seems to be of no value. We shall be told, of course, that literature is important and that its slot on the National Curriculum is assured, but you will wait in vain for the announcement of the establishment of City Colleges of Poetry, or for the opening of the first National Centre for Choral Speaking.

At its best, poetry helps children to become vigorous and adventurous and graceful users of words, nourishes the elusive substance of the human imagination, and shows them how to think well. Ted Hughes summed it up, a long time ago now, when he said:

> What matters most, since we are listening to poetry and not to prose, is that we hear the song and dance in the words. The dance and the song engage the deepest roots of our minds and carry the poet's words down into our depths. And the final sway over our minds that the poet has is largely the sway of the hidden waves of the song, and the motion of the dance in phrasing of the words that it compels us to share as we read or hear it.

I wonder how they will measure that at seven, eleven, fourteen and sixteen?

BfK 47
November 1987

The title catches the rhythms of movement; of sport, of 'Getting Nowhere', of dreaming. And the thoughts and feelings of youth are caught in language which itself dances to a variety of tunes. Berry refers in his excellent introduction to the 'I-can't-read-black-poetry' view. He explains how it can be done and demonstrates it in the poems. I hope the Puffin imprint won't mislead; there's a much wider readership for this, including GCSE and beyond. This is a special collection.

(Adrian Jackson reviewing James Berry's *When I Dance* in *BfK* 64, September 1990)

*Discovering poetry for the first time,
especially when it opens the way
between teacher and class, is exciting.
VAL DOWNES, a primary school
teacher, describes her experience of*

Coming to Poetry

I DON'T SUPPOSE I should have been surprised. After all, I'd seen it work before in my old school. The Rosen, Wright, Patten, Ahlberg magic enticing, and then entrancing, children. There it had been an easier, familiar, friendly commuter-land school and, looking back, of course I remember it working.

Changing schools last Autumn produced one of the most traumatic moments of my teaching career. My new school was a city school with a wide social catchment area though not one with all the problems you can get in the inner city. I was faced with twenty-nine strange third-year faces and any reputation I might have built up in my previous school counted for nothing. It was like starting out all over again, even if I did have a six-year running start. That first morning was a big confidence knock. I knew they'd had an unsettled previous year; I was, for them, yet another new teacher but I hadn't been prepared for the 'we-aren't-going-to-listen-to-you' hostility that greeted me the minute I stepped into the room. By the end of the morning I was feeling awful.

I had a copy of *Quick, Let's Get Out of Here* but no particular intention of using it that day. The afternoon began with a long, unbroken two-hour session with the morning problems persisting. After about forty-five minutes I was at the stage where I badly needed my new class to listen, to hear me. I reached for Rosen, sat them down on the carpet and launched us all into 'Eddie and the Gerbils'.

. . . and suddenly I hear
'Hallo gerbils.'
'Uh?' Ignore it. Munch munch munch.
'Hallo gerbils.'
Better have a look.
Oh no.
He's got a dead mouse in his
hand. Clutching it.
Head poking out the top of his fist,
tail out the bottom. And he's stroking it.
The dead mouse.
And he's going,
'Hallo gerbils hallo gerbils hallo gerbils.'

Illustrations by Quentin Blake from *Quick, Let's Get Out of Here*

Instant attention! I had to read it again and again, and then the bits that stuck, once more. We moved on to other Eddie poems; more bits stuck.

'Time for the cream, Eddie.'
And he goes,
'No cream.'
So I say,
'Yeah, cream,'
and I blob it on
and he goes, 'Oooh.'
You imagine what that would feel like.
A great blob of cold cream.
It would be like
having an ice-lolly down your pants.

That's how it started; quite unexpectedly, through poetry, I began to build up a relationship with my new class – and through the poetry of Michael Rosen in particular. Most days we'd try a new one and always go back to 'favourites'. A momentum slowly began to build over the first half of term. I had to read them over and over again until the children knew parts of them off by heart. The word spread; I would catch them reading to the dinner ladies or sharing them with a friend in a corner of the playground. *Quick, Let's Get Out of Here* became and still is one of the most sought-after books in the school.

Having tasted success, I felt confident to move on to other poets. Brian Patten's *Gargling with Jelly*, Allan Ahlberg's *Please Mrs Butler*, and Rosen and McGough's *You Tell Me* quickly joined the ranks of firm favourites. They started borrowing books, reading them and then telling me which poems I should read to the rest of the class.

My little sister was truly awful,
She was really shocking,
She put the budgie in the fridge
And slugs in Mummy's stocking.
(from *Gargling with Jelly*)

They even made up little sketches which they enacted whilst one child narrated the poem, usually from memory. The final triumph was watching the children choose poetry books, not mentioned by me, as their library books and knowing that at least a third of my class read poetry during quiet reading periods.

After half-term, realising that something special was happening, it became very important for me to discover more about what had occurred, how they set about sorting and selecting material, and what their criteria were for deciding upon a 'good' poem. Borrowing an idea from Andrew Stibbs,* I presented the children with an even wider variety of material and left them to browse. They had to select three poems: one which they would like to copy out and keep, one which they would be happy to read out aloud to the rest of the class, and one which they would recommend to their friends.

I gave them 45 minutes, expecting considerable disruption from pupils I thought would not be particularly enthusiastic. A hushed calm fell on the room; complete absorption! For most of the children, 45 minutes was not being enough. I had to extend it.

What they all had in common was a desire to share the poem which they had chosen themselves. Although I didn't particularly need them to do this, it seemed so important to them that it would have been terrible to have denied them the very pleasure I was encouraging.

Their biggest difficulty was in choosing only three poems; there were so many they enjoyed. To understand a little more about why they had made their choices, I devised a questionnaire for them to complete. I deliberately kept it very short to avoid confusion or boredom. This produced rather limited but nevertheless interesting results. Only five children selected poems that were new to them and these five were from right across the ability range. I somehow expected this to come from the more able readers. The majority of the children included at least one poem that they were familiar with and many, not surprisingly, selected poems that were by poets that they knew and liked.

I asked the children to give reasons for their choices. Practically every child in the class said they enjoyed humorous poetry. No surprise here that children enjoy writing that portrays

* Andrew Stibbs, 'Poetry in the Classroom', *Children's Literature in Education*, Vol. 12, No. 1, 1981.

familiar playground wit. This is something that Roald Dahl achieves so well and both *Revolting Rhymes* and *Dirty Beasts* figured very highly amongst the children's favourites.

> The small girl smiles, one eyelid flickers.
> She whips a pistol from her knickers.
>
> (from *Revolting Rhymes*)

Another major reason given for their choices was that they liked the author. Many children in my class really feel that they know Michael Rosen and are delighted by the fact that he shares stories about his son Eddie with them. Some have even taken the trouble to find out biographical details about Rosen which they then connect with individual poems. Having this familiarity, the children believe in Rosen and read his poetry as true accounts of actual happenings.

Some children said that they liked it when all the poems in one book were by the same author because they were then able to read a collection as a complete book. In contrast to anthologies, which seemed to require a more complex response, collections more readily provided the children with narrative. This was underlined by the popularity of Roald Dahl's *Revolting Rhymes* because they tell a story.

Children's comments also revealed that they identified with certain characters in poems. Most children at some time have either been, or have suffered, a naughty little brother or sister. Brian Patten's 'The Trouble with my Brother' and 'The Trouble with my Sister' were very popular.

> Thomas was only three
> And though he was not fat
> We knew that there was something wrong
> When he ate the cat.
>
> (from *Gargling with Jelly*)

Other reasons given were not quite so universal, but nevertheless interesting. For example, the illustrations and visual presentation were important for several children, especially poems written in the shape of the subject. They enjoyed poems that rhymed, many thinking this to be 'clever.'

The teachers can sit in the staffroom
And have a cosy chat.
We have to go out at playtime;
Where's the fairness in that?
                                                (from *Please Mrs Butler*)

Some children were concerned about the actual subject of the poem; some particularly liked animal poems and those that deal with people.

It's difficult for me to draw concrete conclusions as yet; I'm still learning. I'm now planning to interview small groups of children in much greater depth. It would also be very interesting to repeat the whole experience but using a different group of poets and perhaps being slightly less 'accidental'! The important thing for me, however, was that when I read that first Michael Rosen poem to the children, they were captivated. They hadn't heard the poems before and they didn't know me, and yet almost instantly they responded in a positive way. Given the circumstances, if the children hadn't immediately liked what they had heard, they would not have listened and would have quickly made their feelings known. Rosen was the first step for me and my class in the exploration of many similar exciting poems. Even at this end of the year, they still listen to the same poems and are searching out new ones.

It's been as big an adventure for me too. I came to poetry with and through my children. It's hard to imagine a better way. I'd used and knew some poetry but the light hadn't quite dawned. Charles Causley says that he remembers little poetry before the age of eleven and Joan Aiken recalls being given it as a punishment. Not such bad company.

If poetry is given low priority in schools by teachers, it is perhaps due to their own lack of knowledge of, and exposure to, poetry, and not having the confidence to introduce and encourage it. Children too have been put off poems – often used only as a basis for comprehension work where pupils were literally asked to dissect them. Today, a wide range of material is available and it is fun for the teacher to discover the delights of modern poetry along with the children. Modern poets are able to communicate with children. It is in the interest of promoting this kind of sensitive communication that schools and libraries have an obligation to provide children with access to such books, so that they can extend their own personal reading experience and their enjoyment of poetry. Because of such poets and indeed through them, I was able to communicate with a new and hostile class. For that I am grateful and, as a consequence, my class and I will continue to explore new and exciting fields of poetry. It has become important to us.

BfK 51
July 1988

He was one of the first poets of his generation writing for the young to draw closely on his own childhood experiences (the child in him) and to 'tell it as it was' in the ordinary language children actually use. Up till then (his first book was published in 1974), most children's poetry was rather more formal and dominated by poets (often very good ones) who chose subject matter more remote from children's lives – funny rhymes, the natural world, cautionary verse, magic and the like, mainly written in traditional verse forms. Of course such poetry has its place, but the advent of writers like Rosen has added another dimension and, in so doing, has changed the face of children's poetry.

(Morag Styles, Authorgraph on Michael Rosen in *BfK 51*, July 1988)

The Poetry Library, South Bank Centre, has recently opened a children's section in its new purpose-built library in the Royal Festival Hall. The collection, consisting of about 2,500 modern poetry books for teachers and children, also includes the Signal Poetry Collection, recently rehoused from the Book Trust . . .

(Newspage in *BfK 59*, November 1989)

Taking a Word for a Walk

GILLIAN CLARKE *tells how she tricks children into making images*

YOU CAN DO ANYTHING with images. A poet can make anything, do anything, make us see, hear, feel, smell, taste, imagine anything he or she wants. Sometimes to help children to make really surprising images, I play a trick on them. First I ask them to suggest subjects for poems. In Llannon Primary School, Dyfed, the children suggested 'The Spider'. Then I asked them to tell me as many things as they could think of which are like the spider. I said 'Think of a person who is like a spider. Think of a machine. Think of something to do with the weather, or nature, or your house.' There were many good ideas, like acrobat, architect, builder, electric whisk, sewing machine, knitting needles, God, the moon, a snowflake. Any of them would do but I chose acrobat.

Next I wrote down 'The Acrobat' on a new piece of paper. Secretly I remembered that the children had told me the acrobat is like a spider. The children thought of all the things they could say about an acrobat. I wrote it all down. When the page was full, the poem was ready. I crossed out the word 'acrobat' and wrote 'The Spider' as the new title. That was the trick. They were very surprised, as they had thought their poem would be called 'The Acrobat'. Here it is.

The Spider

Daring and skilful,
determined to dazzle
he performs his tricks on the rope,
turns cartwheels on his wire.

He rides his delicate bicycle

wheels spinning
a tumble-drier
a whirlwind.

He perfects his tricks
walks on stilts on wire
It shines like silver
strong as gold.

He balances to music
drums beating
as he walks on his hands.

Do you think the trick worked? I do. It is exciting to think of
the spider doing all those things in his shining morning web,
just like an acrobat.

Here is a beautiful poem by the six-year-old children in Glyn
Corrwg Primary School in Glamorgan. They said a snowman is
like a candle and thought about a candle first. Then we changed
the title to 'The Snowman'.

The Snowman

He shines like a candle
and melts slowly

He is white and black
and gets smaller all the time

He is as white as feathers
and white horses and snow

He glows in the dark
like a glow-worm

He stands on a flat place
and makes a shadow in the light

He crumples in a circle
like a circus tent

He turns to ice and slush
like a camel's hump

He runs away like milk
and melts like moonlight in sunshine

In the morning he has gone
like the moon

It is true. You can do anything with images. It is like a magic power that anyone can try to use, and often that magic works. If you are a very great poet, like William Shakespeare, it nearly always works. If you are a young poet, it very often works. Here is a poem by Charlotte Poulter, from a primary school in South Wales. In Charlotte's poem, the magic works. She pretends to be something that we can all recognise, and then she transforms the world with a poet's power.

The Sun

I have painted the school in a coat of gold
I have painted the church
It sparkles and glistens
I have painted a house and it shines
I have painted the apple tree
But the apples are green
I have painted a picture-frame
that hangs on the wall
I have painted a girl walking on a road
She has golden slides in her golden hair
The girl walks to school
And the school is a golden box.

Poetry 0–16: A BFK Guide, 1988

The winners of the Faber and Faber Write-A-Story Competition for children were selected according to which entries appeared to have been enjoyable to write. Consequently, the book provides much in the way of light entertainment, but this rather bland collection of mainly escapist fantasies reflects little of the storymaking of children living in a real world of personal and social strife.

Still, there are some gems here. My class particularly enjoyed 'Naughty Mr Nip Nip' – a chilling miniature narrative by six-year-old James Granger. May his pen never rest.

(George Hunt reviewing Ted Hughes' *Winning Words* in BfK 70, September 1991)

Authorgraph
Charles Causley

MORAG STYLES

Mary, Mary Magdalene
lying on the wall,
I throw a pebble on your back,
Will it lie or fall?

When my pebble landed on Mary Magdalene's back I *knew* I was lucky, not just because I was walking round Launceston with Charles Causley as my guide. Not only did I see the ravishing Mary Magdalene church and hear the stories associated with it, but I was also shown eagle one and two, peering down from the top of an elegant house with Britannia beside them. Those familiar with Causley's poetry will immediately recognise the site of two of his best-loved poems from *Figgie Hobbin*, his earliest collection for children.

Launceston, the town where Causley was born, grew up, and where he still lives today, is a fascinating place, the old capital of Cornwall. As the seat of the judiciary, Launceston had a grisly record of public executions and the like. A grim prison dominated the town centre with the remains of a castle and what was once a walled town. Causley grew up in a place where the past cast its spell on the present; the games he played, the rhymes he chanted, the stories he knew backwards were all steeped in the town's riveting and macabre history, relics of which were all around him. Causley's words in the introduction to *The Puffin Book of Magic Verse* seem extremely apt: '. . . folk memories of our long crawl out of the prehistoric cave into the sun of reason will awaken easily.' One brief trip to

Launceston was enough to explain the inspiration and genesis of much of Causley's work.

He is a delightful man, even more fascinating and entertaining than his poetry promised. Any sense of a poet limited by living in a quiet backwater should be dismissed at once. (He has, of course, travelled widely.) The many books covering every possible surface of the Causley study reveal an intellectual with a breadth of interests. He is also modest, down to earth, laughs a lot and doesn't believe in taking himself too seriously, even though he is now Causley, CBE.

Causley attended the local primary school in Launceston of which he was later to be teacher himself for twenty-five years. He was a keen reader from a young age, but didn't remember much exposure to poetry in his early years of schooling except 'a faint-hearted attempt to interest us in Christopher Robin . . . he didn't go down terribly well with me or anybody else in the national school in the late 1920s – he might as well have come from outer space!' Later at grammar school Causley showed obvious promise as a writer and was introduced to the Georgian poets whom he found boring, preferring the resonances of 'Young Lochinvar' and 'Ozymandias'. 'Great stuff!'

What Causley did remember with affection was his old head-teacher (soon to figure prominently in his forthcoming *The Young Man of Cury*), a fine musician, pumping away furiously on the harmonium as he took the whole school for mass singing lessons through the entire repertoire of Cecil Sharp's extensive collection of English folk songs. Causley has always been drawn to the musical side of poetry and he is much admired for his own body of wonderful ballads. He has also devoted a lot of time to writing for music theatre, often composing between books of poetry.

As a teenager in the thirties, Causley and his contemporaries involved themselves in the usual activities of that age group, drinking, dancing and, in his case, playing for the local dance band. But they were well aware of events in Europe and the inevitability of war. 'We all followed the terrible progress of the Spanish Civil War . . . I remember coming home, having my dinner and hearing accounts of the bombing of Madrid . . . you knew it was all going to happen again . . .' What made Causley angry then and still does today is that 'if you had any intelligence

Charles Causley

at all it was perfectly clear what was happening to the Jews in Europe . . .'

It was the fact that poets like Auden, Spender and MacNeice were prepared to speak the truth that attracted Causley as a young man to poetry and he has never moved away from that position. 'The interesting thing about the poem . . . for me . . . is that there's always a sub-text . . . the skin of the poem is never what it's really about . . .'

Causley writes for both an adult and a juvenile readership and doesn't discriminate seriously between the two. His *Collected Poems* contains much of the body of work on the children's list, as well as his adult books. Causley does *not* believe that writing for a younger audience is light relief. He offers them challenges and mystery like the poem 'Why?', based on a childhood memory:

Why do you take my hand, Susanna,
As the pointing flames jump high?
It's only a bundle of sacking and straw.
Nobody's going to die.

It's hard to feel the same about that macabre annual ritual after reading this uneasy poem. As the author says, 'It's a thin dividing line between ecstasy and terror.'

Readers of Causley are drawn to his work because of its musicality and because the poetry feels so rich and deep, although it is often an apparently simple tale on the surface. 'The great problem [in writing poetry] is to achieve these resonances and hints and suggestions and reverberations, and it's an endlessly difficult and endlessly fascinating task to get the thing to work somehow or other . . .' And, of course, he succeeds wonderfully. Causley is now seventy-three, clearly at the height of his power, and there are several new collections in the pipeline.

Causley produced one of the earliest anthologies of contemporary poetry for children, *Dawn and Dusk*, in 1962. Since then, he has compiled three of the finest anthologies of the twentieth century for the young. Clever of Kaye Webb to snap him up for Puffin in the early seventies. *The Puffin Book of Magic Verse* begins thus: 'All poetry is magic. It is a spell against insensitivity, failure of imagination, ignorance and barbarism.' Wow! Causley is a creative and scholarly editor: 'The rule of thumb I had about anthologising was never to make an anthology from other anthologies. It's got to be fresh. I don't think you can do an anthology in under a couple of years. The work should be of the first order. If you think Arnold should be represented, you read the whole of Arnold first.' Bravo!

Causley subsidised his passion for writing by teaching until the early seventies. He insists that he wasn't a particularly good teacher: 'too short a fuse . . . too strong a sense of humour . . .' The more he told me (always deprecatingly) about the way he approached the kids and the curriculum, the more convinced I was that he was a superb, natural teacher. His approach to teaching poetry was simple. Apart from the necessity of reading children a wide range of poetry first, he believed in giving them time, space and freedom. 'I've never set a subject . . . write about something you feel strongly about . . . first-hand experience . . . get it out of life . . . let them make the decisions about it all . . . they know exactly how a poem should look, the shape, how long it should be . . . and they can space out their emotions in a remarkable kind of way, like little bursts of gunfire . . .

I would only put the spelling right so that when the poem was typed out for our anthology, adults wouldn't snigger because of spelling mistakes . . . who worries about that?' Embedded within those apparently casual comments is a whole philosophy about poetry and education.

One thing Causley did like about teaching was the children. 'I was determined to enjoy myself. I never went to school with a heavy heart. I used to set off feeling like a nineteenth-century explorer with a butterfly net . . . and all the wrong equipment . . . as if I was going into undiscovered territory . . . you never knew what was going to happen.' He deplored the large class, the crowded curriculum and too little time, especially for those kids who found learning difficult. Causley didn't think he would have got on too well with the National Curriculum! And he marvelled that it was often the children without many literary skills who wrote the best poetry, 'somehow jabbing down something from their own experience'. A great humanity for, and admiration of, children came over strongly. 'If you get kids on your side they'll die for you . . . they're heroic . . . I love the way they go flat out at things . . . they're economically unsound, physically small . . . and they're often badly treated by adults who fail to understand them . . .'

The main influences on Causley as a poet have been the circumstances of his own life. Living in Cornwall, the feel for the natural world and the sea; the folklore associated with that part of the world; his partiality for music including all kinds of songs; his compassion for the underdog, partly stemming from his working-class roots, his humane beliefs and his hatred of Auden's twentieth-century ogres, particularly intolerance. Then there was Causley's family and his deep attachment to his parents. His father died quite a young man in 1924 from the effects of the First World War. The pain of the experience is suggested in some of Causley's poetry, like this extract from 'Tavistock Goose Fair':

> Today, I hardly remembered my father's face;
> Only the shine of his boot-and-legging leather
> The day we walked the yellow October weather;
> Only the way he strode at a soldier's pace,

The way he stood like a soldier of the line;
Only the feel of his iron hand in mine.

Causley's mother was a great fund of stories and memories, one of the most celebrated of which is 'My Mother Saw a Dancing Bear'. It is typical Causley – a good story, simply told, with a strong, understated message.

> They paid a penny for the dance,
> But what they saw was not the show;
> Only, in bruin's aching eyes,
> Far-distant forests, and the snow.

One of the most remarkable things about Causley is how closely in touch he remains with himself as a child. Perhaps that is one of the reasons why he is such a good writer for children. The final poem in *Figgie Hobbin*, 'Who?', is a good example.

> Who is that child I see wandering, wandering
> Down by the side of the quivering stream?
> Why does he seem not to hear, though I call to him?
> Where does he come from, and what is his name?

Echoes of Robert Louis Stevenson's 'To Any Reader': 'and it is but a child of air. Who lingers in the garden there'. When asked why he doesn't write his autobiography, Causley replies: 'There's not much to say apart from the poems . . . as Rebecca West said, "You can't be sick off the same meal twice!"' This captures Causley so well – his lively sense of humour and his serious commitment to poetry.

> Why does he move like a wraith by the water,
> Soft as the thistledown on the breeze blown?
> When I draw near him so that I may hear him,
> Why does he say that his name is my own?

BfK 64
September 1990

Poetry is a vital dimension;
JILL PIRRIE shows how affirming it
can be in

The Tree and Uncle George:

Green Themes in the Poetry Classroom

ENGLISH TEACHERS DO NOT TEACH environmental awareness.
Rather, they attempt to inculcate it at the deepest level. Poetry,
in particular, imposes constraints of structure, economy, sound,
which enable children to transcend easy sentimentality, look as
though for the first time, and articulate a responsibility for
Earth which has its roots deep within ourselves and our literary
heritage. In the following extract, for instance, the fallen tree
and Uncle George share a deep and elemental source. The same
sun had shone upon them; the same rain had fallen. Now both
have returned to their beginnings:

> The death of Uncle George
> Is woven into the tree's departure.
> The way he used to limp
> Through Henham Woods
> As the rain slowly seeped
> Through his battered raincoat.
> His half-bald head
> Covered in a film of water
> That shimmered in the sun
> Like an over-glazed pot.
> And his worn shoes
> Were the cut-off roots of the stricken tree
> Wedging him firmly
> To the living earth.

Matthew Booley (12 years)

Here the human response to Henham Woods affirms the child's own life source and something of his responsibility to this Earth. The fallen rainforests may seem a far cry from Matthew's blasted tree. In fact, they are inextricably linked. Environmental awareness starts at home; it does not end there.

Sometimes dangers to the environment are natural and the sense of helplessness all the more marked. Dunwich, a Suffolk coastal town, was once a thriving city. Over centuries, the sea has eaten at the coastline until all that remains is a small village. Recently, erosion has been accelerated by the gales which have swept the shores, and man's culpability in the changing climatic conditions is, at least, a matter for conjecture. Here Stephen contemplates the awesomeness of Nature:

> . . . the crumbling cliffs, a line of formless village elders,
> Elders of the village of Britain
> Sat in a never-ending war council against the sea.
> And losing the cold war.
>
> Stephen Gardam (13 years)

Fearfulness, when expressed in and structured by poetry, is so often a necessary pre-requisite to that acceptance and respect which is finally resolved in a sense of responsibility.

Children have all the potential for direct, vigorous writing but they may look without seeing, know without realising. The teacher must provide opportunities for what W Hart Davies calls:

'just looking in a different direction' –

that state of dream-like introspection which is in no sense vague or abstracted. Rather, it is that wakefulness, absorption practised by the poet as he focusses sharply, narrowly, in an attempt at that special kind of thinking which is poetic. Ted Hughes' 'What is the Truth?' is such a dream sequence. God's Son wishes to visit Earth. His Father decides to travel by night because:

In their sleep (men) will say what they truly know.

There follows an inquisition in which villagers are challenged to speak the Truth of a chosen creature. Sometimes they come tantalisingly close to the Truth in startlingly appropriate imagery but, always constrained by their human condition, they must fail. Children engage readily in role play in which they gather on the hillside to speak the Truth before God, Himself. It was within the context of reading this book that my own pupils attempted a 'Green Fable'. 'The Last Elephant', written for this fable, illustrates a child aspiring to 'name' her chosen creature accurately and truthfully, at the same time expressing a wistful sense of its vulnerability.

The Last Elephant
The Elephant came furthest of all.
He followed the Star.
His legs carried his weight for so long
his socks fell down
and made life-long wrinkles.
His ears, ragged,
like a well-worn scarf,
his eyes, brown painted rocks,
smoothed off and gentle
to form great pearls of wisdom,
leading the way across the plains.
His body was as if
he was the most comfortable of all
in his baggy clothing.
His wrinkles were like the ones in the sand,
delicate and always there.

Emma Neilson (13 years)

Two years earlier, Emma had written an 'Elephant' poem. Then, the impetus to write had been released by ivory elephants on a mantelpiece. Repelled and moved by the sight, her words transcend sentimentality as she addresses reality in the uncompromising language of poetry:

The African Elephant Speaks
There used to be thirty
when I was young;
now there are only five.

The rest are dead;
their mothers carried them for nine years.
They wasted their time.
They're on the mantelpiece now,
well, part of them.
The other part is lying on a pile, rotting.
Some were as young as one year,
their little ears flapping
and their bodies wobbling, caked in mud.
Their eyes were like black diamonds,
fitted in wrinkled rock.

Emma Neilson (11 years)

Similarly, Paul mourns the decreasing herds of Highland ox.
On holiday in Scotland he feels first a sense of permanence:

It was wild,
Could have known John the Baptist,
The locusts and honey . . .

Then, a sense of loss:

Suddenly
A crack!
Dove shot out of a nearby forest;
A dog whimpered half a mile away.
And there was a thud
Of rock,
Clay,
And heaving bones.
I never saw him again.

Paul Sparkes (13 years)

Sometimes modern farming methods are the focus. Joanna
writes of the birth of piglets:

In her cot of metal bars,
Rolls of fat, tidal waves.
Underneath, no room for expansion.
A piglet stands in her stiletto shoes,

Her heel stuck through the orange, plastic floor,
A sieve for muck and membrane.

Joanna Tyler (13 years)

As Gareth Owen has said, 'feeling is incapable of direct communication'. It is through concrete imagery, sound and rhythm that it is articulated and released.

'What is the Truth?' ends with the crowing of the cock as the Father leaves this Earth and the Son prepares to remain. Today the crowing of the cock, with all its connotations within our culture, crows for the betrayal of Creation as well as for the betrayal of the Son. And, as Ted Hughes has said, 'those children know it in their bones'.

It is most surely within a context of reading and writing poetry that children learn to know their creation in the literary sense. This precludes the didacticism which all too easily enervates the teaching of moral attitudes and aesthetic values. When the facts have been assimilated, feeling stirred, then again it is poetry which achieves the detachment which confronts reality without concession or sentimentality. This confrontation is the basis of environmental education. And the beginning of hope.

The BfK *Green Guide to Children's Books*, 1991

He can enter the mind of a small child ('View from a High Chair') and enact its insistent thumping for its mother to come and release it in the poem's heavy rhythms. He can describe his son's pain on falling into nettles and, having soothed him, comfort himself by scything them; but 'My son would often feel sharp wounds again.' Some of these will be the wounds of love, first felt (at age 5) for Jessica; and the comfort? '"The pain will go in time," I said.' There are poems which gradually reveal the danger, or at least the scare, of camping out at night, or of climbing a tree. And always the child's predicament is feelingly, accurately created, sympathetically told, and then given a perspective which offers an understanding – though not always comfort.

(Gordon Dennis on Vernon Scannell in *BfK* 79, March 1993)

PART FOUR

Information Books

Perfecting the Message

PAT TRIGGS talks to Aliki about her approach to information books for children

IN 1983 THE BODLEY HEAD publicity calendar had for illustration a lively picture story showing how a book is made. It was informative, colourful and witty; it also contained instructions for cutting and folding which, if followed, turned the illustration into a miniature book. Such thoroughness in pursuing an idea to its logical conclusion is characteristic of the artist who designed and drew the calendar: it was Aliki.

In October *How a Book Is Made*, much expanded from the calendar, is published in book form.

Aliki is an American artist who has lived in London since 1977. She has a string of delightful picture books to her name and has illustrated stories by her Swiss husband, Franz Brandenberg; but in particular she has a unique and distinctive way with information. It is a style which has been developing steadily since her first information books were published in the USA in the sixties.

Returning from Europe to the States, Aliki and her husband settled in New York. She took her art school training into advertising and found she hated everything about it. Looking for a way out, she took her portfolio around the publishing houses. The book business was booming and before long she was being offered the chance to produce a book about dinosaurs. She said, 'I don't know anything about dinosaurs.' The publisher said, 'Great.'

Looking back to that incident and that book, Aliki says, 'Now I know what he meant. I have a friend who knows everything about birds. His books are not successful because he knows too much; he doesn't know what his readers don't know.'

So Aliki started to find out about dinosaurs and the resulting book, *My Visit to the Dinosaurs,* has about it the freshness of a child's first encounter with those compelling, awe-inspiring fossils. How many facts to include, how to present them, what to do about specialised language: these are all problems facing the creators of information books. What goes into an Aliki book is determined by her remarkable ability to see and feel like a child. No matter how exhaustive the research, and it is frequently as extensive and detailed as it would be for an adult book, when the book is being planned, written and drawn, Aliki is writing for herself, but with a part of herself which can still conjure up the perspectives, the preoccupations, the responses of childhood. So that first dinosaur book acknowledges that huge dinosaur skeletons can be frightening, that eating and survival and having 1,600 teeth are interesting. Here also are the first of the little jokes and asides that now regularly punctuate the illustrations in an Aliki book, lightening the tone and offering additional information: in a museum beside a notice requesting 'Quiet', children shout and jump with excitement.

In addition to that carried by the pictures and the main text, information Aliki-style comes in speech bubbles, supplementary hand-lettered text, labels, notices. She knows that children are put off by large, dense blocks of words; spreading the commentary on the pictures among different sources makes it possible to simplify or amplify, to smooth out complications, engage interest, point up details. The readers can take as much or as little as they feel able to handle. 'Books are so expensive,' Aliki says, 'you should be able to go back to them again and again and find new things in them.'

That's a criterion her books certainly meet. In the early days, her response to a request for a second dinosaur book was 'Besides their names, what is there?' Now it's more a case of when to stop. She is a dedicated researcher. On a visit to London (the one that convinced them to stay), the whole Brandenberg family, but especially children Jason and Alexa, got very excited about the Egyptian mummies in the British Museum. 'I was going to do a book just about unwrapping them – then I found there was so much more.' The 'so much more' which found its way into *Mummies Made in Egypt* includes information about Egyptian history and religion as well as highly

detailed accounts of embalming, tomb building, funeral cere-
monies, etc. The illustrations are all in Egyptian style, many
adapted from paintings and sculptures found during the
research. For this meticulous attention to detail Aliki blames
one of her American editors, Barbara Fenton. 'She's the kind of
person who goes inside of you and takes out so much more than
you think you have. She adds so many facets to whatever I
thought I could do. The more questions she asks the more I discover. Now we try to outdo each other with how much more
we can get into and out of a book.'

A Medieval Feast was commissioned in New York and suggested because of Aliki's love of cooking and baking. 'That
book was a direct result of our move here. I wanted to do a
book about England and English history. I visited churches,
castles, houses with my sketchbook. I read and read and read
– there was so much I didn't know about flowers, plants, what
people grew and ate in the Middle Ages. I'm passionate about
gardening, too, so that was another pleasure.'

The problem of how to present all this for children was
solved with the idea of someone coming to visit. 'A neighbour
told me about royal visits and how expensive they were for the
hosts.' There was the shape of the story and the cue for the less
than delighted expressions on the faces of the lord and lady of
Camdenton Manor as they receive news that the king and his
court are intending to stay for a few nights. 'Everything in that
book comes from a specific source except for the kitchen. I
couldn't find a picture of a kitchen. I nearly put a cat in
although I had never seen one in a medieval manuscript. I'm
glad I didn't; I've since discovered that cats were bad luck and
they were never put into pictures.'

With *How a Book Is Made*, Aliki must have won the competition for 'getting things in' hands down. There is everything in
it, from the author getting the idea to the book in the library
and bookshop and eventually in the reader's hands. There is
technical information about computerised typesetting and the
four-colour process, the offset printing press and book-binding,
about selling, marketing and publicity. Yet it remains a book
that can be enjoyed by children of all ages – younger children
can skip the complex bits.

'I did most of the research for the calendar and, being in

A book starts with an idea.

The AUTHOR thinks of a story.
She writes it down.

It is harder than she expected.
Sometimes she can't find the right words.

She has to look things up.

A page from Aliki's *How A Book Is Made*

books myself, I knew some of it very well. But [familiar caveat] I needed to go into some things in greater depth.' The printing process, for example. 'I had to understand it completely. I don't have that kind of mind. I used to draw very superficially until Jason was born. He never sat on a seesaw; he was always underneath it finding out how it worked. I've learned so much from him. For this, I had to understand exactly how the paper went through, why the paint didn't smudge. Lots of people helped me.'

How a Book Is Made has a cast of cats. 'I thought it would make it less serious. It could have been very dreary; I thought the cats would allow me to give it more humour, more lightness.' It also meant not having to draw her editor – though everyone in the book is modelled on a real person and sometimes the resemblance is strong, 'even though I didn't intend it to be'.

Almost the first thing Aliki did for *How a Book Is Made* was to write the book *The Sunny Day* which is described 'being made'. That's typical of a thoroughness that won't sell children short. If the books are successful, it is because so much care and thought has gone into them, often years of thinking and mulling over. 'It takes a long time for a book to come out; the yeast has to rise, you can't force it. When I start I still don't know what will happen until the pen hits the paper. If it's the right time the manuscript comes quickly and I go on to making the dummy, that's the most creative and exciting part. After that it's just a question of perfecting the message.' And perfecting . . . and perfecting . . .

BfK 40
September 1986

'Take, for example, *All About Bread* (1984): it's such a massive subject which you've got to get into thirty-two pages so you've got to become almost an authority before you can say, "Right, I won't have that, but I will have that" . . . and it's always changing. You're always hearing people or talking to people – as well as consulting libraries and museums – because there are always these old boys around who remember all this and in twenty years' time they'll be gone. That generation is still there to draw on. I go down to the pub, to the boozer, because it's the meeting point of any village. Of course, you have to get to know them and it can take a long time, but they'll tell you some lovely stories.'

(Geoffrey Patterson quoted in *BfK* 36, January 1986)

I try to take pains when writing about Islam to make it clear, as far as I can, that I do so as a non-Muslim primarily addressing other non-Muslims. The collaboration and advice of supportive Muslim friends has therefore been invaluable. A decade ago, I worked on a survey of the Islamic world aimed at the middle-school age range. What one of my friends calls the 'insultant' was anything but that. An Arab, educated in both the classical and Western traditions, he was a long-term British resident with an English Muslim wife. Together we went through my MS literally word by word. In some ways it was like the UNESCO experience, looking for the *mot juste* that conveyed accuracy of meaning without leaving either the believer or the sceptic feeling unduly compromised. A crucial passage dealt with the authenticity of the revelations of the Prophet Muhammad, which we finally phrased as follows: 'Muhammad was sitting in a cave on Mount Hira, when he sensed the presence of a strange being. This was perceived by him as the angel Gabriel . . .' 'Perceived' seems a bit heavy-handed perhaps, certainly unpoetic; but perception was what the experience seems essentially to have been about.

(Richard Tames, 'The Truth, Nothing But the Truth – But Not the Whole Truth', in *BfK* 73, March 1992)

Facing the Facts

ELEANOR VON SCHWEINITZ
considers the current state of
information books for children

WHY IS IT THAT MANY of us find it difficult to name an outstanding information book for children or to list half a dozen outstanding information book writers? Would we have the same difficulty if the question related to children's fiction? Why is there such a plethora of awards for children's fiction and only one for information books? And why is so much more critical attention paid to imaginative literature for children?

The Series Format

First, it is only fair to acknowledge the very different talents involved in writing a successful novel and creating an information book. Very few authors have the subject knowledge and the ability both to write lucidly and entertainingly for children and to illustrate their own text. But when they have, a work of truly individual character can emerge with all elements completely integrated.

Most information books of the late 1980s are the product of a streamlined process. Under the control of an editor, the work of writer and illustrator is separately commissioned and brought together by the designer, who often creates a work of considerable visual impact and visual appeal. Nevertheless, many such books are highly ephemeral: within a short space of time they are out of print.

The reason for this state of affairs lies in the economics of information book publishing and marketing. Economics of scale have tended to concentrate output into series, imposing a standardisation of approach that may stifle individual creativity.

This is not to deny that an experienced editor working with a closely knit team can and does produce attractive series books which communicate effectively with their chosen audience. But too often the series format imposes unhelpful constraints, quality varies from book to book, and (perhaps most damaging) information, uniformly packaged, appears undifferentiated. Series publishing has undoubtedly been encouraged by the institutional buyer. Schools and public libraries make up over 80 per cent of the information book market. The publisher consequently sees a large slice of the market defined in terms of educational needs and this may encourage the production of mere project fodder, especially if the consumer shows little discrimination in the selection of material.

For many hard-pressed teachers, information books are chosen from publishers' catalogues, where emphasis is given to the series (indeed some catalogues omit all mention of the author or illustrator). This approach encourages many teachers to assume that a series guarantees a standard quality in all its titles, and time is often too short to re-examine this assumption once the book is acquired.

Range, Scope, Pace

A further assumption – and one that is reinforced by publishers' catalogues – is that series books are suitable for a given age range. Similar page layout, type size and illustration style do suggest a certain uniformity, but closer examination can reveal some startling anomalies.

For example, a current book on money, in a series aimed at seven-to-ten-year-olds, confronts the young reader with the unfamiliar notions of a national economy, capitalism, socialism, inflation, share dealing and the stock exchange. All this in one double-page opening – four short paragraphs and three illustrations with captions.

Problems of this kind most frequently occur in those general catch-all series which include books on an indiscriminate range of subjects – historical, scientific, social, technological. Almost invariably targeted at the junior age group, such series lack any focus – and this can give rise to problems when defining the scope and approach of individual titles.

Thus a book on bridges, in a well-established series for

juniors, covers prehistoric times to the present day in a variety of countries around the globe. This in itself might seem ambitious in a book of thirty-two pages (of which only twenty-four are given over to the body of the text and where up to 50 per cent of each page is taken up by illustrations). But a closer look at those twenty-four pages reveals that bridges are not only considered from a technological standpoint (bridge-building materials and their relation to construction methods and bridge design), but also from a social and economic standpoint (communications and settlement patterns, trade and economic development). There is simply not enough space to introduce the range of factual information involved or explain the many different concepts needed to understand the various topics touched upon. Problems of this kind are less likely to occur in series which concentrate all their titles within a subject area and have a clearly defined approach.

The pace at which information is introduced can be critical in the learning process. Some texts introduce facts with machine-gun rapidity – expecting the reader to grasp new concepts and immediately apply them in the understanding of yet more unfamiliar facts. A successful book will explain, expand, illustrate and reinforce key ideas, often through the close interaction of text and illustration.

Words and Pictures

The relative roles of text and illustration – describing, explaining, exemplifying – vary from subject to subject. Technology makes different demands from the social sciences, for example. The reader's interest may be aroused and sustained by well-chosen illustrations in a book on animal rights, but an understanding of the subject is not dependent on them. Indeed such a notion as 'rights' cannot be directly explained by illustrations, whereas the workings of the internal combustion engine would be incomprehensible without the aid of well-labelled diagrams.

There is a high level of visual sophistication in the presentation of many new series, their initial impact depending on the dramatic use of illustration and graphics in the design of double-page openings.

The quality of illustrations can be impressive, with specially commissioned photographs and excellent artwork and diagrams. But, however good their quality, they must play an appropriate part in *explaining the subject*. The requirements of page design and the placing of illustrative material on the page can sometimes be at odds with this, so that illustrations are used as mere space fillers at one point in a book, whereas elsewhere the text is labouring to explain a complex process that requires far more detailed illustrative treatment than the page design will allow.

can transfer from one to the other without long delays.

In the past steam trains such as this one were to be seen in the city of Montreal.

   The earliest trains consisted of passenger coaches or goods wagons pulled by a separate locomotive. Until about 1900 almost every locomotive was worked by steam. Water in the **boiler** was heated by a very hot fire, fed with coal, oil or wood, and turned into steam at high pressure. This was piped to **cylinders** where the pressure pushed **pistons** to and fro. These were connected to **pivoted rods** which turned the wheels. Modern trains no longer run on steam, because

This is from a recent (1987) book on Railways. It covers a very wide range of aspects and hops from one to the other without much coherence or logic. Among the hotchpotch is this piece of text on how steam engines work. If it is to be included (questionable in a book like this) then it needs a clear, well-labelled diagram to illustrate the process.

Choice of illustrative style can be of crucial importance. Line drawings, diagrams, full-colour artwork and photographs each have their strengths and weaknesses in relation to different subjects. For example, a recent book on road building which uses only photographs would have been much more effective in clarifying its many technical aspects if diagrams and drawings had been used instead. And look at the extract about railways on the previous page.

Captions and labels can both play an important part in linking text and illustrations. But when diagrams use labels which do not match the terminology of the text, is it any wonder that the reader, struggling, let us say, with the finer points of the four-stroke engine, soon gives up – as, for example, the following illustration all too clearly demonstrates:

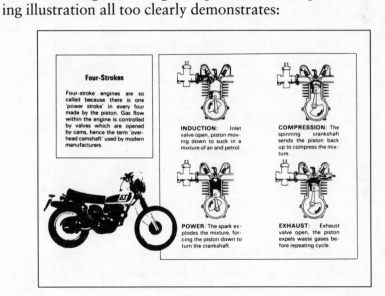

Four-Strokes

Four-stroke engines are so called because there is one 'power stroke' in every four made by the piston. Gas flow within the engine is controlled by valves which are opened by cams, hence the term 'overhead camshaft' used by modern manufacturers.

INDUCTION: Inlet valve open, piston moving down to suck in a mixture of air and petrol.

COMPRESSION: The spinning crankshaft sends the piston back up to compress the mixture.

POWER: The spark explodes the mixture, forcing the piston down to turn the crankshaft.

EXHAUST: Exhaust valve open, the piston expels waste gases before repeating cycle.

Captions can serve a variety of purposes. They may merely identify, they may discuss, explain or question. In each case they can form a bridge between the illustration and the text, facilitating interaction and furthering understanding. However, in books where text and illustration are separately commissioned, they may be so used in the page design that illustrations and their captions have no organic relationship with the text.

Sometimes, in an attempt to make an illustration self-sufficient, the accompanying caption is so long that it becomes difficult to distinguish from the text (especially if a similar typeface and size are used for each). These illustrations with their bumper captions are especially demanding for the reader because they often present difficult concepts in a highly condensed form and in total isolation.

Writing Readable Text

The text of an information book presents a challenge to the writer who must often condense and simplify yet at the same time try to avoid distortion or inaccuracy. A further problem when writing for younger children is that some of them will still be inexperienced readers. Faced with these problems, writers often fail to convey any enthusiasm for their subject. Texts are frequently pedestrian. Vocabulary is restricted. And by deliberately seeking to avoid any structural complexity, sentences and whole paragraphs become stilted, lacking the normal flow of easy communication. The outcome can be a text that 'reads' easily, but fails to communicate coherently with the reader. Some publishers have attempted to tackle the problem by adopting a narrative or first-person approach in books for younger children, but here again there are immense difficulties in finding an easy and convincing style.

Publishers are only too aware of the pitfalls when producing books for younger readers and they have frequently sought the help of educationalists when editing series aimed at the early reader. But the imprimatur of the reading expert is often attached to the dullest texts.

Publishers have responded to the educational research done on readability formulae (with the attendant stress on the length and complexity of words or sentences). But they have neglected the growing number of equally important studies which show that the *way* a text is structured is more significant than the so-called 'difficulty' of individual words and sentences.

Structure, of course, includes the overall organisation of the information and ideas throughout the book. A really well-integrated structure is never easy to achieve – but it is clearly impossible when the content is as wide and multifarious as that of the example on bridges referred to earlier.

Structure can also refer to the organisation of material within short passages of the text. A simply worded paragraph may, in fact, present a formidable barrier to understanding if its content lacks structural coherence – as the following passage (from a series for ten-year-olds plus) demonstrates:

> The music of carnival in Rio is the Samba. The dance of the same name is performed to this music and is made up of tilting and rocking motions of the body. In the parade the samba is usually danced in groups, but can be danced in couples. Today, the parade is as much for the tourists as for the local people. Brazil is the largest Catholic country in the world and after twenty-one years of military rule the people of Rio are poor. They see this as God's will, but everyone is equal at carnival and judged only on their ability to parade. Points are given under headings including songs, choreography, floats and rhythm.

In mainstream (rather than text book) publishing for the secondary-age reader, the uninhibited voice of the author can sometimes be heard. Heather Couper and Nigel Henbest's enthusiasm for astronomy reverberates in their prose and, for once, the browser attracted by dramatic illustrations will not lose interest when turning to the text nor lack clear, accessible information:

> The Sun is now a middle-aged star, about halfway through its life. In about 5,000 million years' time the centre of the Sun will run out of the hydrogen gas that powers its nuclear reactions. The 'ash' of helium from the nuclear reactions will then form into a small dense core at the Sun's heart.
>
> When this happens, the Sun's outer layers of gas will swell up to compensate, and the Sun will grow to a hundred times its present size. Its surface will cool down, to glow a dull red colour. The Sun will then be a red giant star.
>
> The outer layers of a red giant are not stable, however. They pulsate in and out; and eventually the Sun will puff off its outer gases in a ring-like cloud called a planetary nebula.
>
> Left behind will be the Sun's core, now exposed as a tiny, brilliant and very hot star called a white dwarf. The white dwarf will be very dense, and no larger than the Earth. But it will have no supplies of energy. Like an ember on a fire, it

will gradually cool down, and eventually become a dark star except at very close quarters.

Some of the most lively writing can be found in books on controversial topics where publishers have been willing to tackle subjects that give rise to strong emotions and differences of view. The insistence in some quarters that an issue should be considered from all viewpoints and in a dispassionate manner is hardly a prescription for lively writing. And the dutiful drawing up of a balance sheet is unlikely to provoke interest, let alone thought, on the part of the reader. Fortunately there are one or two writers for older children who examine different social and political subjects by skilfully juxtaposing factual statements in a thought-provoking manner and challenging the reader's attitudes by posing questions. Other writers have tackled contentious areas, such as the nuclear debate or green issues, with an open concern which comes through in refreshingly readable prose:

Questions of morality The moral issues surrounding terrorism are not always as clear as one might think. Is all human life equally sacred, or are there circumstances when murder is justifiable? On 20 July 1944, an attempt to blow up the Nazi leader, Adolf Hitler, failed. If the tyrant had been killed, how many innocent lives would have been saved?

Is there a moral difference between murdering an innocent bystander and murdering the soldier of an oppressive army of occupation? Is there a difference between a soldier killing an enemy and a terrorist killing an enemy? Or between the murder of a child and the murder of an adult? Is *risking* human life as evil as *taking* human life?'

Eye-catching Design

Questions of structure and meaning are especially pertinent for those packagers of information for whom 'presentation' would appear to be an end in itself. They are frequently in danger of sacrificing coherence and intelligibility to eye-catching page design.

Many information books divide up their material into standardised sections within double-page openings, each topped by a bold heading. It goes without saying that few subjects lend themselves to being chopped up into these uniform pieces. Different aspects of a subject may have to be condensed or padded out to fill the space available. Each page opening appears to be a self-contained package of information of equal weight to the one before. Any development or flow of ideas between them is obscured by the strident visual messages sent out by the page design.

These are books to catch the wandering eye of the child raised in an age of television advertisements. They are visually exciting and arouse interest but they do little to develop a real understanding of the subject. They may provide a handy sentence or two to copy into a project folder, but, for the browser who gets hooked and wishes to learn, bewilderment may follow. Where is the starting point? How does this illustration relate to that? How does it all add up?

Contents, Index: Retrieving Information

The headings used in these designer books are often catchy, alliterative, or allusive, requiring a certain level of verbal sophistication or prior knowledge of the subject for their interpretation. Some series reproduce a list of these headings on the contents page, to the mystification of anyone expecting to find a clearly structured outline of the subject. See the example overleaf.

The index, together with the contents page, is the main retrieval device of the information book. Educationalists now put considerable emphasis on the need for children to acquire the skills of information retrieval, whether it be to trace information through an automated electronic system or a printed book. Most information books for junior and secondary-age groups have an index but many of them are woefully inadequate. How can we expect our children to become independent learners if we give them useless tools?

There are real difficulties for the indexer of many junior information books. The wide range of subjects touched upon in the text without substantial development poses a problem. Too often an index is little more than an arbitrary selection of terms with no apparent reason for their inclusion or omission.

Contents

Catchy headings for 28 double spreads on the media make for fairly unhelpful guidance for the information seeker consulting the list of contents.

The reader is often directed to a word in the text but finds no real 'information' there or, alternatively, he looks for an expected term in vain. A recent book on the secret service which fails to index the word 'spy' is hardly likely to inspire confidence in the reader.

There is less excuse when this happens in a book for older readers, which is likely to have a far more meaty text. For example, a current book on the media fails to index such key concepts as 'bias' and 'censorship'. It omits important legislation such as the Official Secrets Act, and even significant personalities such as Mary Whitehouse. In fact, of the sixty-five terms in the index, twenty-one are the names of newspapers, although the text deals far less substantively with most of these than it does with the terms that have been omitted.

Even more perverse is the index which includes important terms but conceals them. Subjects are not entered directly in the alphabetical sequence but classified as sub-divisions of broader terms. In a book on the environment, the reader will look in vain at G for 'greenhouse effect' or W for·'whale'. With perseverance they may be discovered: the whale at H (under hunting) and the greenhouse effect at W (under weather).

Yet another fault in many indexes is to list up to twenty or more undifferentiated page references following an entry term. A supreme example of this is in a 48-page book called *Lifeboat* – in which the index has the term 'lifeboat' followed by a string of forty-eight separate page references. To add insult to injury, a further nine entry terms are subordinated to lifeboat (including the term 'crew').

Many books now include a glossary and this can provide useful support to the text. But an entry in the glossary cannot make up for fundamental deficiencies in the text. It is not the place to define key concepts. If their meaning is not made clear in the body of the text with all the means at the writer's disposal (extended explanation, illustration and exemplification), it is hardly likely that all will be revealed through a glossary definition. Nor is the glossary the place to introduce new information which should have been included in the text. In a recent new edition of a book on South African society, in which considerable attention is given to apartheid, the only account of the ANC appears in a brief glossary entry.

Further Reading

Lists of further reading can provide useful suggestions for the reader whose interest has been aroused, perhaps by some aspect of the subject. Some of the titles in a well-established series for older readers provide a model of how this should be done. The selection is imaginative and the succinct appraisals of content, viewpoint, authority, and so on, are sufficiently skilful to whet the appetite. But this is an honourable exception to the usual bare bibliographical listing of half-a-dozen to a dozen books, arranged in author order. It is hard to imagine even the most enthusiastic reader being inspired to visit a library and ask for one of these faceless objects, with no clue but the title to indicate what the book is about, and no indication of the particular features which have led to its being recommended.

A recent book on carnival (in a series for ten-year-olds plus) lists nine items for further reading. About halfway through the list appears: Frazer, Sir J G, *The Golden Bough* (Macmillan), 1936. The young reader who enquires for this at his local branch library is likely to be referred to the central reference library – to be confronted with this thirteen-volume classic (originally published between 1890 and 1915). The compiler of the reading list might at least have had the heart to recommend the abridged one-volume edition.

Much more imagination is shown when it comes to recommending organisations to contact for further information (or to join) and places to visit. These are usually briefly and often temptingly described. Why can't the same be done for the books that are recommended?

Some Improvement. Could Do Better?

In recent years many publishers have responded to the wide concern over social attitudes in materials for young people. Though initially slow to react, they have shown a growing awareness of these issues, in both the subject matter and approach of their information books. In particular, the number of books which support a multi-cultural view of society is increasing.

Publishers have also shown courage in tackling a range of controversial and tricky subjects – such as drugs and AIDS. There is an evident sincerity of purpose in some of these books which is very heartening.

In another welcome development, a few publishers are venturing into the relatively uncharted waters of information books for the nursery/infant age group.

But, overall, the picture is rather a dispiriting one. So many bright and attractive books are fundamentally incoherent; texts are mundane; words and illustrations fail to achieve their full potential because they fail to interact; retrieval devices are seriously deficient.

It is only when teachers and librarians exert pressure through

greater discrimination in their selection of information books
that publishers will be encouraged to confront some of these
questions.*

BfK 55
March 1989

I invited specialist consultants to draw up lists of headwords
in obvious categories but, since the ultimate consumers will
be children, I wanted to know what they were interested in
and what kinds of words they would use for their research.
We also had to resolve the dilemma faced by all compilers of
reference books: whether to be a lumper or a splitter. In other
words do you have separate articles on granite, limestone,
chalk, etc., or lump them all together in a general article
about rocks? In order to throw some light on the problem, we
distributed over seventy notebooks to parents, schools and
public libraries all over Britain, to places as diverse as Belfast,
Edinburgh and Leicestershire. The brief was to record *in the
child's own words* every request for information over a three-
month period. When the lists from the notebooks were col-
lated and analysed, the results were heavily weighted to the
sciences, especially zoology and technology, and very sparse
on literature and the arts. Moreover, in the sciences children
could pinpoint pretty exactly what they wanted to look up. In
contrast, mentions of the arts were much more vague.

(Mary Worrall, 'Creating the Oxford Children's Encyclopedia' in *BfK*
70, September 1991)

---

*We have deliberately not identified the books referred to in this article.
They are mentioned as illustrations of trends evident in many books
from a wide range of publishers.

Very few of the currently available sex education books for this age group contain even a brief mention of AIDS – even those first published or reviewed in 1986. What information is available is partial and selective: warnings against promiscuity, recommendations to abstinence or fidelity with a single partner, identification of gay men as 'high risk'. There is little reference to concepts of 'safer sex', to affected heterosexuals, to assessment of conflicting views among the experts, to specific information about the disease.

(Pat Triggs, 'Information Please About . . . AIDS,' in *BfK 45*, June 1987)

Sifting through recent books from mainstream publishers and from the development education agencies, I did find some encouraging signs that criticism about the presentation of Third World countries is beginning to be taken on board – but in a piecemeal fashion. It is still not possible to recommend without reservations a complete series, or the output of a particular publisher, or even some of the publications from the development education agencies who really ought to be getting it right . . .

(Rosemary Stones, 'How the Other Two Thirds Live', in *BfK 30*, January 1985)

Some Fictions of Non-Fiction

*ROBERT HULL questions some
standard beliefs about the language of
information books*

1. The library will have the books you want . . .

I've made several earnest forays to libraries recently, looking for
non-fiction for children to read – the sort the reader picks up,
gets hooked on, and goes through from beginning to end. And
I've been left with some dismally clear impressions, puzzles for
the teacher and parent in me.

i) Why, even at first and junior school level, are there far
more books that are good to look at than there are books which
children can read? And why so often does quality of text lag
behind quality of image?

ii) Even more acutely, why, in the eleven-to-sixteen age range,
is there a desperate dearth not just of good non-fiction to read,
but often of any non-fiction *at all* to read?

iii) Why are some subjects so much lazier than others that
they ought to be told to pull their socks up?

Have I been to the wrong libraries? Were the good books all
out?

I wonder if part of the trouble isn't the words. It might be
better if we had a less sombre lot of grey-suited terms than
'information', 'facts', 'non-fiction'. The other side has 'story',
'play', 'drama' – it's not fair.

To children, it really wouldn't be fair if, because we ourselves
couldn't shake off a grey Gradgrindian legacy of stern-speaking
about facts, it were to infiltrate books for children, and help
deny them access to the intellectual worlds we say we want
them to enter.

I wonder also, reading so many of these books, or rather

wandering uncertainly about in them, whether our basic hang-up isn't still the feeling that reading is not what one does with a non-fiction book. Perhaps we really still think that a science book for thirteen-year-olds *has* to be arranged 'logically' in chapters which contain 'the' suitable subject matter for that age, and that the essential function of such books is to 'transmit information'.

2. Non-fiction books are for conveying information . . .

The best books I've found – or been offered to read because as parent and teacher I couldn't find them for myself – say, in effect, that the essential job of their kind of non-fiction is not to 'transmit' and 'convey', and that 'facts' are not its defining concern.

The word 'fact' is a thorough nuisance, in fact. Take what sounds like a fully paid-up history fact: 'King Harold was hit in the eye by an arrow at the battle of Hastings.' Definitely a fact; more so than this, perhaps: 'And after the battle were over, They found 'Arold so stately and grand, Sitting there with an eye-full of arrow, On 'is 'orse with 'is 'awk in 'is 'and.'

Yet surely neither is, in itself, a fact; both are statements, for-mulations. The facts are long gone, in 1066. The only thing these statements 'transmit' is themselves. The writer makes statements that refer to (distant) facts, and the statements put together make a world. Which is why I want to say that what the most potent, readable, necessary (and mainly non-existent) non-fiction does is create a world, the world of a writer, a human self.

The books that are a delight to read do exactly that. I found, for example, Fred Wilde's *The Clatter of Clogs in the Early Morning*, published by William Collins, Canada, in which each spread has a reproduction of one of his paintings opposite his text:

At the top of his stick there burned a small acetylene flame made by dripping water on to carbide of calcium. He would push his stick up through the hinged window in the bottom of the lamp, turning on the gas at the same time. The gas mantle would go 'plop', and immediately there was a lovely pool of soft, golden light on the pavement.

'Information' in this book is not a marshalled battalion of 'facts', but a pattern in the intensely aware and informed vision of someone seeing and experiencing things. We meet not 'knowledge', the noun, but the man speaking knowingly, knowledge as adverb, as the accent or attribute of a writer's personality. Of itself, the encounter with such a book should settle an argument for us: we may say that the 'logical' or 'structured' text-book-like book is necessary, but we can never say that books in a particular subject must take that form.

I wish to pursue this fundamental point with reference to a recent picture book from Michael Foreman, *War Boy*, published by Pavilion Books, which like Wilde's also shows how marvellously possible it is for history, at least, to be a compulsive read. It is an account of his life as a young boy in Lowestoft during the Second World War. This, underneath a drawing, is the first page:

> I woke up when the bomb came through the roof. It came through at an angle, overflew my bed by inches, bounced up over my mother's bed, hit the mirror, dropped into the grate and exploded up the chimney. It was an incendiary, a fire bomb.

There's history in the grip of the detail:

> Ivan threw sand over the bomb but the dry sand kept sliding off.

And in sharing the small boy's experience:

> My mother grabbed me from the bed . . . The sky bounced as my mother ran.

And in local significances:

> The Germans were trying to set alight the thatched roof of the church to make a beacon for the following wave of bombers.

And in the comedy:

> At the beginning of the Black Out there were many more casualties in road accidents than from enemy actions . . . Men

People gave up carrying masks after a few months. We were taught to spit on the inside of the mica window to prevent it misting up. Gas masks were good for rude noises and fogged up anyway.

A page from Michael Foreman's *War Boy*

were encouraged to leave their white shirt tails hanging out at night. A local farmer painted white stripes on his cows in case they strayed on the roads.

Foreman's book is what books of non-fiction could far more often be like. It is a young boy's war world, presented with an immediacy that you can't resist; the 'information' about the war is integral to that world, and indeed through this idiosyncratic character adds its uniqueness to our understanding of the war.

3. Narrative is a good dramatic way to convey information . . .

Foreman's text is narrative, and narrative – storytelling – is perhaps the best way to hold the reader's attention continuously. That is, provided it works. Narrative is difficult, and needs a writer to write it; it can't be taken up, as it often seems to be, in the expectation that it will somehow create interest of itself. There are many non-fiction narratives that do not convince, and some that do. The assumption that narrative is essentially a (painless) way of 'conveying information' may well be very unhelpful.

'Informative' but inadequate narrative is so widespread that examples can be found almost at random. This is the first paragraph of *Columbus and the Age of Exploration*, by Stewart Ross, published by Wayland in 1985:

> In the crow's nest the look-out screwed his eyes up against the glare of the tropical sun. Beneath him the little forty-ton ship *Nina* rolled heavily in the Arctic swell. The sailor took a piece of dry biscuit from his pocket. It tasted foul, but there was no other food. They had been at sea for forty days now and supplies were getting perilously low.

The problem here is the writer's reluctance to commit himself to the narrative, and to the viewpoint of his narrator. He has half an eye on the fiction and one-and-a-half on the information; the look-out screws up his eyes to think about the food situation and the weight of the boat. There's no focus; we can't believe it as narrative.

Almost equally at random is some narrative text from a new book for lower juniors, called *Tiny Seed*, by Eric Carle, published by Hodder and Stoughton:

> A strong wind is blowing. It blows flower seeds high in the air and carries them far across the land. One of the seeds is tiny, smaller than any of the others. Will it be able to keep up with the others? And where are they all going?

On the next page:

> One seed drifts down to the desert. It is hot and dry, and the seed cannot grow. Now the tiny seed is flying very low, but the wind pushes it on with the others.

At first it isn't easy to see anything greatly amiss here. The text is 'true', it's 'easy'. But there is a fatal absence of particularity about it – not restored by the non-committal illustrations, in which the seeds look not that different from leaves. We don't know what kind of seed it is: we know only that 'One of the seeds is tiny'; the phrase 'far across the land' leaves us groping for a sharp picture of fields, a ditch, hedges. Then we turn over the page to the most token of deserts. The fate of the tiny seed leaves us deeply unmoved, because the narrative doesn't believe in its own story.

In other words, taking on narrative as a method, to remedy things, only works if the method is well handled. That seems obvious, but it is odd that we so often don't notice what's going wrong. Perhaps this is because we are bemused by the brilliance, often, of the visual component of non-fiction and the professional panache of glamorous packaging into not noticing the grotesque inertia of the text. We may even then also fail to notice that 'simple' text is also frequently difficult – not totally unapproachable, but sufficiently misty and gappy, in a low-key way, to keep the reader just missing the point.

Take for example – it could be many others – another new book in a nature series, *Earth*, written by Alfred Leutscher and brilliantly illustrated by John Butler, published by Methuen. One spread has these bald sentences opposite a beautifully drawn squirrel:

> When autumn leaves fall and decay they add more humus to the soil. In a forest of evergreens, however, there is little humus; the soil is poor and acid. The few pine needles that fall do not add much nourishment. The permanent gloom shelters deer and other shy animals.

. . . And so on.

This is far less easy than it looks. How do children of eight or nine pick up from this context the significance of 'evergreens' – as meaning trees different from trees whose 'leaves fall', while their own 'needles', puzzlingly, fall too? Is 'however' a word familiar to them? How do they know what, or maybe who, the 'nourishment' nourishes (assuming they understand the word 'nourishment')? Will they make the inference that 'the permanent gloom' is produced by 'the evergreens' or treat it as a different entity of some sort, just introduced?

This awkward text cannot tell its story, because it cannot dwell on anything for long. There is too much to do – one spread on farming, one on earthquakes, and so on. For me, it is just not readable. And the reason for that, ultimately, is that it is committed to a notion of 'information' that is diffuse, dislocated, uprooted from the personal intellectual history of the writer. It offers satellite pictures of what we need to see much closer up, out of a human eye in a place.

Compare it with ostensibly more difficult text, intended for older readers, from Richard Adams' *Nature Day and Night* (Penguin 1976):

> I see a grey wagtail bobbing and strutting on a flat stone under a little waterfall. He is bluish grey above and yellow below, very handsome; but it is his brisk, cocky walk (he never hops) and dipping flirting flight, and above all the long tail forever wagging like a clockwork toy, that make him so buoyant and attractive.

4. Some subjects are not suited to non-fiction . . .

I see that Adams writes here as implying an offer of access, through continuous engaged reading, to an intellectual world, and the other way as implying denial. I sense behind all such denials the conviction that the facts matter above all, and a belief that the topic-seen-necessarily-as-facts cannot be also shaped as personal vision. From that it is a step to saying that only chatty areas like history and nature are amenable to humanising treatment through personal, intellectual adventure stories.

This is a dubious argument. Over the years, there have been some fine books on architecture, to take a subject at the border between the two cultures. (Is architecture a science? I'd have thought so. Certainly, if geography and sociology keep putting their hands up saying they want to be, I'm going to let architecture be, too.) This is despite the fact that, apart from the compulsory manic tour of English castles, it's a subject that's historically enjoyed little support in schools.

David Macaulay's *Cathedral* – like his other books – is as much 'technology' as 'architecture', and shows that it is possible to write, for junior school children, technical text that is

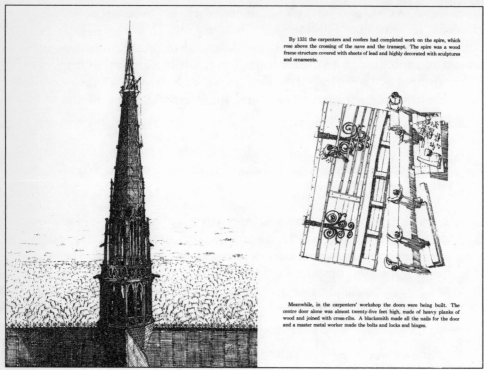

By 1331 the carpenters and roofers had completed work on the spire, which rose above the crossing of the nave and the transept. The spire was a wood frame structure covered with sheets of lead and highly decorated with sculptures and ornaments.

Meanwhile, in the carpenters' workshop the doors were being built. The centre door alone was almost twenty-five feet high, made of heavy planks of wood and joined with cross-ribs. A blacksmith made all the nails for the door and a master metal worker made the bolts and locks and hinges.

Double page spread from David Macaulay's *Cathedral*

effortlessly readable. His story of the building of a fictive 'Chutreaux' is engrossing as narrative, and intimately informative, visually and textually, at the level of (everyone's) mundane questions like, 'How did they get the arches up there?' or 'How do they make bells?' and so on.

Perhaps, some might say, you can only do it in some subjects. With maths, chemistry and physics, especially, text has to be impersonal, objective, etc. This is surely nonsense. Here is some physics:

Go with some friends under the hatches of some big ship and see that you have some small birds with you, and also a small bucket with a hole in suspended high above another one, so that the water will drip slowly from the higher to the lower one. Observe very carefully, when the boat is standing still, the way the birds dart about to and fro in all directions, and the drops fall into the bucket underneath. Get the ship to move as fast as it can and so long as the movement is steady and uniform, you will not see the slightest alteration in the way the birds fly or water falls, and you will not be able to tell from them whether the ship is moving or not.

Physics to *read* . . . from Galileo.

The largest puzzle of all therefore remains: why isn't there, twenty-odd years after the comprehensive idea threw open, at the level of ideology at least, academic subjects to all, more readable non-fiction? Why are books written for seven- to nine-year-olds and later for adults and A-level students, but not – so far as I can see – with anything like the same concern, skill or commitment for children of eleven to sixteen? Do we perhaps not believe that books are the one most effective means of enabling children to enter academic worlds?

If we didn't, it would explain to some degree why – especially in subjects like chemistry, physics, maths, even (amazingly) geography – the dearth of non-fiction reading books continues to block access to those worlds. Is that continued denial a consequence of comprehensive school versions of subjects, in which universality of access was not perceived as a problem? No need for children to read their way into commitment; you were either 'good at physics' – our physics – or not. Perhaps it is this reactionary aspect of the work of comprehensives that has come to roost in the monumental apathies too visible in schools.

5. The textbook has the basic information needed for the course . . .

The contents list of Cotterell and Russell's new *GCSE Social Science* (Heinemann Educational 1988) makes, so to speak, interesting reading. This is Section 1 (nine to come):

Methods Used in Social Science
1.1   The Questionnaire
1.2   Asking Questions: Interviews
1.3   Participant Observation
1.4   Surveys and Sampling
1.5   Secondary Sources: Documentary Evidence
1.6   Presenting the Information

What is worrying is the sense that this all-too-complete course not only can be, but probably has to be, accomplished without independent reading. The subject is already by page 5 defined in such a way as to put pupils' own language resources under suspicion, technicalising words pupils will know, like 'interview' and 'observation':

> The interview is a conversation between an interviewer and a respondent with the purpose of eliciting certain information. Observation is a method in which the researcher becomes involved in some way with the person or group being studied.

The 'Extension Activities' that follow the 'Question' section at the end of each chapter might imply here and there that reading is needed, but of what kind and at what pace is unclear. Nowhere is an actual request made to read a book, only to *Make a study of the upper class* (p. 53), *Make a study of gender socialisation* (p. 57) and so on. The iron insouciance of all this makes it likely that pupils will have their hands, if not their minds, only too full.

6. Exciting works of non-fiction can always be found . . .

Perhaps this close control over secondary-school subjects, and the denial of reading it entails, explains why so many of the good works of non-fiction one finds – on subjects just right for eleven- to sixteen-year-olds – seem to be written and packaged for the sixth form or tertiary level. It is tantalising to see a beautifully produced book, the concept of which is just right for eleven to sixteen, skew off towards that higher level.

One book that I found, for instance, seemed an ideal way in to aspects of (at least) maths and biology. Peter S Stevens' *Patterns in Nature*, published by Peregrine Books in 1976, has fascinating photographs and a very well-written text which one would love to see translated, or rather transposed, for twelve-year-olds:

> The leaves that curl counterclockwise on the left side of the front of the sago palm shown in fig. 54 are opposed by clockwise curls on the right side. Storms spiral counterclockwise

above the equator and clockwise below, just as in a more abstract realm, negative numbers camp to the left of zero and positive numbers to the right.

Time and again, one finds that the fascinating topic is only done in the adults-only version. Whether it's computer graphics, clouds, geology, the working of the brain, the structure of the eye, or whatever, readable non-fiction seems to be far more available for the older student. There are exceptional writers – Asimov, Grigson – who seem to enjoy writing for eleven to sixteens, despite the cultural pressure not to; but I've found it very difficult to discover any really good, new, through-read nonfiction for that older group.

That seems the most baffling of the puzzles. Not far behind is the puzzle of there still being so little really good text for seven- to eleven-year-olds either. Considering the brilliance of the illustration in so much work nowadays, it begins to look like a mystery. Perhaps non-fiction is more mysterious than fiction.

BfK 60
January 1990

For Philip Isaacson, a book about 'buildings' is a book about particular experiences of them. It's about being in the Great Mosque in Cordoba and seeing 'the colours switch so quickly that the arches seem to roll'. It's about looking at Wells Cathedral in the rain, and finding 'the golden cathedral . . . turns blue and green.' It's about awareness and discrimination, standing at doorways that invite us in and peering through fences that suggest we should stay out . . .

Any book is worth having which kicks the stool from under the superstition that non-fiction is packages of facts. But the importance of this book is that it makes ludicrous the notion that anyone can now write for children an 'objective' or merely 'historical' treatment of buildings which is not also a kind of personal statement.

(Robert Hull reviewing *Round Buildings, Square Buildings, and Buildings That Wiggle Like a Fish* in *BfK* 63, July 1990)

It's healthy to have your prejudices overturned occasionally and *Splash!* has caused me immense well-being. Written by two unfamiliar but exotic names and illustrated by a third, preceded by heart-bestrewn dedications and featuring animals in a predominantly pink bathroom setting, the book creates a first impression of unmitigatedly foreign (no, worse, American) soppiness.

Read on, though, and it's a brilliant exposition of the more simple properties of fluids, the ones whose effects are important at plughole level. While Penguin prepares for a bath, his friends discover all sorts of attributes of aqueous matter. It's always container-shaped (a piglet sucks it up through a curly-tail straw), it wrinkles the skin (even on an elephant), things float or sink in it (even soap). Condensation and surface tension are succinctly explained – and how about this for Archimedes: 'Why does the water go up when you get in? Water takes up space. You take up space. You and the water can't be in the same space at the same time, so when you get in the bath the water moves up – and sometimes over.' Eureka! I have found a great book to share with four-and-ups, either in or out of the bath, and one whose gently humorous and utterly straightforward style will permit its enjoyable use with less able children up to twelve.

(Ted Percy reviewing *Splash! – All about Baths*, by Susan Kovacs Buxbaum and Rita Golden Gelman, and illustrated by Maryann Cocca-Leffler, in *BfK 57*, July 1989)

The Birth of a Book

MICHAEL FOREMAN *on the slow emergence of* One World

SOMETIMES A BOOK DEMANDS to be born. You wake up and there it is, slipping out like a baby dolphin, ready-formed and heading for the surface.

But others aren't so smooth. They start as a smidgen of something with an idea beating inside. You pick it up, tickle it and breathe on it, then tuck it away, kangaroo-like, until it needs attention again. Other adventures become more demanding, but all the time the smidgen clings on, close to your heart. Incubating, tugging at you.

Land of Dreams took fourteen years before it saw the light of day. My new book, *One World*, took seven years from conception to finished book, and in the beginning it was quite a different creature.

Several years ago I realised that children were much better informed and more concerned about what was happening in the world than many adults.

For the first time ever, through their access to television, children were able to see what was going on, and know about it directly, as it happened, not the edited text book version or through the filtering process of parents. And not just from excellent children's programmes, like *Newsround*, but also the regular news and current affairs programmes which are part of the home environment.

I see our young sons lying on the floor amid lego and crayons when an item on the six o'clock news suddenly catches their attention, and sometimes their imagination:

'What's that, Dad?'

'What's does that mean?'
'Why are they doing that?'

I remember as a teenager in Suffolk painting 'Ban the Bomb' on the police station. The mother of a friend of mine told me I'd 'grow out of it' and that as I got older I'd understand the ways of the world.

Today's parents are different. The teenage Aldermaston marchers are today's middle-aged. The flower children and young anti-Vietnam protesters are today's parents. They don't tell their children to grow out of it. Many adults have kept faith with their youthful ideals.

It seemed to me that there was a small group of very old people making decisions on behalf of a vast number of other old people which would affect the lives of very young people for a very long time. The short-term plans to comfort the demise of these old dinosaurs would put a blight on the lives of those too young for a voice and with most to lose. Now that children had access to the news, I hoped they'd find a voice.

I decided to do a book which would raise issues children could in turn raise with adults, at home and in the classroom.

During the summer of 1983, I began the first draft of a story that was eventually to become *One World*. The first draft had the working title of 'Hey! I am Me'. It contained a brief history of the world and the growth of the Industrial Revolution and the industrial/military complex, plus a quick tour of the planet and its journey through space – all in thirty-two pages. Needless to say it was confusing and didn't work.

The book was peopled by the old leaders. Only one still holds office, and she needs no introduction. Multitudes of children swarmed through the pages of the book proclaiming 'Hey! I am me', and demanding answers to their questions about their inheritance – the world, and the threat of its destruction.

The book contained scenes of medieval war machines and huge industrial machines consuming vast amounts of energy. Armies of men, women and children toiled in appalling conditions, and generations of children asked, 'Why?'

They were told, 'Sshssh! It's always done that way. Wait till you're grown up. You'll understand.'

I did many versions over the next four or five years but just

couldn't get the balance right. It was either too didactic and
angry, or too diffuse and the point was lost. There were too
many points; I was hitting out in all directions. Publishers
ducked. It contained everything I wanted to say, but was too
difficult to grasp. All spouts and no handle.

Then came the Reykjavik Summit. A world leader did what
General Jodhpur had done in my first book, *The General* (published 1961). He turned his back on the arms race. The other
leaders (who'd been leaning on him) had to step back or fall
over. They had to step back and re-think. The bogie man wanted to boogie.

History went into overdrive. Parts of the book that had given
me such problems were suddenly out of date.

Sometimes a book comes out ahead of its time. It comes out
and nothing much happens. The already-converted notice, and
everybody else ignores it. Then something happens in the world
which prompts similar books and forms a minor genre in which
the earlier book can find a place.

While visiting a school in Germany earlier this year, I was
told that *Dinosaurs and All That Rubbish* is more important
now than when it was first published in 1972. Wrong. It just
gets more attention now.

And much of that additional attention came after Chernobyl.

At 1pm on the day of Chernobyl, I brought the family in
from the garden. I didn't fancy eating our picnic while the
clouds went over.

At 3pm, three-year-old Ben said 'Let's play. Daddy, you be
the bad cloud and I'll be the picnic.' During the course of an
afternoon a catastrophe had become part of a child's imaginative play.

The threat from the arms race faded beside the accelerating
spread of pollution. Even the old leaders made green noises. But
only noises.

I started again, and this time I determined to keep the book
simple.

I always write the first draft of a story in whichever notebook
I'm carrying around at the time. When travelling I never take
anything to read to fill the long hours of enforced idleness.
Train journeys are great for daydreaming. Delayed flights are
good times for people-watching, and the long limbo hours of

Illustration by Michael Foreman from *One World*

night flight, when all you love are a thousand miles away, and you feel weightless, stateless and probably legless after a few airline drinks, are rare opportunities for the brain to float, unfettered and de-ranged, into the soup of ideas. Anyone with a young family will know how rare such moments of real self-indulgence are.

When I'm back home and I feel the story is getting somewhere, I make a little dummy book of folded paper, usually thirty-two pages in length. I write the story through the pages to see how well it fits, leaving space for pictures, and seeing where the breaks come in the text.

When the text is broken up by the act of page turning it reads differently. Turning the page acts as a kind of dissolve. Like the end of a stanza in a poem. So I find it necessary to work and re-work the idea through a series of blank books rather than sheets of flat paper.

Of course, I'm visualising the pictures all the time and decid-ing how much of the idea can be told visually.

At this point I know if it's going to work smoothly or become a case for lengthy incubation. However, even if I think it works well, I'm always in the middle of another book which has to be finished first. So there's always a delay, maybe of months, before I can begin pictures for the new idea. This enforced delay gives time to re-think, and often when I pick up the idea again I find it has lost something – maybe even its life.

So then the initial idea, the spark, lies buried in its notebook. Another spark, another journey, might make a connection, like Frankenstein's monster and the lightning, and the idea begins to twitch again.

This time it wasn't lightning, but a Cornish beach. During the summer of 1989 my sons spent a lot of time exploring rock pools. Suddenly, there it was. A rock pool. A microcosm of the world. Its beauty, its life and its fragility. The simple approach.

'Hey! I am Me' became *One World*.

One World with one child and one small part of the planet. Several versions later I realised it needed a touch of dialogue and introduced a second child.

Of course, there are echoes of the wider world, and beyond. I wanted to keep a sense of the enormity of space and time, and the right of every living thing to its own little bit of that space and time.

It's not the book I set out to write seven years ago, but it's close to what I wanted to say!

BfK 62
May 1990

PART FIVE

Fiction and Fun

*Do some of the things done in school,
primary and secondary, actually
discourage children from seeing books
and reading in a positive way?
JILL BENNETT asks*

Is Your Reading Scheme
Really Necessary?

I TEACH A VERTICALLY GROUPED infant class in an outer London school and for ten years I have been helping children learn to read. Very early on I decided that reading schemes and 'reading books' had no place in what I was trying to achieve.

My chief aim as an infant teacher is to help children become readers who see books as an important part of their lives and who will continue to enjoy literature as they grow up. The best way to achieve this, I believe, is to teach them to read by using *real* books right from the start. As I see it, reading is not about look-say, word-by-word decoding, phonic analysis or a progression from one boring non-story to another through a reading scheme whose controlled vocabulary must be slavishly followed. Reading is, first of all, a matter of getting meaning from print, and children must be made aware of this from the very beginning. The ability to read is developed through reading, and here I see *story* as the basis of everything. I expect my children to learn to read with real books and to enjoy doing so.

As adults, we don't read at the same level and in the same way all the time; at one moment we may be tackling something really difficult and at another relaxing with something completely undemanding. Why should we expect the learner reader

Jill Bennett and her class

to be any different? And yet we often place severe restrictions on children's choice of reading material.

This is not the case in my classroom where, for example, comics, *Mr Men* and Scarry, as well as non-fiction titles, are available alongside the picture books which form the main reading diet of the children. The latter are arranged on a series of shelves with those of approximately the same level grouped together, and this arrangement is explained to newcomers.

At the same time, a selection of the whole range is displayed face out so that a five-year-old may select, say, *Burglar Bill*, which he cannot read for himself, and ask a more experienced friend to read it to him, or merely enjoy browsing through it himself. On the other hand, an older child may return to a well-loved, simple story and read it on his own, or to one or two younger children.

I also have strong views about hearing children read, and each child reads to me every day. But this must not become a 'two pages a day' chore for teacher and child. So, when finding a book to read aloud to me, it is essential that the child chooses one that is within his capabilities, otherwise he will not get the meaning, reading becomes a senseless task and the enjoyment is lost. This approach provides a marvellous opportunity for a teacher to talk with a child about the book he is reading. 'Reading to teacher' then becomes a valuable, shared experience rather than being something children do to 'get on to the next book', 'beat their friends' or 'please Miss'.

BfK 1
March 1980

My father was the sort of man who read *The Field* and *Country Life* and latterly, in his old age, thought there was no greater author than Dick Francis. I shouldn't think he ever read a word of classical literature in his life. My mother played the piano like an angel and used to read biographies, but there was certainly no inclination towards the literary. Also I went to the sort of prep school in the thirties which concentrated on Latin and Greek as a matter of course. That went on till I left public school, so like any classicist – though I'm very grateful for it now – I didn't get a fair crack of the whip as far as Eng. Lit. is concerned till very much later when I went to a college of education, specialising in English, and suddenly studied chaps like Shakespeare at the age of forty-nine or fifty. Of course, as a child I was always keen on reading – mostly the animal stories of Ernest Thompson Seton and Charles G D Roberts, thrilling reading both of them. Then there were the William books and later Sapper and Dornford Yates, but I was very undiscriminating.

(Dick King-Smith in *BfK 45*, July 1987)

How to Organise
an Author Visit

RICHARD HILL

SOMEWHERE IN GREAT BRITAIN a group of hopeful book event organisers is having a conversation something like this:

> *Let's get an author to come.*
> *Great. Who shall we have?*

There follows extended discussion in which names like Alan Garner and Roald Dahl feature largely . . .

> *GULP!*
> *How do we arrange it?*
> *Silence.*

If this scene is at all familiar . . . start here with these questions.

Why?

Why do you want the visit? As part of a book fair? To give the bookshop a boost? To show that authors are real? To create enthusiasm for books and reading? To encourage children to write?

Who?

Who is your audience? Parents? Children? Both? How many will there be? What ages? How organised?

What?

What do you want your visitor to do? Sign books? Perform? Talk? Smile nicely? Tell stories?

Where?

Where will it happen? Library? School hall? Classrooms? Town Hall? Canal barge? Inside or outside? Do you expect your visitor to appear in more than one place?

When?

What is the date? Can it be changed? What time of day? How many times and for how long do you expect your visitor to appear? Have you left enough time to plan it (at least eight weeks – preferably twelve)?

Thinking about all that should leave you ready to go on to:

Who shall we ask to come?

Some authors enjoy meeting their readers; others hate it. Some are marvellous with children; others are disastrous. Some can travel long distances and stay overnight; others are more restricted.

There are hundreds of authors. How can you find one to suit you? Don't worry. Help is at hand.

A new list of authors, illustrators and poets willing to visit schools is now available from the NBL. The list contains addresses and/or publisher contacts, age range preferred, area preferred, availability, and subject of talk. Also the NBL staff have helpfully provided a guide to geographical locations of authors and a listing of at least the last three titles published and presumably in print of each author, illustrator or poet.

And the publishers can give good advice (ask for the publicity person). Maggy Doyle (in charge of Piccolo publicity) gave us this account of a typical phone call.

Ring ring
Book Event
Organiser   'Hello.'
Maggy   'Hello.'

BEO	'I'm organising a book event and wonder if you could supply an author?'
M	'Have you any idea of who you'd like?'
BEO	'Well, anyone you could recommend, really.'
M	'Right. What do you want him to do – sign books or *do* something?'
BEO	'Em. I think the kids will get more out of a visit if they are involved a bit – we'd like someone to do something – but how much will it cost?'
M	'Well, most authors do expect a fee of between £20 and £30 plus expenses but some don't charge anything but expenses.'
BEO	'Oh, I thought we might be able to have somebody free.'
M	'Mm. You may have heard of event organisers not paying anything, but it doesn't happen often. It's mainly at book fairs when publishers take stands and books are in a represented selling situation (s'cuse the jargon). Then we'll ask authors to come along on our behalf and pay any costs ourselves.'
BEO	'Ah. Okay then.'
M	'Now, when is it? How old are the kids, how many in each session, how many sessions, how long is each session? Will books be for sale – if so, through which bookseller? Will books be there or do you want me to supply them? Will you meet him at the station, give him lunch, look after him? What kind of pre-event publicity have you arranged? Will kids have read his books and be familiar with his work or will they be doing a project or other school work about his visit afterwards?'
BEO	'Em . . .'
M	'There's an author [X[who lives near you. He's terrific with kids – he'll leave them with a lasting impression that books are

	interesting, enjoyable, usable and relevant – and we've just published his second book. What about him?'
BEO	'Well . . . haven't you got anyone more famous?'
M	'Yes, we have, but they're often so busy that they don't have much time for personal appearances, and some do feel more at home with adult audiences.'
BEO	'Ah.'
M	'I can thoroughly recommend our new author, though; I've seen him in action, and he doesn't charge a fee . . .'
BEO	'Okay then.'
M	'Right. I'll ring him now and ring you back to confirm. Okay?'
BEO	'Okay. Thanks for your help.'
M	'Okay. Bye'
	Ring ring
BEO	'Hello.'
M	'Hello, sorry, he can't make it . . . now we've got another terrific new . . .'

How much will it cost?

Authors' fees vary (£25 per day plus expenses is average) so it is important to find out what is involved. Be clear about *exactly* what you want an author to do (for example, number and length of appearances, size of audience, etc.) and settle all financial details with the author (or his publisher) *in advance*. You can save on hotel expenses by offering hospitality in someone's home – but *check first*; some authors insist on hotel accommodation.

Can you afford it?

Sometimes authors come *free*.
1. At book fairs, some publishers will provide an author free. (Check and arrange this well in advance.)

2. During Children's Book Week, specified authors agree to waive fees and publishers pay travel expenses. You can get help

from the Writers in Schools Scheme. (Details are available from The Arts Council of Great Britain.)

Under the terms of this scheme, you may normally apply for reimbursement of up to 50 per cent of the fee and also all travelling expenses where long distances are involved.

Fees and expenses should be agreed between you and the writer concerned, and applications should be made in advance of the visit to your regional arts association. It's advisable to contact your regional arts association to find out any regional variations to this pattern.

Similar schemes operate in Scotland and Wales, and lists of Scottish and Welsh writers may be obtained from the Scottish Arts Council and the Welsh Arts Council.

Blueprint for success

In advance

1. Be clear about what you want.
2. Contact authors and/or their publishers well in advance.
3. Make sure that you and the author are clear about fees and expenses, travelling arrangements, times, what he/she will do, etc. Confirm all details in writing (keep a copy) and keep in touch.
4. Arrange publicity: ask publishers for material, get children reading and talking, contact the local paper.
5. Arrange to have books for sale.
6. Arrange a timetable for the day's activities

On the day

1. Look after your author. Writers are human; they need food, drink, rest and reassurance just like the rest of us.

Afterwards

1. Capitalise on the visit in work in school.
2. Write to your author (encourage the children to write too) to say thank you and give him/her some feedback.

*So you've booked the author. You've
got the cash. Is there anything else?
BERNARD ASHLEY (a junior head
and a writer who's done a lot of
visiting) gives us an answer in*

An Author's Eye View

YOU'VE GOT AN AUTHOR coming into the school: a real live writer who does professionally all that writing business the children are doing all the time. After authors, no group has more demands made upon their written output than children in school have, so get your author into the classroom to help them, to show that books come from *people* like him, and like them. Don't throw him away with simply a smile-and-be-nice-to-the-customers stint in the book-shop. Let the children read ahead of the visit, have their questions ready, and generally capitalise on having him in the school.

He will enjoy talking about writing to a group who have actually read one of his books just as much as he will like being celebrated in a corner of the bookshop.

Since he is coming, work at making him special. Get him talked about, from Assembly mentions to break-time chats. In a primary school, you can probably even name the day after him.

Meet him at the school entrance at the agreed time, having provided foolproof instructions on how to get there. (Meeting him at the station or telling him to get a taxi at your expense is a nice courtesy.) Certainly don't leave him kicking around a building being ignored (very easy in a comprehensive). It's good for his soul, really, but he may not feel inclined to come again.

I like a job when I'm in a bookshop. Bookshop stints are all right for illustrators and writers of books on how to make kites – they sit and illustrate or stand and make kites. But a writer of fiction, used to scribbling illegibly in tatty notebooks, needs something public to do. Ask him to tell a story, take money at the till, declare something open – but don't leave him being a Well-Known Figure around the place.

Bernard Ashley

Check with him first whether he minds signing other authors' books. Some people are fussy about it. I sign anything, and others' books get, 'I hope you enjoy X's book' written in them. Be sure to have enough available on sale or return.

Involve your author's publisher. The firmer and surer you are about what you want, the better the publisher will respond. Ask for posters, showcards, book jackets, photographs: and, if they haven't got any on your author, demand to know why not, for heaven's sake. He'll be grateful for that. There he is, pushing himself around, and they haven't got posters . . .!

One 'don't'! Don't greet him with, 'Of course, I haven't read any of your stuff myself, but you're very popular with the children.' (It's the 'of course' that gets him.) If you can't do better than that, don't bother having him. He won't appear to mind your omission, but inside he'll be writing you off as a discourteous charlatan. And don't let him know you asked for someone else but the publisher sent him. He's very sensitive, or he wouldn't be a writer for children.

Overdo the cups of tea, and don't keep on about how good

H E Todd was. Make sure he meets the head – and if you can't say thank you in cash, give him a pen.

He'll treasure it – and he writes with them.

Footnote

Don't be afraid of new names. Being a famous writer doesn't automatically make you good at talking to or meeting people. New writers or less well-known people are often fresher and more enthusiastic – and they may soon be famous!

Think about alternatives to writers or artists. Publishers, editors, designers, printers, bookbinders, booksellers, reviewers and librarians are all part of the world of books.

There are plenty of horror stories about how authors have been treated. There are also plenty about how they have behaved! If you follow our guidelines, you will have done your part. If you feel an author hasn't come up to scratch tell him/her (politely), tell his/her publisher, and tell us at *BfK*. Do the same if the visit has been a great success. Then we'll be in a better position to give each other good advice!

BfK 3
July 1980

Two Writers
Speaking Personally

*'Not to write "politically" would be to
bury the values one cherishes.'
JAMES WATSON on making
connections between the unique and
the universal*

FOR ME, WRITING IS AN INTERACTION between author and reader,
a sharing of things held close to heart and mind. To begin with,
I wrote stories that would be sufficiently exciting to stir in the
young reader something of my own fascination for history. I set
quick-moving adventures in vivid historical settings such as the
Florence of Leonardo in *Sign of the Swallow*, or among the
Minoan splendours of Knossos in *The Bull Leapers*. The aim
was to thrill and at the same time sow a seed-trail in the reader's
imagination, ready to germinate when he or she looked into the
past with a more searching eye.

That old triple alliance of objectives – to entertain, to inform
and (possibly) to educate – forms a reasonable basis for communication over distance and between strangers. For the novel,
however, it leaves out the crucial role of being *in* there; of being
it. In my Spanish Civil War story, *The Freedom Tree*, the central
characters, Will and Griff, find themselves in the cold, rat-
infested trenches of the Aragon front, caught in a blazing cross-
fire. Suddenly, in the pitch darkness, they are eyeball to eyeball
with a youth of their own age from the enemy side, as terrified
as they are.

What happens next, and how it affects the two friends, their
relationship, their attitudes to the conflict and to death is

unique to them and, I hope, to the reader. For a split second, if the illusion has been well-enough staged, the reader *is* the experience: the mediation of the author, words and paper are forgotten in the same way that, with a film, the reality of celluloid, screen and light gives place to a reality of direct identification.

If that amounts to authorial power, then the irony is that the author rarely, if ever, knows what response there has been to that power. Yet the writer is not only talking to, sharing with the reader, but is undergoing his or her own route to discovery. To be interested in history is but a small step to the altogether more dynamic condition of recognising – and perhaps developing – *a sense of history*.

Without a sense of history it is difficult, in my view, to make sense of the present.

Whoever believes that history does not repeat itself is absolutely right if he or she sticks to the pedantry of detail. Hitler was unique; Franco was unique; the bombing of Guernica was unique, and President Pinochet of Chile is unique. Tyranny, however, is not unique; nor are poverty, racialism, sexism or exploitation. That much we can learn from history, though the root causes of such phenomena are admittedly less the task of the novelist to explain than that of philosophers, historians, sociologists and political scientists.

It has often been a source of mild surprise to me to learn that, while the study of politics in school is seen by many as unsuitable fare for education in a democracy, history is bread and butter to the curriculum. How history can be expected to be taught without reference to politics is beyond me, unless the underlying philosophy is that, because history is dead (or even bunk, as Henry Ford would have it), and indeed because it is chiefly about the assertion and dominance of hierarchies (or simply larger-than-life personalities such as Henry VIII and his dreadfully abused wives), *connections* with the way things are today need never be made. *That*, however, is bunk.

Of the many pernicious doctrines that have gathered like carrion on the rooftop of 1984, the one deserving the first dose of buckshot is TINA: the notion that There Is No Alternative may strictly relate to monetarist dogma, but the danger is that the attitude is contagious. Once we admit that 'there is nothing we can do about anything', we are done for – nothing we can do about the suffering of others, nothing we can do about arrest without trial, about torture, about death squads, about starvation. That is the sense of history *some* carry about with them: it was always like this, so carry on regardless.

These are days of pessimism, for TINA rules: yet what sustains my belief – as an individual and a writer – that TINA need not be the measure of history or the order of the day, is a confidence in the staying power of certain fundamental values. That staying power lies with people who, through commitment that is as natural to them as breathing or through convictions forged by circumstance, sacrifice personal safety in the cause of human rights. The tenacity of such people in times of crisis, faced often by overwhelming odds, is the source of inspiration for *The Freedom Tree* and my latest book, *Talking in Whispers*.

In *Whispers*, sixteen-year-old Andres falls into the hands of torturers. Partly through his courage, partly through fortuitous circumstance, the torturers fail to extract the information they require from him; but most importantly, they fail to destroy his spirit. One of the interrogators, the Hog, flings off all control:

> He seized Andres. He roared not as the hog, not as the hyena but as the bull. He seized Andres as if suddenly he were all prisoners, as if he represented every wrong answer, every defiant spirit, every act of simple courage, every refusal to betray a loved one, every resistance to tyranny. He beat him. He dragged him. And yet it was his own cries which were the loudest, his own wailing: his boundless despair.

That is arguably the testament of humanity's faith in the triumph of good over evil.

Yet, it might be asked – for the *young* reader? If it were a universally observed right that children were protected from the realities of the adult world, privileged to escape the hardships suffered by their parents, then it would be perfectly acceptable to have a children's literature wholly given over to the dreamland of messing about in boats on languid rivers and finding secret messages in bottles. Children, though, are and always have been among history's prime victims. The children of El Salvador, Eritrea, Brazil, Indonesia, etc., etc. know that well enough.

James Watson

Our own children have generally been more fortunate: all the more reason for them, I believe, to at least *know* of the plight of their peers; to sympathise, to empathise, eventually to *understand* the connection between the happiness of some and the misery of others; to feel a sense of *solidarity* – if that is not too emotively political a term – with others.

It is that which makes *The Freedom Tree* and *Talking in Whispers* political. They are about uniqueness but they are concerned with universals: of justice and commonality. My fear is that in the age of TINA the young westerner might assume that, because the persecuted have always been persecuted, they can somehow tolerate persecution enough for a general fuss not to be made of it. Such an attitude is *political*, albeit by default or ignorance, and the end of that particular road – as a knowledge of history will graphically remind us – is the concentration camp and the gas chamber.

My Rubber Truncheon Award for the most disgraceful quotation of 1983 goes to Mr Norman Tebbit, who justified his decision not to ban the British export of torture equipment on the grounds that if we didn't sell the stuff, others would. In the context of *that* kind of public morality, *not* to write 'politically' would be to bury the values one cherishes. It would leave the stage clear for pragmatists. Only at the entrepreneur's convenience would two and two make four.

In conclusion, a reminder to myself: to abandon, bypass or censor values as the bedrock of writerly motivation would be a calamity; one of equal severity would be to forget that novels are *stories* about *people*, not vehicles of rhetoric populated with cardboard cut-outs representing types or beliefs. If the pages don't keep turning, the sharing is at an end. In competition with the easy flow of television narratives, the printed word remains the medium that cuts deeper and sticks longer – yet only if it is given a chance.

In *Whispers*, Andres witnesses the burning of his father's and his own books. The flames lick indiscriminately at philosophical tomes and children's books alike. Today's writer is faced with the challenge of producing books riveting enough to hold attention in face of mass media competition. His or her aspiration might also be to write books good enough for burning.

'The classic English children's book is political; mine are not.' JAN NEEDLE on representing the world as he knows it

THE CLASSIC ENGLISH CHILDREN'S BOOK seems to me to be deeply political. It is written by a middle-class person, about middle-class people, for middle-class people. Its politics are hence unconscious, inevitable, and all-pervasive. And because most adults who are actively involved with the children's book – as readers, publishers and critics – are very similar in background, culture and outlook to the people who write it, its politics are invisible.

You will note, I hope, that I referred to the 'English' children's book, not the 'British'. This, I think, makes my point. For not only do the great majority of British children's books come from a tiny group of like-minded and like-cultured people, but they reflect an Englishness that is mind-bogglingly exclusive. Fashionable, now, to pop in the odd (often *very* odd!) black or Asian character – after all, one has to be seen to be 'liberal'. But, tokenism aside, the world of children's books is still overwhelmingly the world of Ransome, de Selincourt, Brazil, Blyton, Old Auntie Thomasina Cobley and all. It is ghetto fiction in which the ghetto, peculiarly, has the power to dominate the population as a whole.

Question: Why is this 'ghetto' so powerful, when the mass of the readership are not 'of' it? Answer: Because not only does it have a virtual monopoly, but our system of education is traditionally (and probably totally unconsciously, by now) geared to the propagation of a set of values which are not 'of' the majority of those who receive it. Even those (many) teachers who crave sufficient alternative material are operating an exam-oriented curriculum. And there aren't any questions on *Grange Hill* on *those* papers!

Illustration: One of my books for younger children, *Losers Weepers,* was heavily criticised in *The Sunday Times* because the dialogue in it is rendered in a (rather generalised) Northern dialect. The reviewer thought it a pity, because it meant 'most children would not be able to understand it'. Being originally from the South, I write about half my books in (equally generalised) Southern speech. No one's told me off so far, surprise surprise.

By a similar process, I think, the books which tend to win 'literary' awards reflect a view of 'literature' which has nothing to do with the taste of their intended audience, but a great deal to do with the Victorian (and therefore, for us new Elizabethans, a political) desire to 'improve' the young. If the dichotomy were not so sad, it would be funny: on the one hand, concerned adults are trying to encourage children to read and, on the other, they are actively disapproving of, if not actively suppressing, the very books which are enjoyed and chosen by kids. It's a good job there is not an equally powerful coterie of mathematicians who disapprove of computers with some equally strange (but, to them, plausible) rationale.

The above is not, incidentally, sour grapes. I've come as close as a toucher to winning two of the big awards, as well as an Other. But the point is this: the criteria by which these things are judged fit perfectly with the ground rules I laid out. The awards circus is a sub-section of society that some people look upon, and refer to, as the children's book mafia. Working honestly, most of them, for what *they* perceive as the common good.

Jan Needle

Having made this rather amazing claim that the classic (or even the average) English children's book is political, let me raise the eyebrows of those who know and love (to categorise) my work even further by claiming that mine are *not*. I'm not talking about all my books (some are merely jolly, or adventures, or just plain daft), but just the ones that are often dubbed 'social realistic', like *Albeson and the Germans*, *My Mate Shofiq*, *A Sense of Shame*, *Piggy in the Middle* and the new one, *A Pitiful Place*. True, they deal with subjects like racism, police brutality, and the Falklands conflict, which might reasonably be seen to be the stuff of politics. But they offer me no 'line'; they have no discernible tendency; they are in absolutely no way didactic. Most of all (as at least one of my publishers would sadly say), they do not bestow upon the child reader an optimism that I, as an adult, believe to be false. It is this false optimism that I hold to be the fundamental political act in the sort of book I have been talking about.

But if this false optimism of the 'classic' English children's book is political, even if unconscious, how can I claim to be non-political by *knowingly* refusing to perpetuate the same lie – while deliberately choosing subjects which may be called the stuff of politics, to boot? Simply like this: I know where I come from, and I know where I am. Within the (desperate) limitations of fiction-writing, I write about people and events which I know. There is no narrow or identifiable political tendency in my books because I do not have one. And I don't write my kind of books as an antidote; I write because they represent the world as I believe in it.

I suspect many people may think I'm being disingenuous – or even mendacious; but I don't think I am. Let me give you a final example. Kenneth Grahame wrote *The Wind in the Willows* (which is one of my favourite books; I love it). Grahame was not being political, but he mirrored his own world unconsciously: a world in which the very rich enjoyed themselves in absurdly selfish ways and the very poor were humiliated or suffered – and in any case misbehaved. I wrote *Wild Wood*, in which the antics of Toad and his friends are seen through the eyes of the stoats, the ferrets and the weasels – the starving rural poor. It is a book about politics, unlike Grahame's, but it is still not a political book, God forbid. And even the *Daily Telegraph* 'loved every word'!

We don't need more politics in children's literature; we need less. If there were more people like me writing more books like some of mine, they would cease to be 'controversial'. Blow the trumpets: and let the ghetto walls come tumbling down.

BfK 25
March 1984

I think writers should always resist attempts to control them, but not shut ears and minds to attempts to influence them, question them or even call them to account. I feel that I will not write anything I am not prepared to defend publicly to parents or any other genuinely interested party.

Writers are like auxiliary aunts and uncles, the friendly, detached, but not uncommitted adults to whom boy or girl can turn for an alternative and enriching view of life. Let it be so. Though let's not be the Christmas visitor who bounces the kids up and down till they are sick on the carpet, then waves goodbye and leaves the parent to clear up the mess.

Our freedom is not separate from the freedoms of the children for whom we write and the people who care for them.

(Robert Leeson, 'A Sense of Power', in *BfK 58*, September 1989)

Orcs in the Classroom?

Over a million boys and girls (but especially boys) have spent a significant proportion of the last two years with their noses buried in a book – a Fighting Fantasy book. How should we react? Be glad they are reading anything? Write it off – along with Blyton and Sweet Dreams – as escapist relaxation? Stay away from an adults-keep-off private preoccupation? DAVID HILL took a close look at role-play adventures and decided to invite the Orcs into his classroom

THE SCOPE OFFERED by these books for classroom work, oral and written, with top-junior and lower-secondary children is enormous. Taking part in a role-play adventure involves children in a wide range of activities: planning, collecting information, asking questions, weighing up evidence, predicting outcomes, giving and receiving instructions, note-making, recording, developing empathy. The kinds of phrases, I realised, that keep cropping up in discussions about developing skills in the English curriculum. Fantasy games are essentially exercises in problem-solving, decision-making and working in groups. All bonus points. But I could see opportunities for more than just developing skills. Through the fun and excitement of the game I hoped to open up possibilities for imaginative experience which could be shared and deepened through talking and writing, and to prepare the ground for a wider range of literary experience.

In particular, I hoped to open the door to contact with the myths, legends, folk tales and fantasies which I feel have so much to offer.

I tried three ways of incorporating adventure gaming books and solo fantasy gamebooks into the English lesson.

1. With the help of a different pupil each lesson, I took on the role of Dungeon Master using the gaming book as my scenario for the adventure. I could enter into the spirit of the adventure and also control the situation without seeming to do so. Everyone got involved and we all shared in the excitement and atmosphere created.

2. The class divided into two groups. Each group represented a corporate adventurer. With me as Dungeon Master, we now had a small group of warrior adventurers setting forth. As each obstacle and monster was encountered, the class decided which group warrior should tackle it. Making the decision involved taking into account the stamina, skill and luck levels of each character – even assessing probabilities!

3. The class divided into groups with a pupil from each group acting as Dungeon Master controlling the adventure game within the group. The children need to be very familiar with the game for this method to succeed. The teacher is less personally involved (not so much fun!) but freer to circulate, observe and help where necessary. With smaller groups some children, of course, find it easier to participate and contribute to the discussion.

Before embarking on the adventure

Make sure that you are fully *au fait* with the rules, especially those linked with combat situations. Have a run through with the class using the combat rules before you set out on the adventure proper.

Ensure that pupils know how to draw using compass directions – N, S, E, W, NE, SW, etc. – how, to carry straight on, turn left, turn right etc. and can put the instructions on a plan. Time spent now will prevent headaches and frustration later on.

The whole exercise of learning the rules, taking the task slowly, is an excellent exercise in personal self-discipline and patience.

Devise a rota for taking the part of Chief Dice Shaker. At

times the fate of the hero is in the Dice Shaker's hands – a situation to revel in!

It is also useful to track down and make the acquaintance of your colleagues in Maths and Geography. They might like to know what you are doing (integration at last!) and you will need graph paper and a compass for keeping a plan of the route travelled by the adventurers.

Buy a couple of extra copies of the book you are using so that the illustrations can be cut out for wall display. Root out the budding artists in the class and employ their talents by making them official picture correspondents with the specific task of providing a pictorial record of the quest. A wall frieze stretching around four walls makes an impressive visual display and can be linked with written work being done, once the adventure is under way.

Illustration by John Higgins from *The Castle of Darkness*

Suggestions to follow up

1. A diary based on each day's journeying. (One lesson constitutes a day. An ongoing piece of work.)

2. Individual mapwork based on what children think the land looks like. This gives a free rein to both artistic and inventive imagination. Some of the place names they invent will often rival those of the fantasy authors themselves.

3. An accurate plan on graph paper of the route taken as the quest progresses. This needs careful monitoring at all stages. The less able pupils, especially in the early stages, will find difficulty in transferring oral directions on to paper.

4. Discussion work on the above will ensure that the pupils know how to read street plans, follow directions and give directions themselves.

5. Children to write their own stories/scenarios revolving around the hero. A few will even write their own computer adventure programme.

6. Children working in pairs become newspaper reporters interviewing the adventuring hero. It can be extended to a cassette audio recording – radio news item; or a video film – a TV interview.

7. Composing a front page of a newspaper based on the homecoming of the hero. (Hopefully not obituary!) A good exercise to show how different newspapers lay out their front page.

8. (a) The hero writes his autobiography or someone writes a biography. A dust-jacket for the cover is designed.
   (b) 'This is Your Life' – drama work.

Themes of work which flow naturally from the above activities include:

1. Discussion work on the themes – 'What is a Hero?' 'What is a Quest?'

2. Discussion work on the theme of leadership and the qualities possessed by a good leader. Group work first.

3. Journeys and quests in myth and legend – Heracles, The-seus, Odysseus, Perseus, Jason, the Grail Quest. (Ideally the teacher should tell some of the stories and not read them. The oral tradition is even more important now that we have entered into the video and computer age.)

4. Monsters of Myth and Legend with a special reference to the story of *Beowulf*.

5. Project work on armour and swords.

6. Work based on *The Silver Sword* by Ian Serraillier. The combined theme of the hero and quest in a real-life situation provides a fine balance to the fantasy aspects of adventure gaming.

Finally – because there is such a link forged between role-playing and fantasy it is essential to have a large selection of books available: fantasy novels, myths, legends and folk tales. These should be on the classroom bookshelf or in the school bookshop – preferably both.

You will soon find that one of the greatest spin-offs of adven-turing is that children, and especially the reluctant reader, clam-our for books which tie in with the theme. One pupil once said to me, 'I likes this. You don't have to be good at CSEs to kill a hydra.'

The potential for learning based on adventure gaming is enormous. I've even done lessons on direct and indirect speech based on the hero relating his adventures and then having them reported in a newspaper; the class actually enjoyed it. Adven-ture gaming makes learning fun and anything which does that can only be applauded.

It also gets pupils of all abilities wanting to read and to enjoy reading. This for all teachers is surely the real name of the game.

BfK 27
July 1984

My Affair with Judy . . .

*NICHOLAS TUCKER describes a
developing relationship between critic
and author*

MY FIRST ENCOUNTER with the best-selling American writer Judy Blume took place in 1976, when I reviewed *Forever*, still her most notorious novel. It describes a brief affair between a seventeen-year-old heroine and a boy of the same age, and was neither brilliantly written nor mere slop and gush. But rather than give a mid-way judgement, I reacted prudishly to the unfamiliar sexual frankness in the story, and perhaps a little jealously too, remembering my own inhibited, unadventurous adolescence. It was, I wrote loftily in *The Times Literary Supplement*, 'A dull novel about two very dull young people . . . who couple and separate like self-lubricated automata . . .' The characters are so flat one might almost be in a sexed-up Enid Blyton plot – *Five Go on an Orgy*, perhaps. But at least Enid Blyton sometimes dealt with feelings; a better analogy might be a so-far missing link in the Janet and John reading scheme: *Come and Have Sex*!

Mine was only one of many hostile reviews that Miss Blume's books have attracted over the years, yet soon afterwards I began to develop an uneasy conscience, particularly when her hardback British publisher told me I had played a part in blocking any quick take-up of the paperback rights over here. In addition, my own children had now read *Forever*, and it clearly had something both they and their friends wanted, since it was widely lent out. This immediate interest in Miss Blume's work is nothing new, especially across the Atlantic. A children's bookshop owner in Canada told me around that time about a successful visit from the author, resulting in a capacity audience of young readers listening to every word with close attention. I also found that my own memories of *Forever* did not simply disappear in favour of better books reviewed since. It did, after all, contain some authentic-sounding dialogue, and the story itself, with its down-beat ending and clever mixture of adolescent idealism and cynicism, was better than I had stated.

When her next two books came out, *It's Not the End of the World* and *Then Again, Maybe I Won't*, I was anxious to be more open-minded. Writing for *New Society*, I raised her ability to see things from a teenager's point of view which, 'plus a fluent, colloquial style, makes it easier for her to cover a range of adolescent preoccupations in a way that appears unforced'. This time, I did not object to the descriptions of voyeurism, wet dreams and various other sexy passages. I also gave my own students who were studying children's literature Miss Blume's powerful story *Blubber*, and, while they were critical of it in parts, most found it extremely readable. Its theme of pointless, cruel bullying in a junior school was well realised, bringing back uncomfortable memories not only of specific incidents of the same type, but also of a whole atmosphere of potential daily insecurity, once an inseparable part of being young and small.

I also liked her latest novel, *Starring Sally J Freedman as Herself*, published over here last summer, and this time, reviewing it once again in *The Times Literary Supplement*, felt I owed her some apology. After commending her professional skill, I concluded, 'Critics such as myself, who have condemned her writing in the past for its sensationalism, may like this present novel.' Curiously enough, the only reservation I felt about it now was that children themselves may find parts of it a little dull, since all the incidents it described were determinedly domestic, with none of the sexual high jinks of former years.

I hope this did not give the impression that I now welcomed Miss Blume back into my critical fold precisely because she had omitted more explicit material in this story. On the contrary, I wish I had praised her more for those earlier novels popular with children but which most critics disliked, since this division between the distaste of adult reviewers and the needs of young readers has always been the key to the different responses she provokes. Adult critics, for example, can be excused for finding

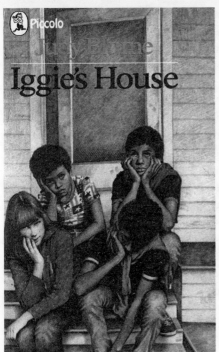
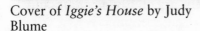

Cover of *Iggie's House* by Judy   Judy Blume
Blume

the technical detail Miss Blume uses to explain and describe period pains, masturbation and so on somewhat tedious. Young readers, though, are often bursting with curiosity not about the facts of life merely as an academic exercise, but also the how, when, where, with whom, how often and anything else that can be thrown in of a reasonably detailed nature. They also want to know how these things work in a personal context, and where better to read about them than in a novel containing adolescent characters themselves very ordinary and therefore easy to identify with?

This was just the type of information Miss Blume handed over in *Forever* and other novels, and young readers were duly grateful.

As well as heart-beats and sparkling eyes, there were discussions of contraceptives, the use of tissues in heavy petting sessions, vaginal discharges ('Just clear ... that's normal.') and what noises people make when they climax. Negative adult reaction to this, I suspect, is not simply based on a distrust of sensational 'problem' novels aimed at the young. There is also a deeper rejection of the whole concept of childhood as a time for intense sexual curiosity. Never mind the fact that Freud first suggested this possibility nearly a hundred years ago, and that dialogue in every school playground and the words and pictures on every school lavatory wall still support such a generalisation. It remains a side – though not, of course, the *only* side – to childhood we do not much want to think about, and children's writers who meet such interest at least half-way have to accept the aggressive critical consequences. How else can one explain the venom Miss Blume has so often attracted, with less competent authors dealing with different topics never suffering from the same disapproving criticism?

I also now believe that the other main complaint about Miss Blume, her selective focus on adolescence as a time for personal problems, is again based on a similar adult unwillingness to face up to the fact that children have always been interested in and sometimes knowledgeable about the more seamy side of life, even from a comparatively early age. Bullying, divorce, dead parents, phobias, racism and savage sibling rivalry, for example, all crop up in various Blume novels. Actual experience of such things is not common to all children, yet the affluent New Jersey environment she writes about, with its family break-ups, drug abuse and psychological stress, is certainly a world that more rather than fewer middle-class children are getting to know about, either at first or second hand. Naturally there are many other things still happening in childhood that make pleasanter reading, but as with sex, one cannot blame children for wanting to find out about the more dramatic behaviour they may be witnessing around them, even if this means choosing novels that offer a fairly one-sided picture of life in the suburbs. Ignoring these issues does not make them go away for some unfortunate children, nor does it mean that others will no longer want to test themselves out in their own imaginations against such upsets.

Not every children's novel that deals with sex and/or personal problems can be justified simply because these are things children feel curious about. Cliché-ridden, falsely perceived, formula novels remain bad whatever situations they describe, and there have been a number like this mostly from the USA and lately from Britain as well. Miss Blume does not come into this category; her dialogue is spare and individual, her jokes are often funny, and the resolutions to her stories are neither sentimental nor fashionably depressing. We should be encouraged that so many children read her, so still choosing books in preference to TV or video at various moments of their lives. There are obvious faults in her writing, and she does not produce novels that both adults and children can share and treasure. But this should not rule out appreciation of her as a serious and successful writer for children, should it?

BfK 27
July 1984

> What *is* the line between selection and censorship – the difference between something that is simply poor-quality and actually offensive, for example, racist and sexist? Or is it less clear-cut? We are very subjective on our part; certain librarians find *Willy the Wimp* and *Willy the Champ* racist and sexist. We do not – but is it censorship for them not to stock these books or is it choice? Once you start on the slippery slope of censorship, where does it stop? If you are looking for it, you can find something you dislike in much of what is available. Who has the right to say one person shall not read something because of their own personal views? The important thing after all is choice.
>
> (Helen Paiba, 'Who Censors?', in *Bfk 58*, September 1989)

Fiction for the Filofax

*CHRIS POWLING reflects on the rise
of the Literary List (kids, for the
consumption of)*

Warning: THE SLAVISH
FOLLOWING OF LISTS
CAN DAMAGE YOUR
READING
Book for Keeps Health Warning

I'M STILL KICKING MYSELF, of course. But when a nice lady from
The Times calls you in the afternoon and actually seeks your
advice, it's hard not to be instantly helpful. Especially when she
tells you she's also enlisting the help of Nina Bawden, Eunice
McMullen, Shirley Hughes, Elaine Moss, Jan Mark, Elizabeth
Attenborough, etc. . . . I mean, it's got to be all right, right?

Even so, by the time she'd phoned me back I was beginning
to feel uneasy. 'Sorry,' I began. 'I'm afraid I can't stick to only
six titles in each age category; kids and books are so diverse.
About a dozen in every section is the smallest number I can
manage.' 'Fine,' she replied. 'That's what everyone's saying.'

And so it turned out. When the article was printed on Friday,
19 February under the headline '*The Times* 50: Books Children
Should Read' it contained plenty of provisos to clear my conscience. 'It would be a thousand pities if any list were taken as a
blueprint of what every child should read at whatever age,'

Elaine Moss insisted. 'Reading should be a pleasure.' Puffin's Elizabeth Attenborough echoed the same point – and showed more presence of mind than most of us by refusing to offer a list beyond the age of fourteen. 'After that they should be reading and trying out absolutely everything.' Nice one Elizabeth, I thought. I wish I'd said that. Still, according to the article, we'd all agreed on one point:

> '. . . we found [the experts] full of healthy misgivings about the whole idea. Unanimously they agreed that any mandatory check list was anathema.' What a relief! That put us completely in the clear . . .

Why, then, was I still so bothered?

Later that week I found out. Apparently *The Times* wasn't the only national newspaper taking an interest in this issue. On the very same day – Friday 19 February – *The Daily Telegraph* had also entered the . . . er, lists. No half-measures with them, though: the piece was called 'The 100 books every school-leaver ought to have read'. There was no nonsense about consulting so-called 'experts', either. Here, augmented by a Tory MP, the team was strictly in-house, two of their own columnists, plus their Arts and Literary editors. This bold stroke in excluding anyone tainted by first-hand experience of children and children's books had brought a marked toughening in 'the cultural content of the satchels that those leaving schools for the last time will carry with them'. For the object of the enterprise was to establish nothing less than 'a core of reading of which those heading for industry, medicine, the law, the Church or perhaps even the dole queue ought to be aware'.

So take a good look at the books they recommend. Two questions seem to me to be prompted at once:

1. If *The Telegraph* list is intended for *every* school-leaver, why is it so highbrow? For the record, I know of at least one middle-aged bookworm – 'literary' by temperament, training and occupation – who's *still* seven titles short of scoring this particular century. Yes, *me*.

2. How, given the list's heavy bias towards the past, do we avoid convincing school-leavers that the only good writer is a dead writer?

The first question points to the sort of debate about what 'literature' actually is that's routine in universities these days.

The second raises the matter of our relationship with it – do we want a mere tugging of forelocks or the sort of active engagement with texts that includes consideration of our own as well as the best of other people's?

Neither question, needless to say, detains our Famous Five at *The Telegraph*. What they're eager to establish is which notches count on a cultural totem pole. This, after all, is only a beginning. Why should they stop at 'The 100 books every school-leaver ought to have read'? Surely we can now look forward to 'The 100 poems every school-leaver ought to know by heart'? Or 'The 100 movies every school-leaver ought to have sat through'? Or 'The 100 paintings every school-leaver ought to have gawped at'? Come on, team. There's work to be done. The filofax generation needs you. This is a show which will run and run – perhaps, with luck and a fair following wind, as far as 'The 100 tunes every school-leaver ought to have whistled in the bath'. If education is a commodity, subject like everything else to market forces, why not offer it in a form that's handy, easy to operate, and above all *testable*?

Hold it, though. Maybe . . . just maybe . . . I'm over-reacting. There does seem some glimmer of understanding in the article that there's more at issue here than an amiable parlour game. 'No one could claim this to be a definitive list,' begins the final paragraph. And, earlier, 'It would be an ideal child who had read the lot and a pretty remarkable one who could score more than 50 per cent.' Really? Now that would explain why, in mid-article, there's a rather startling concession. The list, we're told, is what 'an intelligent school-leaver ought either to have read *or at least to have thought about reading* [my italics]'. Dear me! What softies these hard-liners turn out to be . . .

The truth is, of course, that at *every* age and stage children 'should be reading and trying out absolutely everything'. Lists of 'classics' can be a useful jog to the memory, but following them slavishly is bound to bring the same results as making a meal out of every item on a menu: acute indigestion.

Mind you, there's one strategy I would recommend to *The Telegraph* team. If they're serious about creating a readership for these books, why not ban them completely? It worked a treat with *Spycatcher*.

The *Times* 50: Books Children Should Read

Ages 3-7

(The number of panelists' votes per book is given, right)

Just So Stories Rudyard Kipling	6
The Tale of Peter Rabbit Beatrix Potter	6
Charlotte's Web E.B. White	5
The Very Hungry Caterpillar Eric Carle	5
The World of Pooh A.A. Milne	5
Dogger Shirley Hughes	4
Mr Gumpy's Outing John Burningham	4
Where the Wild Things Are Maurice Sendak	4
Each Peach Pear Plum Allan and Janet Ahlberg	3
Mr Magnolia Quentin Blake	3
Now We Are Six A.A. Milne	3
Rosie's Walk Pat Hutchins	3
Where's Spot? Eric Hill	3

Ages 8-11

The Wind in the Willows Kenneth Grahame	8
The Hobbit J.R.R. Tolkien	7
Tom's Midnight Garden Philippa Pearce	7
BFG Roald Dahl	5
The Iron Man Ted Hughes	5
The Secret Garden Frances Hodgson Burnett	5
A Christmas Carol Charles Dickens	4
The Lion, the Witch and the Wardrobe C.S. Lewis	4
Alice in Wonderland Lewis Carroll	3
Complete Nonsense Book of Edward Lear Edward Lear	3
The Ghost of Thomas Kempe Penelope Lively	3
The Silver Sword Ian Serraillier	3
Stig of the Dump Clive King	3
The Stone Book Alan Garner	3
The Treasure Seekers E. Nesbit	3
The Turbulent Term of Tyke Tyler Gene Kemp	3
The Wolves of Willoughby Chase Joan Aiken	3

Ages 12-18

Eagle of the Ninth Rosemary Sutcliff	6
Treasure Island R.L. Stevenson	5
Brother in the Land Robert Swindells	4
Smith Leon Garfield	4
The Machine Gunners Robert Westall	4

1984 George Orwell	3
Carrie's War Nina Bawden	3
Catcher in the Rye J.D. Salinger	3
The Box of Delights John Masefield	3
The Diary of Anne Frank Anne Frank	3
The Earthsea Trilogy Ursula Le Guin	3
Emil and the Detectives Erich Kastner	3
Goldengrove Jill Paton Walsh	3
Huckleberry Finn Mark Twain	3
Jane Eyre Charlotte Brontë	3
The Hound of the Baskervilles A. Conan Doyle	3
Lord of the Flies William Golding	3
Moonfleet J. Meade Falkner	3
The Owl Service Alan Garner	3
Pride and Prejudice Jane Austen	3

The *Daily Telegraph* Choice

Cornerstones

The Bible (authorised version)
The Iliad by Homer
Odes by Horace
The Canterbury Tales by Chaucer
The Inferno by Dante
Le Morte D'Arthur by Thomas Malory
The Plays by William Shakespeare
Don Quixote by Cervantes
Paradise Lost by John Milton
The Life of Samuel Johnson by James Boswell
On the Origin of Species by Charles Darwin
History of Western Philosophy by Bertrand Russell

Beginnings

The Tale of Peter Rabbit by Beatrix Potter
Winnie-the-Pooh by A.A. Milne
Alice's Adventures in Wonderland by Lewis Carroll
The Wind in the Willows by Kenneth Grahame
The Secret Garden by Frances Hodgson Burnett
The Hobbit by J.R.R. Tolkien
The Lion, the Witch and the Wardrobe by C.S. Lewis
Kidnapped by R.L. Stevenson
Just William by Richmal Crompton
The Adventures of Tom Sawyer by Mark Twain

Fiction in English

Robinson Crusoe by Daniel Defoe
Gulliver's Travels by Jonathan Swift
Tom Jones by Henry Fielding
Tristram Shandy by Laurence Sterne
Mansfield Park by Jane Austen
Vanity Fair by William Makepeace Thackeray
Bleak House by Charles Dickens
Wuthering Heights by Emily Brontë
Moby-Dick, or, The Whale by Herman Melville
The Portrait of a Lady by Henry James
Tess of the D'Urbervilles by Thomas Hardy
The Day's Work by Rudyard Kipling
Chance by Joseph Conrad
A Portrait of the Artist as a Young Man by James Joyce
A Farewell to Arms by Ernest Hemingway
The Great Gatsby by F. Scott Fitzgerald
Sons and Lovers by S.H Lawrence
The History of Mr Polly by H.G. Wells
To the Lighthouse by Virginia Woolf
Point Counter Point by Aldous Huxley
Mr Norris Changes Trains by Christopher Isherwood

Modern Fiction in English

The Power and the Glory by Graham Greene
Decline and Fall by Evelyn Waugh
Afternoon Men by Anthony Powell
Animal Farm by George Orwell
The Catcher in the Rye by J.D. Salinger
Lucky Jim by Kingsley Amis
The Adventures of Augie March by Saul Bellow
Lolita by Vladimir Nabokov
Gone with the Wind by Margaret Mitchell
A House for Mr Biswas by V.S. Naipaul
Hemlock and After by Angus Wilson
Lord of the Flies by William Golding
The Prime of Miss Jean Brodie by Muriel Spark
The Grapes of Wrath by John Steinbeck
Darkness at Noon by Arthur Koestler

Entertainment

Three Men in a Boat by Jerome K. Jerome
The Diary of a Nobody by George and Weedon Grossmith

My Man Jeeves by P.G. Wodehouse
Tales of Mystery and Imagination by Edgar Allan Poe
The Adventures of Sherlock Holmes by Arthur Conan Doyle
The Murder of Roger Ackroyd by Agatha Christie
The Big Sleep by Raymond Chandler
The Thirty-nine Steps by John Buchan

Translations

Short Stories by Guy de Maupassant
Madame Bovary by Gustave Flaubert
The Three Musketeers by Alexandre Dumas
Le Grand Meaulnes by Alain-Fournier
The Plague by Albert Camus
Anna Karenina by Leo Tolstoy
Dead Souls by Gogol
Confessions of the Confidence Trickster Felix Krull by Thomas Mann
Metamorphosis by Kafka
Crime and Punishment by Fyodor Dostoevsky
One Hundred Years of Solitude by Gabriel Garcia Marquez
Confessions of Zeno by Italo Svevo
Dr Zhivago by Boris Pasternak

Poetry

The New Oxford Book of English Verse, editor Helen Gardner
Poems by Keats
Lyrical Ballads by Wordsworth and Coleridge
Don Juan by Byron
Idylls of the King by Tennyson
The Rubaiyat of Omar Khayyam by Edward FitzGerald
Collected Poems by T.S. Eliot
Collected Poems by W.H. Auden
High Windows by Philip Larkin
Les Fleurs du Mal by Baudelaire

Plays

Tartuffe by Molière
Love for Love by William Congreve
The School for Scandal by Richard Brinsley Sheridan
The Importance of Being Earnest by Oscar Wilde
The Master Builder by Henrik Ibsen
The Cherry Orchard by Anton Chekhov

Saint Joan by George Bernard Shaw
Waiting for Godot by Samuel Beckett

Postscripts

Father and Son by Edmund Gosse
Eminent Victorians by Lytton Strachey
Goodbye to All That by Robert Graves

BfK 50
May 1988

'Come to my party' is a theme always running through conversations between young children, so this book is going to
be topical. However, the pictures of the witch and the goblin
are really rather frightening, as is the baboon, the ghost and
the snake. In the light of recent alarm over child abuse and
black magic, I think we adults must be especially careful in
our choice of material for children and so I would hesitate to
recommend this book.

(Moira Small reviewing *Witch, Witch, Come to My Party* in *BfK 73*,
March 1992)

Most children, like many adults – evidence the popularity of
horror films – do get some pleasure from being scared, just
enough. Many of the letters I receive following visits to
schools confirm this. They include the words, 'The best bit
was when you frightened us. It was brilliant!' or similar.

Unfortunately some adults seem to have difficulty with this
idea. I've met a few people responsible for the selection of
books for children who've told me they consider my books
too scary. Quite properly they're exercising their right and
sense of responsibility as librarians or booksellers not to
make my books available to children or their parents. This
doesn't make me wish we'd produced different, less controversial books. It just means I must accept that it will take
longer for children to discover them.

(Rose Impey, 'Too Scary for Children?' in *BfK 61*, March 1990)

Who Reads Teenage Fiction?

ADÈLE GERAS reflects

HERE IS THE FIRST SENTENCE of Franz Kafka's *Metamorphosis*: 'As Gregor Samsa awoke from uneasy dreams, he found himself transformed in his bed into a gigantic insect.'

If his mother had brought him a cup of tea instead of calling to him through the bedroom door, she would have been mesmerised with horror. Just so do some people regard teenagers: as creatures who have undergone a ghastly transformation and are no longer quite of the human species.

I am not an expert on teenagers. I'm not going to discuss their clothes, habits, hairstyles, sexual mores, personal relationships or prospects. I'm going to talk about teenagers and books, and furthermore I'm going to confine myself to those young people who *do* still read. I know many children fall over a metaphorical cliff in adolescence into a reading-abyss, and all I can say to parents of such children is: take them to as many good movies and plays as you can, and do not scoff at talking books on a cassette player. There's nothing immoral about being read to.

It's not enough, though, for a person to read just *anything*. Teachers, librarians, parents and publishers are quite rightly concerned to put good books in front of children, and an awful lot of good books do reach a huge number of people. If, however, your child is engrossed in what you consider to be dross, you should relax and read an article by Peter Dickinson (*Children's Literature in Education*, No. 3, November 1970) called 'A Defence of Rubbish' which is brilliant, and probably the last word on the subject. Still, I shall add a few observations.

1. A Tremendous Amount Of What People Call 'Rubbish' Is Actually Genre-Fiction

There are loud voices raised in anger, that say, 'Romance–rubbish', 'Horror–rubbish', 'Thriller–rubbish', 'Middle-brow women writers–rubbish', and (most Philistine of all) 'American–rubbish'. They are, quite simply, wrong. I speak as someone who read Stephen King, Ruth Rendell and Elmore Leonard before they became big names, and who loved Elizabeth Taylor (the novelist) in tatty library hardback before Virago decked her in their beautiful dark-green covers. These same voices probably also said, 'Humour–rubbish', but this kind of muttering faded into a whisper after the success of Adrian Mole and the Douglas Adams books. If, however, a teenager persists in reading real trash and *nothing but* real trash all the days of her life, she will eventually become a trash-reading adult and then everyone will wash their hands of her, and let her get on with it: strange double standards! You don't hear *Kaleidoscope* on BBC Radio 4 bemoaning the fact that Mills and Boon and Barbara Cartland sell in the millions, but a recent special on Teen Romance had a very tsk! tsk! attitude to *Sweet Valley High* books (which is OK) and failed to mention (which is definitely *not* OK) writers of good romantic books, let alone recommend any actual titles.

2. The Readers Of The Books Publishers Put On Young Adult Lists Are Barely Into Their Teens

I practically live in libraries. In my local branch, all the primary schools come and choose books once a week. Third- and fourth-year Juniors STAMPEDE towards the Y.A. shelves, which are stripped of their juiciest books in seconds. Twelve- to thirteen-year-olds who are readers are already mixing in a lot of books from the adult shelves. (Notice I don't say 'adult books'. See Point 4.) Fifteen-year-olds who are still readers would blush to be seen near a shelf called 'Teenage', 'Young Adult' or any other euphemism the librarians can think up.

3. Girls And Women Read More Fiction Than Boys And Men

And whereas girls enjoy fantasy, horror, thrillers, etc., many

boys wouldn't be seen dead holding any book which has a girl
on the cover. Later on in their lives, alas, it is precisely girls on
the cover that lure certain men into reading certain kinds of
books.

4. Many Books For Teenagers Are Books For Everyone

K M Peyton's *Flambards* was a hugely successful TV serial.
Michelle Magorian's *Back Home* recently became a lovely TV
film. Michael Morpurgo's *Why the Whales Came* is now a film
starring Helen Mirren.

The Railway Children, The Secret Garden, Little Women:
one can multiply examples. Hey presto, the magic of the movies
. . . a book that was only a children's book has become fit for
the grown-ups too! Amazing, but untrue. The truth is: the book
was a fine read for adults all along, but hardly any of them
bothered to pick it up and open it. When I first started to write
children's books, I began to read: Gardam, Paton Walsh, Peyton, Lingard, Bawden etc. and I loved them all. I didn't find
them to read to my daughter (who was only two at the time)
nor for any research purposes. I simply took them from the
library and wallowed in them. Now, I am filled with a kind of
missionary zeal. I go up to perfect strangers in bookshops and
recommend things. I've even been known to take a book from
the YA shelf of a library (sorry, librarians!) and put it in the
adult section in the hope that it might reach the wide audience it
deserves. It's all a question of marketing, I know, but many
potential readers of teenage books are put off by the labelling.
A word of warning here, though, for uninitiated grown-ups:
some of these books may be a lot harder and more demanding
than the Jeffrey Archer, Ian Fleming or Agatha Christie you've
been used to. Beware particularly novels by Alan Garner or
Robert Cormier. You will not be able to skip through them on
your journey to work.

5. Good Writers Do Not Write 'For' Teenagers

They simply happen to write books that teenagers enjoy. Some
of them (J D Salinger, John Steinbeck, George Orwell) wrote
their books for adults. Perhaps writers of books published on
YA lists write for the teenager they used to be, or perhaps (and
this is more likely) *they still* are (give or take a few decades of

Adèle Geras

experience) the same person they were when they were seventeen. The less-than-good teenage books happen, I think, when a
writer sits down and says to herself: 'I'm going to write a book
that'll go down a bomb with all the groovy dudes at the disco.
I'd better go and chat to some real live kids.' That's writing a
book *de haut en bas*, and it shows. Always. Good books, as
Peter Dickinson said recently on the radio, 'come and knock
and knock on the door and demand to be written'. I don't know
what other writers feel, but when I write anything other than a
book for very young children, I forget altogether about my
audience and write entirely to please myself. The ghostly pres-
ences of my English teachers hover over me when I'm correcting,
revising, going over things, but the story, the feelings, the emotions: I'm the one that needs to be moved, enthralled, amused,
involved first of all, or how can I possibly expect that anyone
else will be? I have one word of warning for writers of stories
for teenagers: *beware of being too trendy and up-to-date*. Nothing has less street-cred than yesterday's slang, and you may find

yourself hoist with your own petard if you try to be up-to-the-minute in the matter of pop-groups and so on. I was. I described the hero of one story as looking like the lead singer of Curiosity Killed the Cat. Do you remember them? Do your children? *Sic transit gloria*, etc. The best bet is to do your own thing and hope someone other than you likes it. It's better than putting on a fancy-dress of grooviness which any teenager will see through instantly.

I'd love to start a correspondence. Perhaps *BfK* should allow a page for readers to send in their favourite 'rubbishy' reads. I'll start by nominating the *Whiteoak* books by Mazo de la Roche. There are volumes of them, and they are a saga and a soap opera and, in my memory, wonderful. I haven't dared to re-read these books in case the magic has faded, but I was spellbound at fourteen. Finally, here are twenty English-writing novelists in alphabetical order (leaving out the ones I've already mentioned) to tempt adults, both young and old, and anyone who doubts the existence of the good book for teenagers: Vivien Alcock, Judy Blume (yes), Betsy Byars, Anne Fine, Paula Fox, S E Hinton, Janni Howker, Mollie Hunter, Diana Wynne Jones, Robert Leeson, Penelope Lively, Margaret Mahy, Jan Mark, Zibby O'Neal, Katherine Paterson, Alison Prince, Jean Ure, Cynthia Voight, Robert Westall, Jacqueline Wilson.

Lists are great fun to compile. They are also hell. Look at who I've had to leave out: Berlie Doherty, Dennis Hamley, Deborah Hautzig, Jan Needle, Paul Zindel . . . stop, stop! But do you see *how many* there are?

BfK 60
January 1990

This is a profoundly cruel book, impaling its central character, Chris, on a spike of manipulation, innocence and love. It's
also an agonisingly well-written one, snaring the reader in the
same trap, building the horrifying sense of inevitability from
the moment it begins.

Chris is unwittingly caught up in a gangland war, unsus-
pected in the quiet streets of his Oxford home and symbolised
by the quiet menace of the white Mercedes whose driver's
counterfeit identity draws him into a carefully set trap. He is
led into a morass of betrayal and death in which Jenny, his
girlfriend, loses her life.

The sense of tragedy is felt more keenly because the reader's belief in Chris is unquestioning and because the final sentence of the book is so unbearably poignant – to the last,
Chris remains unaware of the whole sickening truth. *This* is
what the National Curriculum should be putting before our
youngsters – a work of undisputed and breathtaking excellence.

(Val Randall reviewing Philip Pullman's *The White Mercedes* in *BfK 81*,
July 1993)

Very little of what is called storytelling on children's television has anything to do with what is important about
telling stories. Watching someone sitting in a leather armchair
in a Laura Ashley dress reading *Little House on the Prairie*
off an autocue is not the same as having your mum or dad
reading it to you. The thing about storytelling is the relationship between the people involved; an actor reading aloud on
television can't create that relationship with millions of children. David Bellamy, Patrick Moore, James Burke: they get a
relationship because they are passionate about their subjects,
they care, they are committed. An actor reading aloud is
transmitting someone else's story, the result of someone else's
passion, a passion generated while writing the words down,
crossing things out, doing rewrites, finding rhythms for the
page which are quite often different from the rhythms of the
storyteller.

(Tony Robinson, 'Ways of Telling', in *BfK 40*, September 1986)

Kwik? Kwak!

GEORGE HUNT reflects on storytelling on Dominica . . . and its importance in classrooms everywhere

DURING THE EARLY EIGHTIES, I worked as a tutor at the Dominica Teachers' College. My main job was to try to help teachers enliven their children's reading experiences, which in those days tended to consist of recitations from the adventures of Janet, John and other redundant white folk marooned by departing colonialists.

While working in Dominican schools, I'd had some success in persuading children to compose their own texts by presenting them with unfinished stories based on dramatic local landmarks like the Boiling Lake, the Sinking Hole and the Pool of the Drowned Dogs, so one of my suggestions was that Dominican folklore be used in the classroom as a starting point for shared writing. However, my knowledge of this folklore, and of Kwéyòl, the creole language in which it's expressed, was very sketchy, so when the science tutor mentioned in passing the word 'conte', I asked for further information.

The Conte

I learned that conte is a form of oral storytelling, in which the teller recites a tale which incorporates songs, jokes, comical repetitions, satirical contemporary references, flattering remarks to the audience, and whatever else seems likely to please the listener. Without having heard a conte, I was hooked on the tradition already. A conference of head teachers was in preparation, and I pleaded that a conte should be included as an acknowledgement of the oral tradition and, perhaps, as a way of initiating a discussion of how folklore might contribute to

Mr Bertram

education.

On the last day of the conference, Mr Bertram, the long-serving principal of the school in the mountain village of Laudat, volunteered to oblige. A tall and dignified figure, he stood in the centre of the lecture room, surrounded by teachers and tutors who radiated the eagerness of children awaiting a treat.

We weren't disappointed.

The performance began with a salutation of 'Messiez Kwik?' to which the audience responded with a resounding 'Kwak!' We then heard the story of how Anansi humiliated the poseur Rat by tricking him into performing an ostentatious dance on a ballroom floor greased with okro slime. Throughout the story, episodes were punctuated with calls of 'Messiez Kwik?' and enthusiastic responses of 'Kwak!', a device which pulls the audience into the action and helps the teller to structure the tale. In spite of my ignorance of Kwéyòl, I was carried through the story by the narrative power of the teller's words and gestures. At the climax, when Rat writhes into the fandango which will end in a trouser-splitting pratfall and a shamed retreat into holes and corners, the venerable Mr Bertram began to undulate around the room with all the lubricious, rhythmic liquidity of an houri dancing in paradise. Ecstatic laughter broke out, and the story ended with the teller declaring his conviction of the truth of the tale, since Anansi himself had told it him *last week* in the market.

Over the next three years, I witnessed other such marvellous performances . . . but never in a classroom. Once at a somewhat restrained staff party one evening, Ma Lestrade, the college cleaner, took a swig of her severalth rum, said 'Messiez Kwik?' and, after our delighted 'Kwak!', took us on a journey to Hell, accompanying a hapless bride who had inadvertently married the Devil. As I too was on my severalth rum, the details of the story were lost to me, but I do remember a sweet song sung as the river between Earth and Hell was crossed, a wall of drawers full of human offal, and a faithful brother in pursuit of the bride. The climax came with the drowning of the Devil, an episode accompanied by a chilling mime of futile, bubbling struggles. Or was it the bride and her brother who perished? In any case, the story ended with Ma Lestrade rapping her right forefinger against her left wrist, sternly warning the women in the room to be vigilant, as she herself had seen the Devil on the prowl in the market *yesterday*.

Many of the stories featured the grisly inhabitants of the Dominican bush, a mythopoeic landscape of waterfalls, rainbows and jungle-pelted mountains as jagged as a child's drawing of mountains. Here one might meet Papa Bwa, the old man of the woods; or La Diablesse, a cannibalistic beauty whose passion might be assuaged by offering her a lock of freshly plucked hair; or, most ghastly of all, the Soucouyants, women who can peel off their skin and fly through the air as balls of blazing flesh.

Classroom Relevance

Was it because of the macabre nature of so many of the stories that I never heard of them being performed in classrooms? More probably, this was due to a lingering belief that Kwéyòl, a language forged in slavery and frequently used to confuse the oppressor, is a subversive influence which should be kept out of the schools. Once a year, on Independence Day, Kwéyòl is allowed on to the premises, but this token annual airing reinforces an establishment view of the language as a vestige of an impoverished past.

This marginalising of the oral tradition and language of the people is perhaps symptomatic of a more widespread phenomenon in education generally: the tendency, when seeking inspiration, to overlook the marvellous treasures in our own locality. For me, conte provided a glimpse into a book of visions, but for many Dominican teachers, struggling to improve their pupils' mastery of English, it seemed to be an irrelevant relic of a vanishing culture. Similarly, while teaching in London, I've sometimes found myself neglecting surrounding riches close at hand while seeking to engage children in the strange and distant.

I was reminded of this while visiting a neighbour in a geriatric ward recently. The tales he managed to spin from his straitened circumstances were both poignant and hilarious. They were not the sort of tales I would get away with repeating in school though, a point which brings us back to the appropriateness of conte to the classroom or, more pertinently, of the classroom to conte. As with many other forms of oral storytelling – playground gossip, factory floor yarns, pub talk – there is something essentially anti-establishment about conte, an irreverent delight in the vulgar and the bizarre which defies any schoolish constraints. (I once heard a conteur describe a giantess as having 'an arse the size of that wall behind you, and farts that made Hurricane David seem like a breeze'.) Certainly, my attempts to persuade teachers to try to create classroom literature out of conte now seem as realistic as asking them to make a statue of a whirlwind. A written tale is as stiff as stone compared to the live performance with its spontaneous ramblings, pantomime gestures, and interactive calls of 'Kwik?' and 'Kwak!'

Creating a Space for Storytelling

Still, making room on the classroom shelf for La Diablesse and the Soucouyants might help to preserve the vitality of these now threatened characters. On a return visit to Dominica last year, I heard many people express the fear that the recent arrival of round-the-clock American TV must accelerate the decline of conte and of Kwéyòl itself.

I'm convinced that Kwéyòl will survive for at least as long as teachers continue to strive to persuade children to speak 'good

English', but perhaps the future of conte is more precarious. The successful oral story creates a transient magic in unexpected circumstances, but this very transience implies vulnerability. It's the fragile attention of the audience which sustains the spell offered by the teller, a relationship voiced in 'Kwik?' and 'Kwak!' If this mutuality vanishes, then so does the story.

Thus, closer to home, I'll never know the details of how Father Tuohy, the local herbalist, cured my grandma of her spectacular nightmares, nor the ending of the tale told by the town drunk as he wandered down our street years ago, raving of the day when a butterfly 'with wings as wide as a football pitch' appeared in the sky over Prescot. I wasn't listening attentively enough to these tales when they were told, and now it's too late.

Storytelling as a Subversive Activity

But perhaps the ephemerality of individual stories is outweighed by the richness of their source: a universal desire to sing out, from within the iron constraints of the ordinary, a celebration of hilarity and strangeness. This source seems to be inexhaustible, its freshets breaking out in distantly divided places, and proclaiming their common origin through striking resemblances of incident and image. The girl who married the Devil is clearly related to Bluebeard's last wife, but her confrontation with those drawers full of carrion also reminded me of the joiner's mate in one of my brother's apprenticeship yarns, who, while working in a hospital, asked the way to the canteen and was directed into the anatomy lab.

The unruliness of such imagery illustrates its roots in the story-making of people traditionally excluded from formal literature. Perhaps this rebelliousness, together with the desire of almost everyone to share their hopes and horrors in a good yarn, will ensure the survival of conte and related customs throughout the world. Haven't most people, with or without the aid of literature, visited both the remote enchanted harbours and the dead-dog-clogged back-alleys of the imagination, gathering the wordhoard that is shared in story everywhere?

BfK 63
July 1990

Authorgraph
William Mayne

STEPHANIE NETTELL

March 13, 1990

C. Powling Esq.,
The Old Chapel
Easton
Winchester
Hampshire
SO21 1EG

Dear Mr Powling,

*I am sure this sort of thing never works. I shall certainly go
nowhere to accomplish it, and I am sure others would find
it unrewarding to come here. I have not sensed the lack in
my not appearing in your neologies, and the one I did see
had rather small print, but if you find it necessary to molest
my ancient solitary peace for the sake of your new and
madding piece, I am prepared to tolerate for a short time
some person guaranteed not to be strident. My agent,
David Higham Associates, will lead you to a photograph,
for I have none.*

Yours faithfully,
William Mayne

As far as I could see, none of these stone Dale cottages had a name. A solitary figure, long grey hair disconcertingly wild and shoulders hunched in the drenching misty rain, watched me from the grass verge with piercing concentration as I inched along the village street. A local? I rolled down the window.

'Are you – *She?*' it growled* before I could speak.

William Mayne likes to tease.

He also likes to divert you if he senses you might be gaining sufficient confidence to ask a question. 'Shall we have some pudding?' will adroitly intercept, the advantage followed up by a discussion on the merits, *pace* Mrs Beeton, of leaving the stones in bottled greengages. 'I believe the flavour of the stone is the only thing that makes a stone fruit worth having: bottle them in honey with a little water, and leave 'em a couple of years to mature.' We savour the greengages – and with luck the question will have evaporated. The rules, then, say *I* can divert.

It is a distancing typical of the man himself. Yet, like the heart under the Puritan collar or the inspiration of plainchant, beneath the no-nonsense fall of Mayne's style his novels (certainly in the last twenty-odd years) are awash with emotion. *The Jersey Shore* and *A Year and a Day* from the seventies, say, or *Gideon Ahoy*! and *Kelpie* from the eighties – without the stylistic tricks, the dodging and twisting, the slowing of pace, all of which make a protective embankment, emotion would flood them. So in life, perhaps, he dodges and evades his audience, offering mock scowls and diversions.

Perhaps. An enjoyable speculation, anyway. A diverting diversion. (He might fancy such a conceit, but more likely will refuse an interview of himself, on the grounds that it is none of his business.)

---

* 'It growled.' Mayne would not approve. The most characteristic element of his style is the dogged unswerving use of 'said' – almost always in the order 'said Mother' though occasionally a 'she said' slips in. I cannot be dogmatically sure (after all, he admits to around ninety titles – he claims he can't count them because it's so complicated, but I suspect this is for fear of seeming too self-concerned and that he really knows how many), but the most startling departure for me in *Antar and the Eagles* was the first sighting of an 'asked', a 'shouted', 'called' and 'told'. The repeated monosyllabic 'said', blunt, dispassionate, lends not only a typical rhythm to his prose but an emotional distance – that distancing, perhaps, to which some commentators attribute the difficulties young readers can have with his work.

William Mayne

The elaborate letter heading on his reply to *BfK* was designed to mock ours. And, grateful though he is to the PLR office's help – he loses their forms and they simply fill in his titles for him, which, for a writer as prolific as Mayne but without high individual sales, is occasion enough for gratitude – he pursued his complaints about their absurdly long address with a letter to the authorities, purporting to be from PLR and asking for a shorter one, on paper embellished 'Public Ending Right'. Wistfully, he said he had heard no more. ('You weren't put off then?' he asked when I rang for an appointment.)

The computer allows him to play like this. After four years of trading in, upgrading, and taking over his sister's cast-offs, he is in love at the moment with a dainty little Apple Mac, which allows him to make shaded prints of his photographs (a long-standing interest) or a fine production for the printers of a neighbour's book, an updated, century-old local Flora. Best of all, once a week he carts it two miles down the road to the primary school: it's stuffed to the gills with programs to help the secretary and cheery games he has devised for sums, story-telling, writing, drawing. He is just William to the children,

with whom he works in small groups – as we did, the screen
offering me easy or hard 'carries', rewarding my answers with
'Are you sure, Stephanie? Quite right! Well done Stephanie!'
Must be difficult to tell who enjoys it most, he or they . . .

Married for a while 'a long time ago' (about 1970 at a guess)
and with no children (but a whitewashed doorway pencilled all
the way up with visitors' heights), he says his sole point of reference can only be 'oneself as a child'. Yet throughout his work,
small children offer sharp-focus, sidelit views of life that suggest
he listens hard and with fondness:

'I'll be better when I'm several,' said the little brother. He was
nearly four. (*Netta*)

'You haven't got two colours on the same,' she said. 'Except
one sock matches the other.'
'They both do.' (*No More School*)

'I remember. It was before I knew about money, a long time
ago.' (*The Jersey Shore*)

'If I put [the straw] in my mouth the milk can look down it.'
'At night I have to go to bed . . . Do you know what happens
to me Johnny? I go to sleep. My eyes go out.' (*Plot Night*)

And many other more complex thoughts from older children.

An escaping wriggle. 'If you do put in a real quote, someone
says, "That doesn't sound natural, would you mind taking it
out?" What they actually say sounds much too precious.'
Almost pinned down. 'If a character is going to talk a certain
way they will and that's that.' Gives up. 'The bits of books I
always liked when I was little were the bits I knew were *true*,
but hadn't seemed to one's parents or teachers or acquaintances
the sort of thing worth having regard for, and which you
couldn't tell *them*.'

It might be a comfort to some child to know that its way of
thinking is not necessarily wrong because it's not the 'right'
way – I don't want them to think the accepted way has any
more value at all than their own way. So if they can see

people in books making efforts at saying things and not actually getting into a lot of trouble for it, or perhaps being brought round to another point of view, then that can possibly take away some pain from the reader in another instance.

Today it's not so difficult for children to say what they think more clearly to adults, because teachers are to some extent teaching through what they get from children rather than just imposing on them. The difficulty lies in pure organisation – if you've got twenty-five of them each saying their thing, sometimes you've got to flatten them a bit. I actually believe they're still listening if you're telling them a story and they're talking to their neighbour – I can tell you a story and stir a pan and talk to the telephone, it can all happen if you get the balance right – but if there are twenty-five of them you must impose some external structure on them.

He dismisses his own schooling ('I gave up thinking school was any good at fourteen, though social pressures didn't allow one to abandon it') at the Cathedral Choir School, Canterbury, though it wove itself into the fabric of his life – the choir-school novels, his musical interests, while even today we are playing (in twinky-twanky tones on the computer) a carol he composed for the children and their instruments. He himself tried teaching (and the BBC), though any reckless forays into direct questioning about what he did on leaving school are met with a 'can't remember' muttered into the lunch – a delicately laid out salad of mushrooms and home-made bread with rocket (no lettuce, nor dandelions – gold in every bank I'd passed – because their milky sap gives you fibrositis), chives, marjoram and parsley. And Wensleydale cheese.

The garden where the salad grew falls steeply away behind the house before merging into the daleside that sweeps, green and grand, up to a high bare skyline (not gardening, he says, but civil engineering). In front it shelters from the public road (of course) behind the post office. He has lived in the village thirty years, seventeen in this house, converting it little by little from the original hall or chapel, re-levelling floors, opening out a wall here, building stairs there: we are eating in the cellar, with a gleamingly clean electric Aga, having coffee in the stable above with an open round stove for cheer, while upstairs in the now divided hall his desk looks out both sides to the glories of Wensleydale. A hardy, energetic man, only paint and wall-paper defeat him – luckily it's not that type of cottage.

He's found himself turning into a squire figure: chairman for seven years in the days of parish meetings, he came to be responsible for the painstaking formation of a parish council (absorbing four or five meetings, sorting out their objections and difficulties). 'Someone has to do it or it doesn't happen – like the Commons Registration Act about rights over land.' For years he prepared maps and deals with commissioners, ensuring no one would lose their rights: 'These things were not always written down before, and one has got to have an agitator some- where – oh, I'm terribly bossy. Well, not that bossy – a little bit bossy. I was bossy there, just after Christmas . . .' and he retold the Battle of the Institute Floor, when, as a trustee of the hand- somely renovated (largely due to him) village hall, he had sur- vived the wrathful hurt of the three ladies he had prevented, in the nick of time, from zealously scrubbing the new floor. 'It's all right for someone to be bossy if they dislike it – that means they're doing it because they *care*.'

Time-consuming to lay pipes and drains, surely? 'Actually I was quite pleased when one morning I told our "foreman", a well-established resident who knows about such things, "Look, I can't help you tomorrow because, you know, I'm just a work- ing lad . . ." "Oh," he said, "you don't seem to go away very much, what do you do?"' He rubs his hands gleefully. 'Just the right attitude – no one knows what I do.'

This, in spite of his local roots going deep. Born in 1928 'just down the river in Hull – this is my drainage basin', he grew up not far away by Nidderdale. Having relished the soft pillows of rain rolling down the dale ('I've no time for this "what lovely sunshine" nonsense'), he later perversely ponders on returning to the warmth of Australia, where for some years he struggled to teach creative writing to college students whose best work was often their letter explaining their absence from class – and himself wrote the nostalgic West Country stories, like *A Year and a Day* and *Max's Dream*. But then agrees he would surely wither away. The intricate shading of family relationships is a recurring theme of his work, and his own family – five children of a doctor, now eighty-nine and in trouble the previous day for burning down his bed with an electric blanket – recur in his conversation: his father would like to believe he has only four children, refusing to speak to William because he has had to take charge of his affairs.

Despite total trust in his agent for over twenty years, Jacqueline Korn of Higham ('a stalwart, no one better – how else can one tell whether to stick out for another ½ per cent?'), he is clearly very much in command, casting a shrewd eye over accounts, insisting on wrong texts (for Nicola Bayley's *The Patchwork Cat* in 1981) being pulped, and breaking away from Julia MacRae when he no longer felt comfortable.

He has never written for adults, though a novel like *The Jersey Shore* (with a grown-up low-key jacket he designed himself – 'Well, they needn't have used it') appeals strongly to them. 'Adults can read my books if they like, it doesn't matter. I'm not interested in what they think.' So he won't, like so many, move over? 'Ah well, it's like the people at Portland Place who all want to move over to Lime Grove if they can. They've forgotten which is the truly superior medium, they've forgotten where the backgrounds are better.' The young reader's imagination should be working like a radio listener's? 'Or like the typesetter's. The typesetter of the *Hob* stories was extremely disappointed with the pictures – his own were much better, you see.'

BfK 63
July 1990

The Need for Story

TREVOR DICKINSON HMI

SOME THINGS STAY THE SAME because they're rooted in the deep-est fabric of our human being. One of those constancies is the need for story, story told and, more recently, for story read.
    Barbara Hardy wrote:

> We dream in narrative, remember, anticipate, hope, despair, believe, doubt, plan, revise, criticise, construct, gossip, learn, hate and love by narrative.

The printed word ('writing to keep it to remember', as a child once called it) has meant that we can draw out stories, daily, freshly from further and further afield. The printed word and our growing capacity to read it have together given us the chance to shake off what R K Narayan in 'A Tiger for Malgudi' describes as 'fetters and shackles for the rising soul, minds over-burdened with knowledge, facts or information'.
    At the same time, however, it has to be understood that the reading of story is not mere escape. The reading of story is part of the effort to understand more clearly what is simply 'known'. Story is part of the vast evidence about life and those who live it. Story is the agent of Rudyard Kipling's 'six honest serving men' in 'The Elephant's Child':

> They taught me all I knew
> Their names are What and Why and When
> And How and Where and Who.

Since story is a fundamental question-raiser, I would argue that those who don't read stories, those who neglect the importance of story-reading, are dangerous to us all. Our children and the adults they become need to be able constantly to ask the right questions about life and its living. They need the best language in which to frame those questions and in which to understand the answers.

It's for these reasons that all our children need to be surrounded by rich print worlds – which places special obligations, of course, upon school and public libraries. They share a particular responsibility to demonstrate, through their book provision, that the adult world deeply cherishes its children. That essential demonstration pays dividends, I believe, in helping the growing of children into adults who, touched from their earliest years by the sad and joyful magic of books, have been given the chance to be creative, imaginative beings, more fully conscious of, and more sensitive to, the needs of the many living worlds about them. I know that being a reader doesn't guarantee that we know *ourselves* or that we're more sensitive to those who share our space. Nonetheless, I can't escape the faith that our sustained contact with the efforts of good writers to grapple with life's eternal questions at least gives us a chance to be a little better. It gives us less excuse for not being so.

For the children we teach and provide for in our libraries depend on our having in mind for them some noble, adult-reading destinations. What kinds of readers do we want our present children to be when they are forty or fifty or sixty or more years old? What aim should we have, at the outset, for them all?

I'm not thinking of reading benchmarks for eleven-year-olds. Indeed, I'm convinced that there are deep dangers in meeting some books too soon, emotionally unprepared for and switched off, perhaps for ever, by a particular book's adult concerns. For instance, I'm eternally glad that I met *Huckleberry Finn* first in my twenties rather than at twelve. By the same token, I'm ever guiltily sad at my grammar school teaching struggles to teach *Silas Marner* to twelve-year-old boys and girls whose tedium was matched only by their sour distaste. I was fifty-five before I read the novel again – reduced to tears on some un-Eliot Greek island. My regret is that few, if any, of those I taught will have ever returned to the book.

No – what I seek to pursue is merely the thought that teachers and librarians should believe that all those in their care may have one day the potential to read, say, *Hard Times*. For some of their children, they may believe that if their adult reading is lame, they will, nonetheless, have the capacity to listen to and understand the novel – as illiterate audiences heard and understood Dickens. From the beginning the assumption has to be made by teachers and librarians that one day each child who stumbles into the nursery classroom or the children's library is entitled, at the age of fifty or sixty, to meet, say, Ronald Bottrall's poem 'Belfast' (and, pray, reflect upon it as a piece of bizarre, sad history):

> It doesn't matter if you are a child
> Or an old woman,
> There is no time to look at the sun
> Or enjoy the privacy
> Of cellars, attics and cemeteries.
> In the morning
> And the afternoon and the evening
> Things happen.
> You put out your hand to greet a friend.
> Before you can reach him
> He has exploded into fragments.

With Bottrall's poem just read, it will be as well if the future reader can quietly lean for some consolation upon Dostoyevsky's *Brothers Karamazov*:

> Love will teach us all things: but we must learn how to win love, it is got with difficulty: it is a possession dearly bought with much labour and in long time; for one must love not sometimes only, for a passing moment, but always: even the wicked can do that.

From the beginning, teachers and librarians should have for children the aspiration that, one day, they might meet with delight the work of, for instance, R K Narayan or Shusako Endo or Ngugi or Margaret Atwood or Gabriel Marquez or Elizabeth Jolley or Primo Levi or Janet Frame or . . .

The beginning needs an end. But what of the beginnings? To make their way to the writers like those I've just mentioned, to

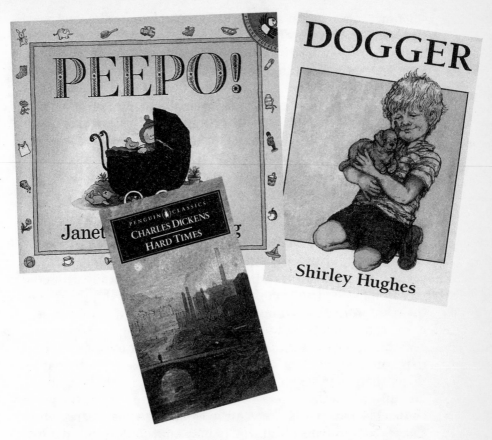

Covers from *Peepo* by Janet and Allan Ahlberg, *Dogger* by Shirley Hughes and *Hard Times* by Charles Dickens

their successors in the year 2000 and beyond, and to the great writers of the past who will continue long to have their tomorrows, today's children need good starting points. They need starting points beyond the last visible reading scheme. They need to start perhaps with the Ahlbergs' *Each Peach Pear Plum*, a book in which text and illustration sing so richly together. They might start with the same two authors' remarkable history book *Peepo*. They might move to John Burningham, perhaps to the unending delight of the questions in his *Would You Rather?* or to the moving comedy of Shirley Hughes's *Dogger*. A little older, some will still be caught (and carried forward) by the poignant magic of the classic *Velveteen Rabbit*.

Some, older still, may identify with and be oddly comforted by *The Shrinking of Treehorn*. At, perhaps, twelve or so, the road will, for some, be brightened by the outstanding poetry (and art) anthology *Talking to the Sun*. The picture story books *Rose Blanche, Are We Nearly There?* and *Piggy Book* will continue to speak volumes to sophisticated young readers in their late teens. With luck, few of them will be disengaged from encounters with Anne Fine or Robert Westall or Susan Cooper or Jan Mark or Katharine Paterson or Cynthia Voigt or James Berry. This is not an 'approved' list: there's too much to choose from. The roads (diverging 'in a yellow wood') may lead to Jeffrey Archer or to Chinua Achebe, to Frederick Forsythe or to E M Forster, to Robert Ludlum or to Doris Lessing.

These roads are not the same. It would be dangerous to be dogmatic about the needs for the readers our children become to take 'the road less travelled by'. In plucking authors from the air I don't intend an excess of worthiness. The light, the trivial, the comfortable (and comforting) are not barred. None of us, I hope, can be serious all the time. To meet a range of genres and generations of writing is essential. But I cannot escape the belief that some writers *are* better and more necessary to humanity than others. I argue merely that every effort should be made to give all our children an unblindfold chance to choose the wiser route. My faith is that, given the right start, the clearest, best signposted, and most beautiful of maps, few of our children will go astray.

With retirement looming, I begin to grasp a truth which, had I been sharper, I would (I should) have grasped too many years ago. It's summed up for me in a poem by Gillian Clarke, called 'Miracle on St David's Day'. In that poem she gives an account of her reading poetry in a mental institution and of being interrupted by a man who hadn't spoken for forty years. He interrupts to recite faultlessly Wordsworth's 'Daffodils' he learned in school as a child – and Gillian Clarke comments:

> . . . he has remembered there was a music
> Of speech and that once he had something to say.

At the heart of what I seek to say here is the belief that in presenting our children with the best, most considered of language in the best of books, teachers and librarians are enabling them all to possess a music of speech, giving them all an improved chance of something to say and the means by which to say it for themselves.

My slow realisation, however, helped by my repeated reading of Gillian Clarke's poem (in which, simultaneously, I find ever something new and contentedly discover the same), is that of knowing now, as never before, that our children can never escape us. We can escape them – and do. But our children are ours forever, touched for better or for worse by the what and how of our teaching. We have, as teachers, as librarians, as parents, that terrifying obligation and proud privilege of making sure that our book-touch is benign and lasting. Our unremembered children will then be ever in our happy debt.

I end with a reflection on reading by E B White, whose *Charlotte's Web* continues to instruct and delight children as much now as it did when first published almost forty years ago.

Reading is the work of the alert mind, is demanding, and under ideal conditions produces finally a sort of ecstasy . . . The experience of reading has a sublimity and power unequalled by any other form of communication. It would be just as well if educators clung to this great phenomenon and did not get side-tracked.

BfK 64
September 1990

Dear *BfK*

Hold it right there! Before you go any further into gutting more fiction for its mathematical and scientific core curriculum attainment targets, please reflect on the fact that some of us actively refuse to allow course books to examine or assess children through our texts, considering fiction written for pleasure to be available principally for entertainment. There are bonuses to fiction, of course, and you know that I can speak at length about them: but such secondary use should always be firmly in the hands of the reader.

They're big on 'unit studies' in Strathclyde – where a reception class I saw was so busy mining the cross-curricular ore from *The Lighthouse Keeper's Lunch* that it took the best part of half a term for the children to get to the end of the story. I wonder if they cared by then?

But well done or poorly, please don't spread this approach to books through *Books for Keeps* of all places – the magazine born to support those who first treated good books properly by encouraging private ownership. Ownership has two meanings: the physical and the spiritual, and this second is as important as the first. What a child does as the result of reading or sharing a book should be his or her concern (within the law). School mathematics and science can be exciting enough, and there are many cross-curricular ways into both areas without doing our books to death. If you suggest in your pages such activities with any of mine, I'll sue for misuse.

Bernard Ashley, Letter to the Editor, in *BfK* 56, May 1989)

Ten Golden Rules for Critics of Children's Books

ROBERT LEESON

I WAS A CRITIC before I was a published writer and can say truthfully that one reason why I began to write children's books was a critical dissatisfaction with existing input.

So I know the game from both sides and, in twenty-five years as a literary editor, I often acted as umpire. During those years I worked out Ten Golden Rules for reviewers . . . because it turns out that what annoys the author often bothers the editor. And a well-made review ought to help and please the author, too.

Here they are:

1. Don't skim read – a critic's vice. Read to enjoy.

2. Know the publishing history of author and book, or try to find out.

3. Do not say, 'I could do better', or worse, 'anyone can write this stuff', unless you have tried.

4. Beware of using your review to show you know more than the author.

5. Beware of taking against a book, then rationalising a personal dislike into objective criticism by nit-picking.

6. Beware of making statements about what is in the book which you cannot back up if challenged.

7. Don't review too many titles at a time, even if round about Christmas time the literary editor becomes desperate.

8. If reviewing several books, you may look for a common theme. This makes for an interesting review. But recognise when the theme wears thin and don't fit books into an argumentative framework where they don't belong.

9. Don't make gratuitous attacks on the style of the book when what you dislike is its content.

10. Write usefully first and foremost – to inform is the first function of a review. Let wit follow wisdom.

And, I might add an eleventh rule – if you aren't ready to sign the review, don't attack the book.

Follow all these rules, and you'll be at peace with yourself. It won't guarantee that all the authors will love you. Some of them are quite unreasonable . . .

Some More Golden Rules

Are these notes enough? And how do they work out in practice? For a personal comment, BfK *went to a children's author who has more experience than most in being on the receiving end – JEAN URE*

I HEARTILY ENDORSE ALL TEN of Bob Leeson's Golden Rules, but would like to amplify one or two and add a couple more to the list. If I use reviews of my own books to illustrate my points, this is simply because I tend to read my own reviews with a more jaundiced attention than I do other people's. I don't think I can be alone in this . . .

Golden Rule No. 10: 'Write usefully first and foremost.' Yes, most certainly – but that doesn't mean do a re-write of the blurb and call it a review! This is a particularly annoying habit. Expound the plot by all means, but unless there's a critical summing-up or expression of opinion this doesn't qualify as a review.

Golden Rule No. 6: Not only 'beware of making statements about what is in the book which you cannot back up if challenged', but *don't make authoritative pronouncements if you're not prepared (or haven't the space) to back them up at the time.*

Here I speak from recent experience: the wound is still raw! I had a review which was truly excellent (in other words, *favourable*), fulfilling all the reviewing criteria that even the most demanding of authors could lay down – until it came to the punchline. The punchline was: 'If only Ms Ure had a literary style to match her insight she would be right up in the first ranks of writers for the YA.'

Now, I accept that it's any reviewer's right to find fault. What I do *not* accept is that it's a reviewer's right to cast a slur on a writer's style (by which very largely hangs or falls a writer's reputation) without giving at least some examples by way of justification. Reviewers are not there to play God. We all *know* opinions are only personal opinions, but personal opinions can be devastating, and I take it as no part of a reviewer's brief to devastate, certainly not without good *and demonstrated* cause.

Golden Rule No. 3: Under the heading of reviewers' claims to being able to do better than the author under review, I'd instance the following: 'a brilliant and powerful book in many ways – but I'm glad it's not my name on it.' This, by implication, is saying that the reviewer is every bit as capable as the author of writing a brilliant and powerful book – and so indeed he may be, but is it seemly so to puff himself up whilst reviewing another writer's work?

Two other Golden Rules which I find it difficult to encapsulate but feel I must attempt . . .

Extra Golden Rule (i): Don't be dogmatic. By this I mean, don't put forward what is essentially your own reading of the work as if it's a statement of fact, for example: 'Comprehensive school teachers might like to read this book because it has been carefully thought out with their needs in mind.' Oh? Who says so? The reviewer says so! But what right has a reviewer to make any such assertion? Reviewers should stick to reviewing and not make unwarranted assumptions.

Finally, Extra Golden Rule (ii): Don't review a book solely in terms of your own ideology. This is perhaps a refinement of Bob's Golden Rule No. 5. I include it as a separate issue only because I've noticed a growing tendency for people with axes to grind, albeit perfectly good and respectable axes, to lose all sense of perspective.

When writing books, I do not consciously consider that I must take care not to offend any of the currently accepted canons. I am, after all, writing novels, not polemics. My own philosophy of life will inescapably come across, and this, I believe, is as it should be.

I recently learnt, however, from the US *Interracial Bulletin* that my philosophy, as perceived in a light-hearted book called *A Proper Little Nooryeff*, is shot through with 'subtle bigotry' . . .

> For instance, Jamie is convinced to help with the ballet show not because of the artistic value of ballet [oh boy!] nor even because of the exercise he would get [but Jamie, think of the exercise!] but because the show's proceeds will go to persons with disabilities. [Bad, bad, bad!] More specifically, the money will go to Fairfield, a segregated [no, they don't mean racially] institution where his cousin resides . . . it is never mentioned that the money would be more appropriately raised for a program which encourages mainstreaming, employment, accessible recreation or independent living.

Along the way, with almost total disregard for any other qualities the book may have, I'm also taken to task for classism, sexism, remedialism and sissyism . . .

> The greatest failure of the book is its finale. The fact that Jamie has survived the ridicule of ruffians doesn't convince him to pursue his talent openly and with pride. In the end, he worries about how he will face his sex-polluted slob of a best-friend, Doug. Does Jamie fear that Doug will think him a sissy, or perhaps worse, gay?

Yes! Yes! Yes! He does! *Imagine* . . . the horror of it!

We come here to the age-old question . . . is one delivering political messages or is one writing books about people living in the real world? The standard retort, of course, is that OK, in the real world people *might* be classist, sexist, racist, genderist, sissyist, homophobe, but we, the right-minded ones, are trying to change all that. Should we therefore be including such wrong-thinking characters in our books?

My answer is a very firm yes, we should – but not without making it very clear where we personally stand on such issues, which is precisely what I did in *Nooryeff*. Unfortunately, the most well-meaning and high-minded of people, such as I'd suppose the reviewer for *Interracial Bulletin* to be, can be as riddled with prejudice as any blimp. If I had space I could refute every one of the charges made against *Nooryeff* save for the handicapism, to which I plead guilty. But let us think . . . how could I have handled it?

Anita:	But, Jamie, it's for charity! It's for Fairfield.
Jamie:	Sod Fairfield. The money would be more appropriately raised for a program to encourage mainstreaming, employment, accessible recreation or independent living.
Anita:	Oh, Jamie, you're so right! We should not be supporting these segregated institutions for people suffering from cerebral palsy.
Jamie:	Now that you've seen the light, I will dance for you.
Anita:	Oh, Jamie!

See what I mean?

The question inevitably arises: how much notice should a writer take of reviews?

I don't feel inclined to lay down rules about this. There are writers who claim – indeed, I know one personally – to be totally incurious about their reviews and pretty well impervious to either praise or criticism. I find this difficult to comprehend, but who shall doubt that this is their right? For myself I readily confess to being made of weaker stuff. After twenty-odd years as a professional writer I still remain naively eager to hear other people's opinions of my work. I *care* what my readers think – and my readers include my reviewers. I am made happy by good reviews, cast down by bad ones; not, after all these years, to any incapacitating degree, but sufficient for me to take note of what reviewers say . . . usually.

For instance, I largely (largely but not *entirely*) dismissed the above-mentioned *Nooryeff* review on the grounds that it came from the standpoint of ideology rather than literature.

On the one occasion when I did take criticism to heart, it rather rebounded on me. This was when I allowed myself to be riled by a scathing review of *Nooryeff* in the then *Gay News* (ideology again) in which it was somewhat irritably suggested that the book would have been far more interesting had I made my *'butch, attractive, muscly, fantastically gifted, sexy ballet dancer'* gay. Now, I had originally toyed with this idea, but dismissed it as being too much of a stereotype: *Gay News* made me wonder whether perhaps a straight ballet dancer was a stereotype? Thus, in the original draft of the sequel, I did the next best thing and made my fantastic, etc. hero bi-sexual. Unfortunately, there was such an outcry at my publishers – 'Not *Jamie!*' they wailed – that I was forced to listen to editorial pleadings and have a rethink: my hero reverted to being madly butch.

Gay News, had, I think, folded by this time, so I never got a scathing review, which I should have enjoyed; instead I received a panic-stricken letter from my US editor saying that the ending of the book would have to be changed or they would be inundated with hate mail from the gay lobby. (The sequel, by the way, was rather aptly named *You Win Some, You Lose Some . . .*)

So have I learnt *nothing* from reviews during my ten years as a children's writer? I've learnt what sort of books win prizes, what sort of books reviewers wet their knickers over, what sort of books put their hackles up, what sort of subjects throw them into a state of uncritical swoon – but as regards my own personal writing, I'm afraid the answer has to be no; not a lot. Perhaps I'm asking more of reviewers than they feel able (for a whole variety of reasons, space and economics not least among them) to give. But then this entire article has been intended as a plea for both *more* reviewing and more *critically informed* reviewing, which must surely be in the best interests of us all . . . isn't it?

BfK 66
January 1991

They find him.

(Val Randall reviewing *Star Trek III: The Search for Spock* by Uonda N McIntyre in *BfK 29*, November 1984)

Reasons for the low standards of kids' fiction are legion: nepotism, various problems with 'established authors', reliance upon classics or folk tales. But one major factor encouraging people's belief that any idiot can write stories for children must be the growing trend of publishing books by celebrities. Take *The Old Man of Lochnagar*. I know HRH wrote it for family amusement, that royalties go to charity, but one expects a future king to have a little pride. Perhaps worthy causes outweighed personal considerations? Yet a sponsored leap from Beachy Head would produce just as much cash. And if, like most sponsored activities, this would-n't constitute an outright public good, at least it wouldn't be a positive mischief. Chances are, *anyone* reading *Lochnagar* could do better themselves, and that can only harm the general standing of children's literature.

(Steve Bowles, 'Celebrity Snares', in *BfK 7*, March 1981)

SAT Upon

LIZ WATERLAND

ALEXANDER SPOTTED it straight away. 'Are you doing our tests?' he said with interest. 'What tests are those?' said I. He explained he'd heard on the telly that all seven-year-olds were going to be tested 'for the government' and he'd been waiting to have his. Well, I had to come clean and admit that there would be some tests and that this time, when he read with me, I would be looking out for how many words he could read without my help. What, I wondered, did he think of the idea? He smiled engagingly . . . 'It seems a bit silly. I've read with you lots of times; you ought to know how I can read by now, I should think.'

And so, of course, I do. I know Alexander's reading very well. I know he has a taste for the quirky and the unusual; he has just read *Tales of a One Way Street* and admired the way the stories seem ordinary and then 'sort of turn round and surprise you'. I know he reads a book a day and an extra one on Saturday 'because I read one at the library while Mummy does the shopping' and I know that he reads fluently and skilfully . . . especially when reading silently which he prefers because it's quicker.

He read beautifully, as I knew he would, and gained his Level Three label with ease. Good old Alexander! A few more like him and I could tackle the Level Twos. Let me think . . . half an hour or so for each Level Three, say fifteen minutes for each Level Two, an open-ended amount for Level One. I should have SAT on them all in about fifteen teaching hours. It's a good job I'm not the class teacher with all those writing, spelling, maths and science assessments to make as well. At least it's only the admin that's going to the wall, not children's learning.

What's it all in aid of? It isn't for the children's benefit that normal service was suspended for five weeks; they're having their most lovely term snatched away from them. The summer term of their top infant year, when so many of them grow up before our eyes and revel in their new powers, the term of outings and trips and drawing cowslips and ladybirds, the term when just a bit more teaching will give little Zoë (summer-born and struggling) the confidence to read for herself and will teach David to skip at last. All this is wasted and lost . . . the time that for us and our 'big children' will never come again.

Certainly it can't be for the teachers. Run ragged by the need to respond to every bright idea Elizabeth House dreams up, peering out from under expensive heaps of files and booklets, told how to do their jobs by people whose only contact with teaching is that they once went to school, trying to do it all in thirty hours (less administration, form-filling, oh yes, and the reading SATs). Would we have chosen this as the culmination of our children's precious infant schooling, the way we'd want to remember April, May and June and the children whose company we're privileged to have shared?

For the parents then? For their 'right to know'? Parents who've been in and out of school since their child started with us? Who have a knowledge of their child down to the number of teeth he's lost and what are his favourite songs? Are they really to benefit from being given a number which is supposed, by the time it's been 'resolved' and averaged and weighted and summated, to tell them all about their child's abilities in the complexities of language and science and maths? We might as well sort them by their zodiac signs. At least that would give twelve categories instead of only three. 'Your child is a Two in English' has all the subtlety and nuance of assessing the bouquet of a bottle of wine by smashing it over the waiter.

I do think Alexander had it bang to rights when he described it as being 'for the government'. What the motivation is, I'm not sure. Is it to be seen to be *doing* something about something? Is it to discredit teachers? Is it to keep parents quiet about resources? Is it, even, out of genuine concern for small children? I don't know. But I do know that it's cost a fortune which could have provided another teacher in every school, or extra books or computers or visits to museums. I do know that it's taken up

SuperSAT?

time which could have been spent on reading books or sewing or learning how to write in italics.

And yet, surely *something* can be said for it all?

Well, of course, the choice of books is interesting. If your child has spent two years working her way through *Gayway* or *Ginn 360,* it will be a shock to be presented with the readerly requirements of much of the literature of SATs. (We actually had a different problem at Level Two. So many of the books were familiar to our children, I had a job to provide some of them with a choice that would fulfil the need for a book they didn't know well.)

Yes, the books were, on the whole, all right. What we were asked to do with them, however, was very odd. The idea that, say, *The Very Hungry Caterpillar* was only suitable for the emergent reader and couldn't be offered to a child at the independent reading stage, while *The Little Red Hen* is presented as only suitable for Level Two readers, is exactly the opposite of the apprenticeship model of reading, in which a good book is seen as valuable at any of the levels of reading development. Surely Level One can be assessed with *The Little Red Hen* and Level Two works just as well with Eric Carle? That, after all, is what multi-layered books such as these are so good at, enabling

Covers of *The Very Hungry Caterpillar* by Eric Carle
and *Joe's Cafe* by Rose Impey and SuePorter

all children to interact with them and to show what they can do. The notion of books as rungs on a ladder which you leave behind as you progress past them is exactly what we've been fighting *against* for so long. Here it is again pretending to be valid for telling about a child's reading ability.

Still, the SAT has put a model of reading assessment into every school which is certainly better than using the Richter Scale approach which might have been chosen. (This, of course, is the system in which the assumption is made that knowing a child's reading age tells you something about his reading development, attitudes and skills. It's about as meaningful as thinking that knowing what an earthquake measured on the Richter Scale will tell you what it was like to live through it.)

Even then, though, this small benefit has been spoiled by the sloppiness with which it's been organised. The child who can read and understand *Little Bear* is a quite different reader from the one who can tackle *The Sick Cow*. The ability to read *Joe's Café* is no indicator of an understanding of *A Necklace of Raindrops*. The skills needed, the sophistication, the vocabulary are not the same. Should we choose to test the children on the easiest option offered to us so they can do their best, or should we use it as a learning experience and challenge them? (You must be joking . . . *we want good scores for our school!*)

Sloppiness even characterises the marking system. 'Errors' are only counted if the teacher intervenes to tell the child what the error is. Keep quiet. No 'Teacher tolds', no failure. It's a good job we're all honest and conscientious and wouldn't dream of allowing a child to read nonsense for the sake of claiming another Level Two.

Not to be too grudging, though, I admit to reading about a school which took part in last year's trials. The staff were so taken by the miscue analysis model of assessing reading, they've carried on using it ever since. Certainly, if it is really new to a school, it can't help but be a good thing for the teachers to be introduced to the notion of looking at a child's strategies and behaviours as a way of learning about them. Just as it must be a good thing for reading schemers to be introduced to the notion that you don't need one to help a child to learn to read.

I suppose, too, there's some good to be found in the pathetic sight of parents fighting to buy the government- approved books. Anything which gets parents into bookshops and Maurice Sendak into children's homes can't be all bad. (Even if I had to find out what books I was supposed to use for the SAT via a crumpled cutting from a parent's newspaper. Contempt for the professional can hardly have been more clearly expressed.)

Despite all this, however, I do know that very soon, perhaps not next year but certainly soon, the whole thing will disappear. It will have cost billions and it will be ended. There is no way in which this farce can be sustained year after year. It's too expensive, too impractical, too pointless. We shall have the dubious satisfaction of being in on the largest and most costly failed experiment in education ever. When the collapse comes and the statutory orders are withdrawn and the SATs are no more, we'll go back to asking teachers to know about children and tell what they know to parents. We may be more definite about how we know it and how we are going to tell it . . . but that is no bad thing. We may have new insights into the good, the bad and the ugly of assessment and reporting . . . that won't be bad either.

What we will have returned to, though, is what Alexander knew all along – the idea that the only way to know a child is to work with him and alongside him while he learns, and that the only way to say something about a child's reading is to read things with him. All we can ask is, 'How long, Lord, how long?'

BfK 69
July 1991

This is a thin, one-idea story with little character development, though its theme will entertain young readers and have a more pointed topical relevance for teachers: Guy's school is taken over by government-appointed robots who make the children sit in silence in neat rows, learning grammar and history dates and poetry by rote. After strict tests, the children are priced according to how they score.

Hmmm . . . don't show this one to John Patten.

(Linda Newbery reviewing Jon Blake's *Roboskool* in *Bfk 81*, July 1993)

Smiling at the Crocodile

*MARY HOFFMAN tells the story of
the sequel to* Amazing Grace

WRITING A BESTSELLER is easy – because you don't know you're doing it. Writing a sequel to a bestseller is a totally different matter. The day I wrote down the text for *Amazing Grace*, I wrote another story, since bottom-drawered, and the outline for a third, which became the modestly successful *Leon's Lucky Lunchbreak*. I had no idea then, or even later when I saw Caroline Binch's first wonderful picture of Grace and her grandmother, that I had written my breakthrough book.

I don't think that sank in till I went on holiday to the States last April and agreed to do a few signing sessions in bookshops while I was there. Americans take children's books and their writers a lot more seriously than the British do. *Amazing Grace* had a review to itself across three columns in *The New York Times*, from a journalist who found more in it than I had remembered putting there.

Queues of eager children who kept me in a Denver bookshop for several hours contrasted with the two or three who'd gathered in my local North London one a few months earlier. When I got back to England, my editor at Francies Lincoln, Janetta Otter-Barry, dropped the casual remark, 'It's a pity you don't want to do a sequel', and I had to do some serious thinking.

I'm not keen on the modern desire to turn every good thing into a series. *Back to the Future* was a perfectly constructed film, and although the next two were mildly enjoyable, we didn't really need them. Sequels are what readers construct in their heads after putting a book down. Who wants *Son of Heathcliffe*, *Return to Bleak House* or *Ulysses 2*? But there are one or two successful follow-ups, notably *The Growing Pains of Adrian Mole*. Could Caroline and I match Sue Townsend?

An original sketch by Caroline Binch

The desire to do so is understandable: the satisfaction for readers of more-of-the-same comfort, which can so easily lead to indistinguishable and undistinguished writing like the 'Babysitters Club' books; for publishers writers and illustrators, the assurance of a ready-made market at least initially. Spin-off publishing and merchandising is where the big money is – just think of *The Snowman* or *Spot* and sequels are the most basic spin-off of all.

Why resist? Well, is it going to be a real book? Is there a genuine second story to be told about this character or will you just apply the formula, take the money and run? The original book had some clear underlying messages: all stories are for all people, girls can be strong, being black is something to be proud of, life is what you make it, don't let people put you down, go for it. . .

If you read the newspaper coverage, both quality and tab-loid, of the recent PEN survey, you might think I wrote those lit-tle slogans down on my cuff and consulted them every few min-utes at my word processor. Actually I was only wearing a towel, being in a women's health club at the time, and I just started to write 'Grace was a girl who loved stories' without knowing what was going to come next. Not quite as ultimately life-changing as 'In a hole in the ground there lived a hobbit . . .' but almost as unplanned.

The sequel wasn't ever going to be that relaxed. The family who modelled for Caroline's pictures had moved back to The Gambia in West Africa. Grace was approaching nine years old and the difficulties seemed enormous. But Frances Lincoln is a very enterprising person as well as a company, and she and they all seemed inspired by the first book's message that we could do anything we wanted, if only we put our minds to it.

What clinched it was a story which suddenly started to nag at me to be told. Grace was now a role model and heroine for thousands of children. She was from a warm and loving family, but in the original book there was no mention of her father. How would an imaginative, story-loving child like Grace react if she had an absent father? How would she feel if she went to visit him and met his second family? She could feel torn in two or she could come to feel like the link between the two halves of her family. If she could pull off that transformation, she could help and encourage many children who find themselves in that situation today.

'Write it, put down the phone and write it now. We need it!' said my Denver bookseller friend when I outlined the plot to her. Thus encouraged, I flew to The Gambia with Caroline one cold, grey morning last December. It was an overwhelming experience, I had never been to Africa, never met the people whose faces I had grown to know so well from Caroline's pic-tures, never spent more than an hour or two with Caroline her-self, come to that.

We landed, three hours late, in brilliant afternoon sunshine and were met by drums and dancers and a terrifying figure called Mama Para. We were to see him a few times again in other entertainments. It is a Christmas character, basically benevolent, but must surely cause a few nightmares among Gam-

bian children? Grace, whose real name is Salan, had gone to the
airport to meet us at the right time, but because of the delay,
was not there when we arrived. Her mother, Lorraine, was, and
I searched her features for the Ma of the book as we drove the
dusty road from Banjul airport to Bakau, where they live.

One of the well-intentioned ideas I had had for the second
book was to show modern Africa – tall white buildings, thriving commerce, anything to get away from the mudhut and
famine images which is all that many British children, even
black ones, see of that continent. But The Gambia is not Kenya
or Nigeria. Its only profitable trade is the tourist one and there
is a big contrast between the hotels and the rest of the buildings.
You see sheep and chickens wandering about the roads of the
capital Banjul and only a few of those roads are metalled.

So that was one good intention out of the window! The
Africa I saw was startling. To Western eyes homes made up of
odd bits and pieces, dirt roads and shoeless children made a
strong first impression. It would be dishonest to pretend otherwise in my case. But very quickly your eye begins to take in
other things. Palm trees, baobabs, casuarinas, hibiscus, vul-
tures, batik butterflies and, above all, colours. Vivid blue skies,
purple flowers trailing over our hut-style room at the hotel,
cloth of every shade and pattern worn by men and women, particularly spectacular on the women with their matching head-
cloths twisted into elaborate and becoming styles, piles of pink
papaya and red water melon on our breakfast table . . . it was
like living in a kaleidoscope.

Before I left, a colleague of my husband's, who'd recently
come back from The Gambia, had said it was a dangerous place
for Westerners and that there were armed guards on the hotels.
What with that and the injections against yellow fever, cholera,
hepatitis and meningitis and the course of anti-malaria pills I
was taking, there had been moments when I wondered if this
sequel idea had been such a good one.

All this had dispersed by the time we woke the next morning.
We met Salan and she was just like her picture. Fortunately she
hadn't grown too much. She thought it was great fun that we
had both come to see her though she wondered why Caroline
hadn't brought her son, Joe. Right outside our hut was a clear,
turquoise swimming pool under a leaning palm tree and Caro-

line and I soon discovered that 'Gambian Time' always meant
we had time for a swim before any morning appointment,
which might take place up to two and a half hours later than
arranged.

There were certainly no armed guards on our hotel – it was
entirely open-plan with no guardable outside door anyway. We
never felt a moment's unease the whole time we were there. Of
course, we were taken around by Lorraine, who works on the
local paper, and knows a lot of people. But even when we left
the hotel on our own and were besieged by the young hustlers
who want to sell you cheap cigarettes or be your guide for the
day, we had no trouble explaining that we knew where we were
going and what we were doing, accompanied by lots of smiles.

We had some memorable experiences. We met Lorraine's
boss, the Liberian editor of the ambitiously named *Daily
Observer*, which still only comes out three times a week. Kenneth Best and his wife had fled from their own war-ravaged
country two years before and had made a new life for themselves. In their offices, we met a young man who'd invented a
bush telephone and made a prototype out of wood and bits of
Walkman. Everybody joined in on testing it out, delightedly
speaking to one another from room to room. Caroline and I

Illustration by Caroline Binch from *Amazing Grace*

were interviewed by a young reporter about the new book. The whole building was alive with enthusiasm and interest – no jaded Wapping hacks these.

We visited Salan's school and met her headmistress, Mrs Ndow, another impressive figure – a retired civil servant, who had started teaching poor children in the streets of Serrekunda, The Gambia's most populous town, and ended up starting three schools in Bakau. They have virtually no children's books in The Gambia and our slender gift of British paperbacks was well received.

We played in the warm Atlantic ocean outside our hotel with Salan and her friends and talked to Lorraine about her own experiences of coming back to The Gambia after a childhood in Britain. Caroline and I went on our own on a 'Roots' trip up-river to Juffure, supposedly the village of Alex Haley's ancestor, Kunta Kinte. And we wished we had not. The report in the *Sunday Times* in February this year that Haley had made most of his book up and plagiarised some of the rest didn't surprise me at all. Self-appointed 'policemen' swatted children away from us with tree branches and then expected to be tipped for it. Pre-arranged photo-sessions with a village chieftain and an old woman descendant in Kinte Kunta (Kinte's compound) were designed to put money in the baskets of those individuals, not the villages. We got back on our pleasure boat to eat a lavish lunch and felt too sick to enjoy it.

The people of The Gambia aren't starving; they have enough food. But they are desperate for education, books, writing materials and for someone to take an interest in them. 'You will forget me,' said a girl of about eleven on the jetty at the fishing village of Albreda. I had nothing left to give her but she has been with me ever since.

Happier trips were to the incredible wildlife reserve at Abuko, Serrekunda market and Lorraine's family compound in Banjul. We also spent some social time with Nana, a powerful figure in the books and as lovely off the page as on. By now, Lorraine was a firm friend and Caroline and I were getting on famously. Apart from a terrible sleep problem over the last few days caused by the multiple early-morning chorus of the Muezzin, church bells, exotic birds and, even more maddening, British birdwatchers – 'Have you got the binoculars, Kevin?' –

all before 6.30 am, we were having a great time.

On our last morning, we gave way to the importunities of two 'guides' who had been promising all week to take us to see the crocodiles. There is a sacred crocodile pit in Bakau, where women go to pray if they have fertility problems, and where men take their business worries. We walked to it through back streets, far away from the world of the hotel and supermarket. Charles and Moses told us about a young girl of eighteen who had just died in the village, days after giving birth to twins. Everyone was rallying round to look after the babies. Charles said he was himself a twin, one of several sets his mother had had. No crocodile pit for her.

When we got to the pit, we couldn't believe what we were seeing. There were no fences or barriers. 'Go on, touch them,' our guides encouraged us. There was one huge beast, known as Charlie, crossing the path ahead of us. He sank down on the edge of a very smelly canal. 'It's all right, this is a holy place,' said Charles, so I knelt down and touched the crocodile's sun-warmed scales and held his back leg. Caroline did it, too. If he had decided to turn his massive head and jaw round on us there would have been only one kind of sequel. But he didn't. It was a tremendous last experience of The Gambia.

Back in England, I wanted to squeeze all this into my book. The first draft was a bit like a travelogue. But I soon realised that, although The Gambia had been a wonderful bonus and Caroline's new pictures were going to give the second book added vitality and glamour, the story I was going to tell could just as easily have taken place in a wet week in Neasden. I would have to find other ways of raising awareness of the little girl in Albreda. It wasn't the job of Grace's new story.

It doesn't have an official title, as yet, though I call it 'Grace Unlimited'. It's a family story and as much concerned with Grace's inner world as the first book, but is longer and for a slightly older readership. I've made a few changes at the sugges-tion of my American publishers. They want to know things like, why isn't Grace at school? How come she can just go and visit her Dad in The Gambia? British readers take a lot more for granted, but these changes were easy to accommodate. Now all we're waiting for is Caroline's second trip to take the final photographs.

By autumn next year we may know whether we've got
another bestseller. But I know already we've got another real
book and that's what counts. Favourable reviews would be
nice, but I'll be convinced we've succeeded when we get the first
letter from a child like the one I had this morning from a little
girl in Michigan. Too bad I shan't ever get one from a little girl
in Albreda. She has no pen or paper and, even if the book
becomes available in The Gambia, there is no way she could ever
afford a copy. A satisfactory sequel for her is a much harder
undertaking than writing a book.

BfK 80
May 1993

A Last Word

On the Importance of Books in Schools

MICHAEL ROSEN

IN THE LAST FEW YEARS a change has taken place in the relationship between schools and books.

I was at school between 1950 and 1964. I'm fairly certain that at no time before the sixth form did anyone either direct me towards any books to read outside of school, nor for that matter did they ask me what I was reading in my own time. My schools were state infant, junior and grammar schools in a largely middle-class area in North-west London. It's important to be clear about this because it's now become commonplace for politicians and journalists to refer to some kind of educational golden age where there was 100 per cent literacy, where everybody could read, did read and schools were 'doing their job'. In the schools I attended, this most certainly wasn't the case. There was a resistant cluster, who as I remember couldn't read at all – they were omitted when we read round the class out of 'Beacon Readers'. There was another group who found it very difficult – they stumbled and ground to a halt in these read-around sessions and the rest of us were given the space to snigger at them. In the fourth year at my junior school, there were two classes of over forty children. Something like twenty-five of us passed the 11-plus. Because my class was where the twenty-five lived – the 'A' stream – most of the time in school was spent doing maths. All of every morning in fact. This was because the 11-plus was one third maths and one third formal logic, intelligence tests.

In essence, then, my primary school, along with hundreds of

others, didn't see how what we would in normal speech call a 'book' had much of a part to play in education.

Later, at my grammar school, books – albeit often of a very specific kind – put in more of an appearance. We were encouraged to use the school library, there were class readers for English – *Jim Davis* by John Masefield, *A Midsummer Night's Dream*, the New Testament in RE and text books, text books and text books. These we had on one-term or one-year loan, we put our names in them and they covered Maths, Geography, History, the Sciences and languages. I recollect one English teacher urging us to read out of school, but he himself didn't initiate any discussion around our home reading or introduce books to us in lesson time to read at home apart from the class reader.

Luckily, my out of school literacy experience by this time was very wide-ranging, supported and scrutinised by my parents: 'I think it's time you gave Thomas Hardy a go.' 'Alec McCowen is playing Malvolio – I think you'll like it' . . . That sort of thing. However, it wasn't until I reached the sixth form that I was exposed to any kind of home-school continuum in reading: Mike Benton, producer of many school anthologies of poetry since then, taught me English and sent us off to the library to read criticism. Only then was I initiated into using more than one text for essays: *Cambridge European History* and Brogan on French history, for instance.

I labour this point in order to show that the misty-eyed view of education, especially grammar-school education, that we hear from such people as Kenneth Clarke has to be qualified. . . . At my grammar school, over 60 per cent of the students left in advance of the sixth form, before these later initiations I've just described came into play. In other words, the formalised and structured use of a variety of books to support learning in schools only arrived when the school population had been weeded down to less than 10 per cent of pupils in state schools.

Between the time I left primary school in 1957 and the arrival of what Professor Ted Wragg has called Mad Curriculum Disease, huge changes took place in attitudes to literacy, children's books and children. These changes can be traced by taking a quick look at the new and expanded institutions that grew up at this time: school libraries in every school, class libraries, school bookshops, professional school librarians, a library support service from local libraries, teacher–parent reading programmes, the National Federation of Children's Book Groups, Children's Book Week and so on.

Magazines and book clubs grew up to support and inform these changes: *Books for Keeps*, *Books for Your Children*, *Dragon's Teeth*, *Letterbox Library* and the now defunct *Children's Rights Workshop*. Why am I describing what is to many of us so familiar? To remind us, to remind myself that all these features that surround us and support the reading of books are relatively new, were fought for by educationists, librarians and parents spending many, many hours of unpaid time.

The domination in children's books of all kinds by white, middle-class lifestyles, heroes and heroines, Anglocentric perspectives on the rest of the world, white view of the Third World – all these were challenged. One of my Christmas presents as a child had been the Puffin book, *Malay Adventure*:

> Here and there they passed a group of broken-down huts, located beside a filthy pool of stagnant water, which smelt most foully.
>
> 'How can anyone bear to live there?' asked Brian.
>
> 'Only a Chinaman could,' Chapman admitted, 'it would kill anyone else. But they don't seem to mind either dirt or discomfort. As for smells, the worse they are the more they seem to like them.'
>
> 'Perhaps the Chinese nose is fitted with a special filter,' suggested Willem.
>
> 'Perhaps so, but it must be a particularly effective one – a semi-permeable membrane, maybe.'

In these times of mocking PC – political correctness – it does us no harm to remind ourselves that this was the political correctness of only a few years ago.

But let me return to the changes – totally out of reach of government directives – autonomous networks of information and self-education that sprang up around teachers' centres, libraries and teachers' associations like the National Association of Teachers of English, and magazines.

It'll be seen in years to come, more clearly than now perhaps, that all this had a profound effect on what was written, who was writing, what was published and who was reading. We were on the verge, or perhaps in the middle, of a truly popular culture.

Yet this same period has been characterised recently in precisely the opposite terms – as the lost generation, a time when the adults concerned with children's literacy have failed. Let two things be said here:

1. There is no valid evidence whatsoever for this.
2. Any changes in literacy cannot possibly be attributed to one or other teaching method since the number of variables affecting children's literacy is so great – numbers of children for whom English is a second language, the increase or decrease of home support, the rapid turnover of teachers in one area as opposed to another and so on.

More than that, the teaching methods described under such headings as 'progressive' or 'look and say' are in fact so diverse that one-to-one correlations are not worth the paper they are written on.

We can be certain of one thing, though: this government, in spite of all the rhetoric concerning literacy levels, has declared war on the reading of books. Let's look at their weapons:

- the closing of public libraries
- the elimination of the library support services
- the forced amateuring of school librarians – professionals can't be afforded
- budget restrictions on school book buying as documented by the NAS/UWT and the Children's Book Foundation
- the domination of fixed courses of study, set texts and testing that limit casual and pupil-led reading and browsing
- the contract arrangement with teachers that has resulted in a huge decrease in after-hours cultural activities
- the elimination of text books for home reading and the consequent rise of the work-sheet.

This list is having and is going to have more effect than the sum of its parts. We are at this moment witnessing the elimination of

Michael Rosen

a cadre of expertise that has informed and supported teachers in the hunt for books to suit the individual children in their classes. This matches the return of an idea of children's literature based on English Heritage – the idea that we are not entitled to be full members of British society unless we've been forced to read *Wind in the Willows* and, as Norman Tebbit would put it, support the England cricket team no matter what culture we belong to.

In addition, school budgets available for buying books are now less. This has a direct class effect. Schools in middle-class areas get subsidised to the tune of thousands of pounds. My step-daughter's school has raised something like £15,000 for a new school library from parents. Schools in working-class areas just have to lump it. At the secondary level, the removal of 100 per cent coursework at GCSE, the arrival of compulsory

Shakespeare for thirteen- to sixteen-year-olds, the narrowing down of set texts are all acts that discourage, not encourage, autonomous reading. This is matched by the elimination of coursework in other subjects, too. In order to do his coursework project on Science, my son had to read a book on the thyroid gland – not a text book – and a chapter in a text book from the library on the endocrine system. For his empathy work on the London Blitz, a six-page diary – he read six or seven eyewitness accounts bought from the local community bookshops, THAP and Centreprise, and a chapter or two from A J P Taylor.

All this is under attack as we restrict our children to the photocopied sheet, the worksheet, the set text, the removal of coursework, and the constant testing and examining.

It's a dispiriting picture. Middle-class parents like me can and do compensate like crazy. We pile off to our local bookshop and buy the text book that the teacher is photocopying page by page. We buy one or two more in order to show our children that knowledge is not finite, absolute and restricted to one authority. We take our children to the theatre so that the cloze procedure on Shakespeare – 'To be or not to blank' (fill in the missing word) – is supported by flesh and blood actors and emotions. We pull books off our shelves and say: 'First World War? Try Siegfried Sassoon.' With our smaller children, for every Peg and Jack and Jack and Mac they are sent home with by curriculum-dominated teachers, we read ten real books. We get in the *Beano* and *Snap*, and Tintin and Asterix, too.

In summary, what is happening is that the access to books for working-class children is being limited by the day. That moment, that beginning of a child's literary popular culture, is being wiped out. If there aren't the librarians, school bookshops, flexible school curricula and knowledgeable teachers to introduce, say, *No Hickory, No Dickory, No Dock* by John Agard and Grace Nichols, or *Daz 4 Zoe* by Robert Swindells, then the vast majority of children will not come across them in their lives. Yet it is books like these that made and make children's literature what I keep calling a popular culture: wide-ranging, inclusive, with roots in popular speech and popular forms of discourse.

Now, let's get this into perspective. No one will die as a result of all this. The world is in a terrible condition and we are living in Britain at a time when people can die of hypothermia while there is coal in the ground and miners are out of work.

Nor for that matter is the class-effect of what I've described particularly new. Schooling in this society has always meant the classing of children. It is through the school system from private, through the selective, the religious and the sump schools that children are graded to slot into society's class system. Within schools, the streaming and classing of pupils goes on apace with assessment hitting kids so often and so fast it is occupying weeks and weeks of teacher/student time at all levels. My stepdaughter, aged fourteen, will have been assessed six times in two years by the time she is sixteen.

What's more, the reading of books is no guarantee against barbarism, nor is the not-reading of books evidence of barbarity. The man who rang me recently one night at 9.35 and said, 'Is that Michael Rosen?', 'Yes', 'You filthy fucking Jew . . .' (I then put the phone down) would, if true to type, be highly literate in racist, fascist and antisemitic literature. Clearly, compassion, courage in the face of brutality, honest-dealing, and a whole gamut of desirable actions do not depend on our being active readers.

What follows from this is that in opposing what the government is doing to the reading of books for all children, and working-class children in particular, we have to be quite clear, and much clearer than we have been in the past, about why we are defending book-reading.

We can say that the book has a kind of informal autonomy not matched by other media. You can take it with you, you can skip-read it more quickly on a first reading than a film, TV or radio. You can mark it and refer to it, and read from it more conveniently than other media. You can scan a range of books, their content and their style more quickly than, say, a pile of videos. You can cross-check, cross-reference more easily when you're considering anything you're interested in, whether it's for a formal essay or for your own interest. In other words, books can put you just that bit more in charge of the form.

It's also now commonplace in theory to dwell on reading as a creative act – an imaginative re-creation of text with the tools of previous texts and knowledge doing the work. All reading – no matter how directive and limited – relies on shared meaning. If

I say: 'Do you know the joke about butter? No? I won't tell it to you or you might spread it . . .' then clearly for the joke to work you have to know what butter is.

This re-creative act has been described in wholesome terms on its own merit. In addition to this, it has been said that reading opens up new possibilities. As we read, we are able to try out emotions and actions in the safety of our own home, as the ads used to say. It provides a safe context to experience the dangerous, the absurd and whatever emotion the text suggests without having to suffer or get egg on our face. What would it be like to face up to something really dangerous like a wolf in your grannie's bonnet? What would it be like to discover that your father was killed by your mother's present husband? Read and find out.

I would agree with all these defences, these 'apologies' for literature, but as educators, writers and mediators I think we should be saying more than this.

The government, through its English studies junta in particular, is positing a model of reading based on authority. The set text, the cloze procedure and the removal of the expertise to help teachers and pupils into personable reading, is a way of suggesting that books are sites of authority that should not really be challenged. The close-ended questions of the worksheets are the same. 'Describe socialisation', for example. No suggestion here that socialisation is itself a problematic concept.

Hence the 'good things' about reading I've mentioned – the re-creative, possibility-opening, autonomy-encouraging features – are not sufficient to oppose the authoritarian mode.

What we need is more cogent defence of reading than we have so far. And we can only find this when the humanistic arguments we have used so far – autonomy, re-creation, imagination, possibility-showing – are put into the context in which the options and choices available to us in society are seen as differentially distributed. What those of us who create and mediate writing for children need to proclaim is that:

1 We have to make as wide a range of experiences as possible available to children – ones that include all the cultures and classes of the children themselves. This doesn't simply mean writing them, it now means fighting to save every part

of the elaborate support structure I described earlier, because it's mainly through that structure that children receive the multi-cultural, the offbeat, and the dissident. They could not find those texts without the support structure.

2 In a society where it's possible for there to be miscarriages of justice like the Birmingham Six, swindlers like Robert Maxwell or for millionaires to sack miners, and the stroke of a pen to turn away asylum seekers . . . in a society like that, we are in desperate need for millions of people with the ability to interrogate texts – where text means every form of discourse from the teenage magazine to the politician's speech, the benefit entitlement form, or *Hamlet*. Of course, in one sense, we interrogate every text from the moment we hear and read. What I'm talking about is a widening and deepening of that interrogation which can only come about if we are given a wide and deep range of texts, where we can learn how to cross-reference from non-fiction to fiction, from TV to poetry, from one text to another that directly contradicts it.

I once came home with an essay to do on the Chartists. 'What's your essay?' my father asked. 'Why Chartism failed.' 'Failed?' he said. 'Failed? Who said it failed?'

The moment we learn that authority does not lie in one source; that it doesn't necessarily lie in one book, one film, one magazine or one politician's statement, then a qualitative change comes over us. It makes it more possible for us to question what we read and learn.

We are moving into a situation where children are to be presented with absolute truths absolutely – single texts, compulsorily read. And yet it is clear every day that single truths are not the way of the world. Open today's paper and discover that the man our leaders told us was second only to Hitler in his barbarity was being supplied with arms by these very same leaders so that he could kill civilians. And more, our leaders bust a gut trying to prevent us from knowing about it.

We are in desperate need for millions of people to interrogate this and imagine new possibilities, alternatives, other ways of going on. A humanistic defence of literature is not sufficient to bring this about. We need to insist that reading means: cultural cross-referencing, contrasting of oppositional texts, resourcing alternative views and making space in classrooms for the socialised interpretation of multiple meanings.

That's what we need in an unequal world and it's something we have to organise ourselves into getting.

BfK 79
March 1993

Now is the time to reveal my guilty secret . . . I'm not just a mother who dislikes *some* book events. I'm an English teacher with a passionate interest for a whole range of book-related activities for pupils aged five to sixteen. *Underlying all that I've done has been my firm conviction that books should be sold in schools for their own sake, not to raise money. Consequently, anxiety over which option gives the highest rate of commission to the school is, in my opinion, the wrong priority.*

The guiding principle should be how we can persuade children to read for pleasure. Ignoring all the debate on how and why children learn to read, it's incontrovertible that if children develop the habit of reading they have a hobby and means of relaxation which they can pursue, no matter what their academic achievements and future employment. Selling books should, therefore, be just one of the many strategies schools adopt to encourage children to become readers. The pleasure of owning a book to which you can return at any time, which you can lend to others and which is *yours*, not the school's or the library's, is one which *should be experienced by all children, irrespective of any financial benefit to the school.*

(Pat Clark, 'How Fair is Your School's Bookfair?' in *BfK* 76, September 1992)

The Library That Doesn't Exist . . .

As part of her prize for winning this year's Library Association Carnegie Medal, Berlie Doherty is allowed to give £1,000 worth of books, donated by Birmingham-based Peters Library Service, to an organisation of her choice. Appropriately enough, perhaps, since her winning book was called *Dear Nobody* (Hamish Hamilton), Berlie donated her gift to a library that no longer exists. It used to be at the top of my street until the local council closed it down eighteen months ago. Andrew Milloy, who oversees young people's services in Sheffield, commented: 'It's a challenge to the local council to re-open the library in Eccleshall, but whatever their decision the books will provide a valuable resource and will reach a great number of schools through the schools library service.'

(Newspage in *BfK* 77, November 1992)

. . . And Now the Bad News

Did you see the reports, last month, that total spending on books and equipment for five- to eleven-year-olds now runs individually to less than the weekly cost of three Mars bars? What, then, are the statistics for the school system as a whole? The following paragraph comes from a recent press release by the Publishers' Association. We'd like to have offered our own gloss but words fail even *BfK* when faced with facts like these:

'School book sales in the United Kingdom fell by 4 million in cash from 109.1 million to 105.1 million to the beginning of September 1989 as against the previous year. The number of books purchased fell by 2 million from 32.6 million to 30.6 million. On average, every class of 20 children lost six books. Throughout the 1980s, the number of books bought by British state schools has fallen by 35 per cent.'

Depressing, yes? Especially since, with LMS already upon us, it's not hard to guess what the Official Alibi will be . . .

(Newspage in *BfK* 63, July 1990)

The International Federation of Library Associations' most recent conference was held in Moscow. After a peaceful sunny weekend, we awoke to a gloomy Monday morning and the news that there had been an overnight coup. There were tanks on the streets outside our hotel. The Kremlin was sealed off and there was a complete news blackout . . .

We survived on stories: from colleagues, from people on the streets. Stories helped me to make sense of what was one of the most emotional weeks of my life. Stories helped me to reflect on my experiences. Stories helped me to share my understanding with other colleagues, with family and friends . . .

My abiding memories are really of the people, their warmth and anxiety to have a true democracy, where their opinions are heard. They know that life will be hard and nothing can change overnight.

Most of all, I appreciate how vital is our right to information. How crucial it is for all of us to defend in our own democracy, the structures, currently under threat from central government cuts, that give us free access to information and books: the school and public libraries.

(Judith Elkin, 'Moscow: August 1991'; in *BfK* 72, January 1992)

Contributors' Biographies

BRIAN ALDERSON has been Children's Books Editor at *The Times* for longer than he cares to think. His experience of the vicissitudes of this journalistic occupation contrasts with labours undertaken in parallel on the history, bibliography and criticism of children's literature. He has also translated stories by the Grimms and Hans Christian Andersen, and adapted stories from *The Arabian Nights* for children.

BERNARD ASHLEY works and lives in South London, not far from where he was born in 1935. He is headteacher of a junior school in Charlton and writing is his hobby: novels, short stories, picture books and TV scripts. He's a family man with three sons and three grandchildren.

JILL BENNETT is deputy head of a primary school in Hounslow, Middlesex. She is author of *Learning to Read with Picture Books* and has compiled some twenty-five poetry anthologies. In 1990 she won the Eleanor Farjeon Award in recognition of her services to children's literature.

GILLIAN CLARKE is a poet who works often with children in schools. Her latest collection of poetry is *The King of Britain's Daughter* published by Carcanet, and is a Poetry Book Society Recommendation. Her translation of Welsh traditional stories for children, *One Moonlit Night*, was published by Gomer Press in 1991.

TREVOR DICKINSON taught in England and Canada, before

becoming Sheffield's English Adviser in 1968 and an HMI in 1971. For his last five Inspectorate years until 1991, his major concern was for school libraries. In 1990 he was awarded an OBE, and in 1991 an honorary fellowship of the Library Association.

VAL DOWNES still teaches at Staple Hill Primary School, Bristol, no longer as the language post-holder, but as a part-timer due to the arrival of her two daughters. Poetry is still high on her agenda when, each September, another new sea of faces greets her.

MICHAEL FOREMAN studied at the Royal College of Art. He's been an art director of *Playboy*, *King* and *Ambit* magazines and has made animated films in Scandinavia and for the BBC. He's written and illustrated many children's books and won numerous awards including the Francis Williams Prize (twice), the Kate Greenaway Medal (again, twice), the Emil/Kurt Maschler Award and the Bologna Graphics Prize.

ADÈLE GERAS has published over thirty books for children and young adults. Her most recent works include the Egerton Hall trilogy (*The Tower Room*, *Watching the Roses* and *Pictures of the Night*) and *The Fantora Family Photographs*. She lives in Manchester.

ERIC HADLEY is a principal lecturer in the Faculty of Education at Cardiff Institute of Higher Education. His business – though he didn't realise it at the time he started – is teaching reading, which is what he's done for the past twenty-five years, to children and adults. His greatest satisfaction lies in the four books he's written for children – *Legends of the Sun and Moon*; *Legends of Earth, Air, Fire and Water*; *Ivan the Fool and Other Stories* and *Tales of Four Dervishes*.

ERIK CHRISTIAN HAUGAARD was born in Copenhagen in 1923, but left Denmark one week before the German occupation. He studied at Black Mountain College, from 1941–42, then served as an airgunner in the RCAF 619 Squadron, from 1943–5. In 1949, he married Myrna Seld, and lived in Spain,

Italy, Israel, Denmark, England and Ireland. In 1981, Myrna died, and he subsequently married Masako Taira, in 1986. Since then, he has lived in Japan and Ireland. His books have received many awards and prizes, among them The Globe Horn Book Award, Jane Adams Award, The Phoenix Award and the Danish Cultural Ministry Prize.

RON HEAPY is still working with talented authors and artists at Oxford University Press. He's still surprised by what they will get up to next. In his spare time, he grows flowers and works with children in plays and musicals.

DAVID HILL was Head of English at a comprehensive school in Plymouth in 1984. Since then we at *BfK* have lost touch with him – where are you now, David?

MARY HOFFMAN is the author of some fifty children's books. In addition to writing picture books, junior fiction and a few non-fiction titles, she acts as educational consultant to BBC TV and some publishers. Keeping a balance between the two kinds of work provides a fruitful tension – the best kind!

SHIRLEY HUGHES was born on the Wirral and trained in Liverpool and Oxford. From the fifties, she freelanced as an illustrator, and began writing picture books when she had a young family of her own. *Dogger* won the 1977 Kate Greenaway medal, and in 1984 Shirley was given the Eleanor Farjeon Award for distinguished services to children's literature.

ROBERT HULL taught for twenty-five years in state schools and is now a freelance writer and lecturer. He is the author of *The Language Gap* and *Behind the Poem*.

GEORGE HUNT has been working in education since 1977. He has taught at a variety of South-East London primary schools, and at teacher training establishments in Dominica, Bedford and Reading. He's currently a lecturer in Language in Education at the University of Reading.

LISA KOPPER was amongst the first illustrators to tackle successfully the difficult area of multi-cultural imagery in the early eighties. Since then she has collaborated with many writers to produce a wealth of work for children's books and television. Her first solo book, *Daisy Thinks She Is a Baby*, was published in the autumn of 1993 by Hamish Hamilton.

ROBERT LEESON is a writer, critic and journalist. He's the author of over fifty children's books – historical, fantasy, sci-fi, school and comic. His work also includes promoting children's creative writing, raising funds for Third World libraries and being a lay official/negotiator for The Writer's Guild. In 1985 he won the Eleanor Farjeon Award. He's married with a son and a daughter.

MARGARET MEEK SPENCER joined the Department of English in the University of London Institute of Education in 1968. Her teaching life has been influenced by the significant growth in the understanding of children's language and thought, the production of books for children, the professional importance of the London Association for the Teaching of English and the SLA, of research in classrooms and extended studies of children's learning to read and write. Her books are *Learning to Read*, *How Texts Teach What Readers Learn* and *On Being Literate*. She was awarded the Eleanor Farjeon Prize for services to children's literature in 1970. On her retirement in 1990 she became Emeritus Reader in Education.

JAN NEEDLE (born 1943, resident of Lancashire) has written about twenty-five books for children, including *Wild Wood*, *My Mate Shofiq*, and *Wagstaffe the Wind-up Boy*. Sadly for his bank balance, his output has remained deeply unrespectable where kiddie-lit really matters – in the eyes of certain adults. Ho-hum.

STEPHANIE NETTELL has spent a working lifetime in literary journalism including fourteen years as Children's Books Editor of *The Guardian*, judging and chairing its annual prize – as well as many others. In 1992 she was awarded the Eleanor Farjeon Award for distinguished services to children's books. Married to writer Alex Hamilton, she has two grown-up sons.

JACK OUSBEY has taught in primary and secondary schools, and a college of education. He was an inspector with the Nottinghamshire authority, before devoting his time to writing, reviewing and running in-service events. He also works as a consultant and writer with Ragdoll, a children's television company.

JILL PIRRIE teaches English at Halesworth Middle School. Her pupils have consistently won awards in national competitions like the W H Smith 'Young Writers'. An anthology of Halesworth children's poetry was published by Bloodaxe in 1993. A second edition of Jill's book, *On Common Ground*, has been published by the World Wide Fund for Nature.

CHRIS POWLING is the author of a number of stories and novels for children, ranging from beginner readers to teenagers. He's taught all age levels in the state system and is currently a senior lecturer in English at King Alfred's College, Winchester, as well as being a regular contributor to radio programmes on children's books, a consultant for a national children's book club and, of course, the editor of *Books for Keeps*.

JAMES RIORDAN earns his bread and butter as Academic Head of the Department of Linguistic and International Studies at the University of Surrey. Any jam on the bread comes from writing short stories for children and collections of folk tales. His books include *Woman in the Moon and Other Tales of Forgotten Heroines* and a modern version of *Gulliver's Travels*.

MICHAEL ROSEN writes books, performs in schools and occasionally on TV and does radio programmes for Radio 4 and BBC World Service. All this keeps him busy – but not enough to stop him watching Arsenal and wrestling with his children.

ELEANOR VON SCHWEINITZ lectured at the School of Information Studies in the Polytechnic of North London for just over twenty-two years. She was one of the original panel of judges for the *Times Educational Supplement* Junior Information Book Award and is currently Information Book Reviews Editor at *Books for Keeps*.

MORAG STYLES is Language Co-ordinator at Homerton College. She has devoted much of her professional life to poetry, running workshops for children and adults, editing anthologies and writing books for teachers about poetry in the classroom. She's co-editor of *After Alice*, essays exploring aspects of children's literature, and *The* Books for Keeps *Guide to Poetry, 0–16*.

PAT TRIGGS, retiring early, exchanged Bristol Polytechnic and editing *BfK* for freedom, freelancing and financial uncertainty. She tried 'perfecting the message' herself in *Toybox Science* (A & C Black) which made the *TES* Junior Information Book Award shortlist – encouraging for a beginner. Still much involved with schools through consultancy – helping, she hopes, to preserve good teachers and good teaching from the preoccupations of blinkered know-nothings dispensing policy.

NICHOLAS TUCKER taught English in comprehensive schools in London before qualifying as an educational psychologist. He is now Lecturer in Developmental Psychology at the University of Sussex, with a special interest both in children's reactions to literature and in the history and present-day status of childhood itself. He has written five books for children as well as books about children's literature, including *The Child and the Book: a literary and psychological exploration*.

JEAN URE lives with her actor husband, five rescued dogs and two rescued cats in a Queen Anne house in the centre of soulless Croydon. Her interests include reading (of course!), walking the dogs and listening to music. She's a vegan and a committed worker for animals rights.

MARTIN WADDELL was born in 1941 and escaped education. After failing to make the grade as a professional footballer he began to write and has been writing ever since. Many books, a clever wife, three large sons and an interesting life have been the result to date. To be continued . . .

LIZ WATERLAND has been a teacher of three- to eleven-year-olds for twenty-six years and a headteacher for two. Her main interest is in helping children to achieve literacy as early and as pleasurably as possible. She daily becomes more bolshy in defence of young children's interests in the education system.

JAMES WATSON combines writing with full-time teaching. He's director of BA course in Media and Communication, run in partnership between West Kent College and the University of Greenwich. He has written several plays for radio but his chief work is as an author of novels for young teenagers. *Talking in Whispers* (1983) won him The Other Award and the Buxtehuder Bulle Prize for books for young readers.

VICTOR WATSON is Head of English at Homerton College, Cambridge. He has a special interest in the history and nature of children's books from the early eighteenth century to the present, and a particular enthusiasm for William Blake, Lewis Carroll and Arthur Ransome.

A Skeleton Book List

As a magazine concerned for the most part with newly available children's hardbacks and paperbacks, *Books for Keeps* offers full book information (including price and ISBN) at the end of each article. We soon, however, discovered the impossiblity of such a policy in a compilation like this which spans more than a dozen years of book trade endeavour. So we've kept the list below to a minimum. It's not intended as an academic reference point but as basic First Aid, giving hardback details only, for readers keen to follow up a particular article. If more information is needed, a local library or bookshop is almost certain to be able to help.

Classics, Folk and Fairy Tales

Needle on Treasure Island – Jan Needle
A Fine Boy For Killing, Wild Wood (ill. William Rushton) and *Another Fine Mess* are all published by André Deutsch. *Losers Weepers* is published by Methuen.

Hans Christian Andersen – Erik Haugaard
Andersen: His Classic Fairy Tales – ill. Michael Foreman, Gollancz

On the Permanence of Pooh – Chris Powling
The 'Pooh' books are all published by Methuen

The Limits of Delight – Margaret Meek
The Wind in the Willows was first published in 1908 but
Shepard's famous illustrations were not added until 1930. It is
available in a variety of editions.
Kenneth Grahame – Peter Green, John Murray
Secret Gardens – Humphrey Carpenter, Allen & Unwin

Picture Books

A Question of Images – Lisa Kopper

All the *Jafta* titles are written by Hugh Lewin, ill. Lisa Kopper
and published by Evans or Bell and Hyman

The Flow of the Images – Brian Alderson

The Caldecott Tradition for Today's Children
The following list has been compiled with the wholly practical
aim of recommending some of the picture books in 'the
Caldecott tradition' that are available in bookshops or
libraries today. The titles have been selected and classified to
show the tradition at work in different kinds of picture books.
Sing a Song For Sixpence – Brian Alderson, Cambridge
Nursery Rhymes – Quentin Blake, Cape
Gregory Griggs and Other Nursery Rhyme People – Arnold
Lobel, Hamish Hamilton
Rhymes without Reason from Mother Goose – Wallace Tripp,
Worlds Work
Over the Moon – Charlotte Voake, Walker
Each Peach Pear Plum – Allan and Janet Ahlberg, Viking
Kestrel
A Was an Apple Pie – Tracy Campbell Pearson, Bodley Head
Sing a Song of Sixpence – Tracy Campbell Pearson, Bodley
Head
Hector Protector and As I Went Over the Water – Maurice
Sendak, Macmillan
The Three Little Pigs – Erik Blegvad, Julia MacRae
The Great Big Enormous Turnip – Tolstoy, ill. Helen
Oxenbury, Heinemann
The Little Red Hen – Margot Zemach, Viking Kestrel

The Old Joke Book – Allan and Janet Ahlberg, Viking Kestrel
Mr Magnolia – Quentin Blake, Cape
Johnny Crow's Garden – L Leslie Brooke, Warne
Hairy MacLary from Donaldson's Dairy – Lynley Dodd,
Spindlewood
Pat the Cat – Colin and Jacqui Hawkins, Bell and Hyman
This is the Bear – Sarah Hayes, ill. Helen Craig, Walker
Diana and her Rhinoceros – Edward Ardizzone, Collins
Johnny the Clockmaker – Edward Ardizzone, Oxford
Little Tim and the Brave Sea Captain – Edward Ardizzone,
Viking Kestrel
The Snowman – Raymond Briggs, Hamish Hamilton
Mr Gumpy's Outing – John Burningham, Cape
The Winter Bear – Ruth Craft, ill. Erik Blegvad, Collins
The Big Green Book – Robert Graves, ill. Maurice Sendak,
Puffin
See Mouse Run – Sally Grindley, ill. Priscilla Lamont, Hamish
Hamilton
The Sly Old Cat – Beatrix Potter, Warne
Mr and Mrs Pig's Evening Out – Mary Rayner, Macmillan
Tom's Cat – Charlotte Voake, Walker
John Brown, Rose and the Midnight Cat – Jenny Wagner, ill.
Ron Brooks, Viking Kestrel
The Elephant and the Bad Baby – Elfrida Vipont, ill.
Raymond Briggs, Hamish Hamilton

Working with Charlie – Ron Heapy

All of the following titles are illustrated by Charles Keeping
and published by Oxford:
The Highwayman – Alfred Noyes
Beowulf – Kevin Crossley-Holland
Sammy Streetsinger
The Wedding Ghost – Leon Garfield
The Lady of Shalott – Alfred Lord Tennyson
Adam and Paradise Island

Writing Texts for Picture Books – Martin Waddell

All of the following titles are written by Martin Waddell and
published by Walker:
The Hidden House – ill. Angela Barrett

The Park in the Dark – ill. Barbara Firth
Once There Were Giants – ill. Penny Dale
Can't You Sleep, Little Bear? – ill. Barbara Firth
Farmer Duck – ill. Helen Oxenbury
Pig in the Pond – ill. Jill Barton
The Happy Hedgehog Band– ill. Jill Barton

Poetry

Taking Care of the Small Box – Jack Ousbey

'Poetry and Children' by Leonard Clark, *Children's Literature in Education* – ed. Geoff Fox, Agathon Press
Selected Poems – Gillian Clarke, Carcanet
Vasco Popa in *Poetry in The Making* – Ted Hughes, Faber
Listening to Poetry, Here Today – Ted Hughes, Hutchinson Educational
Poems of Love and Death – George MacBeth, Secker & Warburg
Katerina Brae – Christopher Reid, Faber
The Fiction Makers – Anne Stevenson, Oxford

Coming to Poetry – Val Downes

Quick, Let's Get Out of Here – Michael Rosen, Deutsch
Gargling with Jelly – Brian Patten, Viking Kestrel
Please Mrs Butler – Allan Ahlberg, Viking Kestrel
Revolting Rhymes – Roald Dahl, Cape
Andrew Stibb's 'Poetry in the Classroom from *Children's Literature in Education*, Vol. 12

Taking a Word for a Walk – Gillian Clarke

This article comes from:
There's a Poet Behind You – ed. Helen Cook and Morag Styles, A & C Black

Authorgraph: Charles Causley – Morag Styles

Collected Poems 1951–1975 – Charles Causley, Macmillan
Early in the Morning – Charles Causley, Viking Kestrel
Figgie Hobbin – Charles Causley, Macmillan

Jack the Treacle Eater – Charles Causley, Macmillan
The Puffin Book of Magic Verse – edited by Charles Causley,
Viking Kestrel
The Puffin Book of Salt-Sea Verse – edited by Charles Causley,
Viking Kestrel
The Sun, Dancing – edited by Charles Causley, Viking Kestrel

The Tree and Uncle George – Jill Pirrie
What Is The Truth – Ted Hughes, Faber

Information Books

Perfecting the Message – Pat Triggs
All of the following titles are by Aliki:
My Visit to the Dinosaurs – A & C Black
Fossils Tell of Long Ago – A & C Black
Digging Up Dinosaurs – The Bodley Head
Mummies Made in Egypt – The Bodley Head
A Medieval Feast – The Bodley Head
How a Book Is Made – The Bodley Head

Some Fictions of Non-fiction – Robert Hull
War Boy – Michael Foreman, Pavilion
Cathedral – David Macaulay Collins

The Birth of a Book – Michael Foreman
One World – Michael Foreman, Andersen Press

Fiction and Fun

**Two Writers Speaking Personally – James Watson, Jan
Needle**
Jan Needle's titles mentioned are published by André Deutsch
James Watson's titles mentioned are published by Gollancz

My Affair with Judy – Nicholas Tucker
All the books mentioned are published by Heinemann, except *Forever* and *Are You There God? It's Me Margaret* which are published by Gollancz

Authorgraph: William Mayne – Stephanie Nettell
All of the following titles are by William Mayne:
No More School – Hamish Hamilton
Drift – Cape
Gideon Ahoy! – Viking Kestrel
Kelpie – Cape
The Patchwork Cat – Cape
Hob Stories – Walker
Netta – Hamish Hamilton
Antar and the Eagles – Walker
Men of the House – Heinemann
The Farm that Ran Out of Names – Cape
A Year and A Day – Hamish Hamilton
The Jersey Shore – Hamish Hamilton
Plot Night – Hamish Hamilton
Max's Dream – Hamish Hamilton

Some More Golden Rules – Jean Ure
Jean Ure's titles mentioned are published by Bodley Head

Smiling at the Crocodile – Mary Hoffman
Amazing Grace – ill. Caroline Binch, Frances Lincoln

A Last Word

On the Importance of Books in Schools – Michael Rosen
No Hickory, No Dickory, No Dock – John Agard and Grace Nichols, Viking Kestrel
Daz 4 Zoe – Robert Swindells, Hamish Hamilton

Acknowledgements

The editor and publishers would like to thank all our contributors for permission to use material in this collection. Writers, illustrators and publishers alike waived any payment and wished the project well. *Books for Keeps* much appreciates their generosity. We've made every effort to trace copyright holders who are acknowledged in the list below. Please let us know if anyone has been omitted so we can correct this at the first opportunity.

Photographs: We'd like to thank the following for the photographs used: David Hill, Peter Walsh Photography, Walker Books and, in particular, the indefatigable Richard Mewton. Please contact *Books for Keeps* for any further information.

Michael Foreman for the use of the illustration on page 16 from *Hans Andersen: His Classic Fairy Tales* published by Gollancz
Curtis Brown, London, for the illustration on page 21 from *Winnie the Pooh* by A A Milne published by Methuen
Macmillan for the use of the illustration on page 33 from *Alice's Adventures in Wonderland* by Lewis Carroll
Hodder & Stoughton for the use of the illustration on page 36 from *Peter Pan and Wendy* by J M Barrie
Lisa Kopper for the use of the illustration on page 43 from *Jafta – The Wedding* by Hugh Lewin
The Bodley Head Children's Books for the use of the illustration on page 44 from *Amber's Other Grandparents* by Peter Bonnici
The Bodley Head Children's Books for the use of the illustration on page 48 from *Chips and Jessie* by Shirley Hughes
Walker Books for the use of the illustration on page 50 from *Two Shoes, New Shoes* by Shirley Hughes

Cambridge University Press for the illustration on page 55 from *Sing a Song for Sixpence*: *The English Picture Tradition*
Oxford University Press for the use of the illustration on page 61 from *The Lady of Shalott* by Alfred Lord Tennyson
Walker Books for the use of the illustration on page 65 from *The Hidden House* by Martin Waddell
Walker Books for the use of the illustration on page 66 from *The Park in the Dark* by Martin Waddell
Methuen for the use of the illustration on page 77 from *Mother Goose*
Blackie Children's Books for the illustration on page 85 from *Something I Remember* poems by Eleanor Farjeon, ed. Anne Harvey
Quentin Blake for the use of the illustrations on page 90 *Quick, Let's Get Out of Here* by Michael Rosen, pub. Deutsch
The Bodley Head Children's Books for the use of the illustration on page 116 from *How A Book Is Made* by Aliki
Pavilion for the illustration on page 136 from *War Boy* by Micheal Foreman
Collins for the use of the illustrations on page 140 from *Cathedral* by David Macaulay
Andersen Press for the use of the illustration on page 148 from *One World* by Michael Foreman
Armada for the use of the illustration on page 174 from *The Castle of Darkness* by J H Brennan
Piccolo for the illustration on page 179 from *Iggie's House* by Judy Blume
The Bodley Head Children's Books for the use of the illustration on page 211 from *Dogger* by Shirley Hughes
Puffin Books for the use of the illustration on page 211 from *Peepo* by Janet and Allan Ahlberg
The National Museum of Wales for the Penguin Classics cover of *Hard Times* on page 211 showing a detail from 'The Nant-Y-Glo Iron Works', a watercolour by George Robertson
Puffin Books for the use of the illustration on page 225 from *The Very Hungry Caterpillar* by Eric Carle
Orchard Books for the use of the illustration on page 225 from *Joe's Cafe* by Rose Impey and Sue Porter
Caroline Binch for the loan of her original sketch on page 229
Frances Lincoln for the use of the illustration on page 232 from *Amazing Grace* by Mary Hoffman
Cover design by Alec Davis – designer of *Books for Keeps* since Issue 1.

The Children's Book Magazine
has been published six times a year – in January, March,
May, July, September and November – since 1980.
If *The Best of Books for Keeps* has whetted your appetite
and you haven't yet come across the magazine itself, why
not let us send you a free copy?

Write to *Books for Keeps*
             6 Brightfield Road
             Lee
             London
             SE12 8QF

or telephone 081 852 4953 where you can also place a
subscription.